SALAFISM AND THE STATE

D1566424

NIAS – Nordic Institute of Asian Studies
New and Recent Monographs

NIAS Press is the autonomous publishing arm of the Nordic Institute of Asian Studies (NIAS), a research institute located at the University of Copenhagen. NIAS is partially funded by the governments of Denmark, Finland, Iceland, Norway and Sweden via the Nordic Council of Ministers, and works to encourage and support Asian studies in the Nordic countries. In so doing, NIAS has been publishing books since 1969, with more than two hundred titles produced in the past few years.

UNIVERSITY OF COPENHAGEN

norden

Nordic Council of Ministers

Salafism and the State

Islamic Activism and National Identity in Contemporary Indonesia

CHRIS CHAPLIN

 niasPRESS

Salafism and the State
Islamic Activism and National Identity in Contemporary Indonesia
by Chris Chaplin

Nordic Institute of Asian Studies
Monograph series, no. 155

First published in 2021 by NIAS Press
NIAS – Nordic Institute of Asian Studies
Øster Farimagsgade 5, 1353 Copenhagen K, Denmark
Tel: +45 3532 9503 • Fax: +45 3532 9549
E-mail: books@nias.ku.dk • Online: www. niaspress. dk

A CIP catalogue record for this book is available from the British Library

ISBN 978-87-7694-304-2 (Hbk)
ISBN 978-87-7694-305-9 (Pbk)
ISBN 978-87-7694-717-0 (Epub)

Typeset in 11 pt Arno by Don Wagner
Printed and bound in the United Kingdom by Printforce
Cover design: NIAS Press

Cover illustration: worshippers at Istiqlal mosque,
Jakarta, 2013 (photo by the author).

CONTENTS

FIGURES

ARTWORK
by Izabela Chaplin

Acknowledgements

This book would not have been possible without the assistance of countless of people, to whom I remain indebted. The book is admittedly many years late, and has gone through numerous iterations. The seed from which this project grew was planted during my studies at the School of Oriental and African Studies and London School of Economics, but really took off several years after I graduated and began working in Indonesia. Through countless conversations with friends amongst Jakarta's vibrant NGO community, I became fascinated with the role of religion, faith and national belonging in 21st century Indonesia. As I began to formulate my thinking, I became interested in pursuing the topic further, and it inevitably became the basis of a doctoral research project.

I was lucky enough to conduct my doctoral research at the Department of Sociology and Department of Social Anthropology at the University of Cambridge. These departments offered a fantastic learning environment, and I'm beholden to all the staff who provided support throughout my studies. Through their assistance I was able to secure funding to conduct field research through both the graduate board of studies and the Evans Fund. Special thanks must go to Humeira Iqtidar and Kostas Retsikas for their insightful comments during my doctoral studies. However, the biggest thanks is for my PhD supervisor, David Lehmann. His expertise, patience, insight, support and engagement in this project pushed me to expand upon my initial research questions, and think of Salafism, religion and sociology in ever more innovative ways. His faith in this project will not be forgotten.

My initial field research was conducted in Yogyakarta and I am grateful for the support and encouragement I received from everyone at the Department for Postgraduate Studies at Universitas Islam Negeri Sunan Kalijaga. The assistance and workspace provided by them was invaluable. In particular, I express my gratitude to Noorhaidi Hasan, whose own work on Salafism continues to be an inspiration. Without his guidance and assistance, I would have never got this project off the ground. I also express my thanks to Ratno Lukito, Ahmad Yani Anshori, Khoiruddin Nasution,

Ocktoberrinsyah Rinsyah, Fatimah Husein and Syaifudin Zuhri – all of whom provided insight, recommendations and fascinating intellectual conversations throughout my time at Sunan Kalijaga. My knowledge of the Islamic sciences pales in comparison, and they were always patient when answering my questions, no matter how simple my enquiry. A special thanks must also be reserved for Nia, whose research assistance – not to mention countless pieces of advice – was of tremendous importance. Nia engaged with Salafi women in a way that I could not. Her acumen greatly enriched my ethnography by offering a comparative lens on gender roles within the movement that I would not have seen otherwise. I must also thank all those interlocutors without whose engagement I could not have conducted my ethnography; I have kept their names anonymous throughout this book, but their warmness and patience will not be forgotten.

Upon completing my initial fieldwork, I didn't return to Cambridge but rather ended up in Jakarta, where I spent almost a year typing up interviews, analysing field notes and writing (and re-writing) chapters. Over time I would continue to return to Jakarta, which became a base from which I refined and expanded upon my research. There are, again, too many names to mention here, but I'm especially grateful for those who spent hours drinking coffee and writing together at Anomali throughout 2013 and beyond. Arthur and Nico – thank you.

As the heart of Indonesian political life, Jakarta is home to numerous academic institutions and think tanks filled with people who have provided support, feedback on drafts, and well-received comments. I owe a deep gratitude to researchers at the Pusat Pengkajian Islam dan Masyarakat UIN Jakarta, the Wahid Institute, Pusat Studi Agama dan Demokrasi – Paramadina, Amnesty International, and the Institute for Policy Analysis of Conflict. The wealth of knowledge individuals from these institutions have, and their engagement on issues concerning religious tolerance and democracy, is something I deeply admire and benefited from. A special thanks must go to Ismatu Ropi, Ahmad Suaedy, Papang Hidayat, Ihsan al-Fauzi, Nava Nuraniyah and Sidney Jones.

After finalising my doctoral work, I was fortunate enough to be offered a postdoctoral position at the Royal Netherlands Institute for Southeast Asian and Caribbean Studies (KITLV) in Leiden. The institute offered a fantastic environment to expand upon my initial fieldwork and test some of my theories with colleagues. In particular, I'd like to thank Gerry Van Klinken and

Henke Schulte Nordholt for their insight, faith and hospitality, as well as to Yayah Siegers and the rest of KITLV for their assistance during my time in Leiden. I'd also like to thank all the PhD students and researchers attached to the KITLV at the time: Retna Hanani, Prio Sambodho, Wija, Vita Febriany, and Willem van der Muur, whose own work inspired me to think in new ways about my own. Finally, I've reserved special mention for Ward Berenschot and David Kloos, as they kindly provided feedback on a draft of this manuscript when it was near completion. It has, without a doubt, become a much more thorough work thanks to you, and I'm forever grateful.

During my time at the KITLV I was fortunate enough to meet a wide range of academics from across the world. As part of my postdoctoral research, I spent most of 2016 in Makassar, South Sulawesi. While this book is not based on my research in Makassar, I reflected on its draft chapters during conversations and presentations at the Universitas Islam Negeri Allaudin. I thank all those at Universitas Islam Negeri Allaudin for their hospitality. In particular, Syarifuddin Jurdi's mentorship and kindness will never be forgotten. I have fond memories of retreating to the hills of Malino to write draft papers together Pak! While at the KITLV, I was fortunate enough to meet Greg Fealy, whose work on Islam in Indonesia has inspired me ever since my academic career began. Greg read the entire draft of this manuscript and provided comments and suggestions that greatly improved this book. For this, and for all of Greg's assistance in arranging panels, reviewing articles and sharing advice, I express my deepest gratitude! Closer to home, I would also like to express my gratitude to the Saw Swee Hock Centre for Southeast Asia at the LSE, who provided me with a visiting fellowship back in 2017. I benefited tremendously from the resources available at the LSE, and would particularly like to thank Daniela Lai and Indraneel Sircar for their insightful discussions on methodology and research. A special thanks must also go to Michael Buehler and Daniel Peterson. Our long conversations on Islam, politics, and Indonesia remain a source of inspiration to this day.

In turning this project into a book, I must express my gratitude to the anonymous reviewers, and the editorial team at NIAS Press. In particular, I remain indebted to Gerald Jackson, whose constructive comments and patience as I worked through drafts have strengthened this work.

Finally, there are numerous friends and family who have supported me throughout this book. There are too many to mention, but I think it only right to name several who tolerated my constant musings concerning Salafism, provided much needed breaks during fieldwork and ensured I remained well supplied with good meals and conversation. I'm thinking specifically of Olof Blomqvist, David Chaplin, Lauren Van Staden, Sophie Crocker, Arthur Van Witzenburg, Arthur Betts, Luke Phillips, James Hanley, Jon Napier, Carole Reckinger, Joanna Lanceron, Tim Cowan, Nico Prins, Hugh Lovatt, and Matt Phillips. A further thanks must also go to my parents, John and Izabela, sister Marianna and brother-in-law Harry, as well as my amazing nieces and nephews. I would also like to give special thanks to Pak Din and Nigel for allowing me to send countless books back to the UK via their living room, and the inspiration they have always provided me with. In many ways, their own stories of adventure motivated my own ethnographic engagement.

But perhaps the biggest acknowledgement must go to Angela, without whose support, patience, insight, closeness and humour – not to mention our countless trips and walks – I could have not finished this book. She is one of the greatest intellectual minds I've ever engaged with, and also the kindest and most thoughtful person I know. When I first met Angela, we were two PhD candidates fresh back from our different research trips, struggling to make sense of all the ideas and memories we'd just returned with. She is now my wife and best friend. Thank you, Angela!

Notes on Transliteration, Spelling and Illustrations

For most of the Islamic terminology in this book, I use a transliteration system as set out by the *International Journal of Middle East Studies* (IJMES). However, because Indonesian uses Roman script, I refer to the Salafi organisations as they refer to themselves. This may create a degree of confusion. For instance, propagation, or calling one to the faith, will be referred to as *da'wa* (per the IJMES transliteration system) unless it is part of an organisation's name, such as the *Dewan Dakwah Islamiyah Indonesia* (Indonesian Islamic Propagation Council), who spell *da'wa* as *dakwah*. The reasons for this are two-fold: first, I believe it respects the spelling selected by those I studied; second, it shows the multiple spellings and transliteration systems at play in Indonesia. This is important when analysing the different networks within the Salafi movement, as they can often be distinguishable from each other via transliteration. For example, two rival sets of scholars in Yogyakarta refer to themselves as either Ustadz (preacher) or al-Ustadz (*the* preacher); a minor but noteworthy difference when attempting to recognise where one's loyalties lie.

When spelling Indonesian phrases, concepts or popular names, I adopted the Enhanced Indonesian Spelling System, released in 1972 to replace the Soewandi spelling system. Consequently, I refer to the former presidents as Sukarno and Suharto rather than Soekarno and Soeharto, and to Yogyakarta rather than Jogjakarta (for example). Exceptions to this rule will only exist when referring to a name or organisation that continues to use the older form of spelling.

All photos featured within this book have been used with permission. Illustrations presented within each of the three vignettes are original line drawings created by Izabela Chaplin especially for this book.

Abbreviations and Acronyms

At-Turots	Yayasan Majelis At-Turots Al-Islamy (Majelis at-Turots Al-Islamy Foundation)
DDII	Dewan Dakwah Islamiyah Indonesia (Indonesian Islamic Propagation Council)
FKAWJ	Forum Komunikasi Ahlus Sunnah wal-Jama'ah (Forum for Followers of the Sunna and the Community of the Prophet)
FKKA	Forum Kegiatan Kemuslimahan al-Atsary (Al-Atsary Forum for Muslimah Activities)
FPI	Front Pembela Islam (Islamic Defenders Front)
HMI	Himpunan Mahasiswa Islam (Islamic Student Organisation)
ICBB	Pesantren Islamic Centre Bin Baz
ICMI	Ikatan Cendekiawan Muslim Indonesia (Indonesian Association for Muslim Intellectuals)
JSM	Jama'ah Salafiyyah Muhtasiba (loosely translated as the Salafi Jama'ah that practice hisba)
LDK	Lembaga Dakwah Kampus (Campus Propagation Board)
LIPIA	Lembaga Ilmu Pengetahuan Islam dan Arab (Institute for the Study of Islam and Arabic)
MEDIU	Al-Madinah International University
MUI	Majelis Ulama Indonesia (Indonesia Council of Ulama)
PKS	Partai Keadilan Sejahtera (Prosperous Justice Party)
UGM	Universitas Gadjah Madah (Gadjah Madah University)
UNY	Universitas Negeri Yogyakarta (Yogyakarta State University)
YBPM	Yayasan Bina Pengusaha Muslim ((Muslim Businessmen Foundation)
YPIA	Yayasan Pendidikan Islam al-Atsary (Al-Atsary Islamic Education Foundation

A Religious Gathering (by Izabela Chaplin)

The Distinguished Shaykh

Bantul, Yogyakarta, February 2012

The small, scenic country road leading to the Islamic learning centre was busy. Buses from across Java were arriving and unloading passengers, predominantly men in their late teens to early forties, onto the narrow road leading to the school. The bus drivers proudly hung signs and banners from their windows announcing where they were from: schools from Central Java, Islamic radio stations from West Java or Sharia businesses from the local universities of Yogyakarta.

This scene was exceptional. The road – little more than a single car's width – was clearly not built to handle such traffic. Crisscrossing a landscape of lush green rice fields and sloping hills, the flow of people and buses was out of place; an element of chaos in the otherwise pristine and calm surroundings. Adding to the commotion, motorcyclists – myself included – zigzagged through the moving crowd, directed by men dressed in parking attendant jackets over long, flowing Islamic robes, to a makeshift car park at the entrance of a nearby Islamic medical facility.

The cause of all this commotion was the arrival of Shaykh Abdurrozzaq bin Abdul Muhsin al Abbad, a leading scholar at the Islamic University of Madinah

1

and mentor for many prominent Salafi scholars in Indonesia. Al Abbad was visiting the Islamic centre, a Salafi-Islamic school set up by Indonesian scholar Abu Nida in 2000. It was a special occasion. The centre had just been awarded official accreditation by the Islamic University, and al Abbad was there to deliver the keynote address. The centre had spared no expense for the occasion. Outside the modern mosque complex, two large screens projected an image of the makeshift stage to the overflow audience gathered outside. The event was to be broadcast on several Salafi radio and TV stations. Banners announcing al Abbad's presence and the accreditation hung from the archway at the front of the school, and flyers about the event had been distributed.

After I parked my bike, I was greeted by Yasir, the school's English language teacher. Dressed in crisp white religious robes and exuding the sweet smell of the fragrances popular with many Salafi men, Yasir was beaming. He led me past the separate entrance for women – blocked from view from the main road – to a seat outside the main mosque building. Seating me next to a group of his older students, he spoke proudly of what a great moment this was not just for the school, but for the local community. Now Bantul, where the centre was located, had a world class, internationally recognised school!

When Yasir excused himself to attend to other guests, his students returned to their conversation about football. Soon we were joined by several young men who had recently arrived by bus. They'd made a beeline for us, or me more accurately, as I clearly was an oddity at the event. 'Are you Muslim?' they asked in English. I answered no, at which they laughed and switched the conversation to Indonesian saying they hoped Allah would show me the way. We continued to chat – where are you from, what did I think about Islam, what did they think of Yogyakarta. At one point, one of them suggested I watch videos of Yusuf Estes, the former Christian pastor from the US turned Muslim preacher.

By 8:30am, half an hour after the talk was scheduled to start, the buses had offloaded the final passengers and approximately 300 men were present. Most were dressed in short trousers and the Islamically inspired shirts popular amongst many Salafi activists. There were, however, several notable exceptions, most of whom wore the more traditional Javanese songkok (black hats) with sarongs. A hum of feedback from the PA system unintentionally announced the event was going to start, and Arif, the school's principal, asked everyone to sit. There was a brief welcome by a representative from the local regency office and then some opening words by the school's founder, Abu Nida.

Abu Nida needed no introduction. He was known as the 'grandfather' of Yogyakarta's ever-expanding Salafi movement. He was a great speaker who could hold audiences for hours. But this wasn't one of his lectures and he was not the star; the crowd was there for the shaykh. Al Abbad was a large, stocky individual with a thick beard. He had tutored many leading Indonesian Salafis during their studies at the Islamic University of Madinah. Because he could not speak Indonesian, he proceeded to give his talk in Arabic, with Arif interjecting every minute or so to provide a translation for audience members who did not speak Arabic – seemingly the majority, given the fastidious notetaking that occurred during Arif's translations.

The shaykh lectured on the topic of mukmin (mu'in or piety). He did not draw from the Hadith which he had dedicated his life to studying, instead making references to the contemporary world. He stressed the audience's need to be careful not to contaminate their keimanan (faith) with worldly desires that would cause fitnah (sedition). He emphasised that mukmin was something one needed to constantly guard and care for. It was like the fig tree; one needs patience and special care for it to grow. But when it does, it develops branches, roots and fruit. Prayer, study and introspection were like water to the fig tree.

The majority of the audience was enthralled with the shaykh's words and sat quietly despite the strength of the sun now beating down on those outside the mosque complex. But not everyone was convinced. After the shaykh had finished speaking the floor was opened for questions. An old man, dressed in traditional Javanese clothing, warily rose to his feet and addressed the shaykh in a mixture of Indonesian and Javanese. Arif, himself from outside Java, politely asked the man to speak Indonesian to avoid confusion and the old man broke into a slow, rhythmic Indonesian. He reflected on the differences between Indonesia and Saudi Arabia, commenting that on Java, the rice field was a more appropriate metaphor for faith than a fig tree. This caused a stir amongst the audience.

'Is he Imam Syafi'i?' the individual in front of me asked openly to both no one and everyone. There was anxiety in his voice. I knew that 'Imam Syafi'i' referred to those who followed the Syafi'i school of Islamic jurisprudence and commonly denoted someone from Indonesia's largest Islamic organisation, the Nahdlatul Ulama, which bitterly opposed Salafism. As the murmurs from the audience got louder, Arif called for order but to little avail. Those around me began to stand and move to the front to get a better look at what was going on. I too tried to move, as the surge of people blocked my view. But almost as quickly as the furore began, it was over. The microphone was switched off and those on stage quickly

3

dispersed. By the time I could see the stage again, neither the shaykh, Arif, Abu Nida, nor the old man were there. There had been no conclusion to the talk.

The audience began to scatter and mill around the mosque, passing the time before the Dhuhur prayer. The hasty end to the talk had caught all of us off guard. Was it a reaction to the old man's hostility? Was he even being hostile? I wasn't sure. Later, I asked Yasir what had happened. The old man hadn't been argumentative, he insisted, but admitted that it wasn't uncommon for people to misunderstand Salafi intentions. 'We look different ... and have beards, and, if we are honest, we dress the same as more violent groups, so there is confusion,' he added.

The reaction of Salafis to the supposed Imam Syafi'i signified a broader unease I had noticed during my fieldwork. In the month after the shaykh's visit, Nahdlatul Ulama launched a campaign to train its members on how to combat Salafism in their strongholds of East and Central Java. Salafis have, in a similar manner, taken issue with the teachings of Nahdlatul Ulama, deriding the way the organisation revered Islamic scholars 'like saints.' Yet the unease I witnessed ran deeper than inter-organisational rivalry; it represented competing visions about what being a Muslim in modern Indonesia meant.

This point was vividly apparent during my visits to the areas immediately surrounding the Islamic centre. In one village I came across a mosque caretaker who had stubbornly refused funds from the Salafi centre to rebuild his mosque after an earthquake in 2006. Speaking from outside his patched-up one-story mosque, he proudly stated he didn't want their money lest they 'take it [his mosque] over.' He continued: 'They don't speak Javanese ... nor do they join the pos ronda [communal guard duties] ... they are foreign and stubborn.'

There is a real grievance here. Many in the vicinity of the Islamic learning centre pointed out that those from the school didn't follow the communal practices expected by Javanese people. Yet as much as detractors accused Salafis of touting a foreign Islam, the Salafi vision of Islam and society was closer to Indonesian Islamism than many like to admit. The Salafis had come from Indonesian universities, been inspired by ideas of building a modern Islamic society, and aimed to use their higher levels of education to provide welfare, social services and high-quality education. Salafi Islamic doctrine may be uncompromisingly strict, but their efforts to assist society were there for all to see. Over time, I came to realise that the threat posed by Salafism was more existential: it represented a clash between opposing visions of what is meant to be a modern Muslim in Indonesia today.

Introduction

Since the resignation of President Suharto in 1998, public religious activism across Indonesia has flourished. Generally speaking, society has become more visibly pious and the county is now home to an eclectic but growing range of Islamic media programmes, halal-certified consumer products and financial services. The variety of products and preachers available also means that Islamic activism has not only become more noticeable, but also much more diverse and personal. If one was a pious Muslim in Indonesia 50 years ago, then one would most likely had been affiliated with Muhammadiyah, Nahdlatul Ulama or another of Indonesia's well-established Islamic organisations. However, as the opening vignette alludes, the country now hosts a variety of sometimes conflicting and contentious Islamic traditions, doctrines and movements.

In this far more variegated religious landscape, Indonesians themselves often seek out Islamic tenets or personal communication with popular preachers, many of whom run their own TV programmes, blogs or businesses. In scholastic accounts of contemporary Islam, this process has

Figure 1. Demonstrators in Freedom Square, Jakarta, 2 December 2016 (photo by Zarqan)

been described as the commodification of religion (Kitiarsa 2008) and the objectification of Islamic authority (Eickelman & Piscatori 1996). Beyond being offered distinct choices of how to express one's faith, Indonesians are also provided with a rich tapestry of competing visions of how to create a truly Islamic society. The religious clothes one wears, products one buys, or place where one lives are all deeply personal choices, acting as markers that differentiate oneself from other Indonesian Muslims.

Adding to this diversified field, Indonesia has seen the growing popularity of globally expansive movements, such as Hizbut Tahrir, the Muslim Brotherhood and Salafism; all of these have increased their public presence over the late 20th and early 21st century. As across much of the Muslim world, these movements – like the revivalism that they are part of – are particularly popular amongst younger Muslims, especially those who were brought up in the decades following the Iranian revolution and Afghan–Soviet war.

It is difficult to quantify the exact scale of this revivalism in Indonesia, especially with regards to the more conservatively inclined movements involved. However, one need only to look at the growing stature of TV channels, websites and schools promoting these doctrines to grasp their significance. To give an illustration of this growth, the Salafi-influenced organisation Wahdah Islamiyah has, over the past 20 years, expanded from a small foundation with a handful of schools in South Sulawesi to a nation-wide organisation consisting of 120 branches, 170 schools and a university, a humanitarian wing and cable TV channel (Chaplin 2018). Additionally, Din Wahid's rich study (2015) of Salafi schools documents the increased sophistication of Salafi education across 50 Salafi institutions, many of which have grown in size during the post-Suharto era. Although no accurate figures of Salafi followers exist, other conservative Islamic movements have registered several thousand followers. Before the Indonesian government banned Hizbut Tahrir in 2017, it claimed to have over 30,000 members nationwide (Osman 2019). These numbers are most likely inflated, but Indonesia was nonetheless recognised as Hizbut Tahrir's largest global chapter.

The above figures may seem insignificant in a country of approximately 225 million Muslims, but they have clearly irked Indonesia's much larger Islamic organisations. Indonesia's largest organisation, Nahdlatul Ulama, has spent considerable resources training their members to counter Salafi preaching, and forcefully cultivated an understanding of Salafism as a radical and violent Islamic cult that aims to bring Sharia law to all corners of Indonesia (Idahram 2011). More so, commentators frequently draw a direct line between increasing religious intolerance in Indonesian society and the ability of these global movements to promote their views in public (e.g., Banker 2019; Scott 2016).

This is not without justification. Not only have attacks on Indonesia's LGBTQ, Shi'a and Ahmadiyah communities increased in recent years, but there have been over 100 convictions for blasphemy since 2005 (Amnesty 2014). In addition, Buehler and Pisani (2016) have recorded over 442 Sharia inspired by-laws that have been implemented since the fall of Suharto. If academics previously painted a largely benign image of Islamic mobilisation during Indonesia's 20th century, then the current century has comparatively been described as one of an Islamic 'conservative turn' driven, in part, by globally expansive Islamic movements (Van Bruinessen 2013b).

Conservative Islamic revivalism has been a concern amongst scholars of global Islam, politics and the humanities for several decades, not least due to fears that such movements are prone to political violence. In fact, a Google NGram search of book references shows an eightfold increase in the use of the term 'Salafi' from 1980 to 2008, rising precipitously after the attacks on the US on 11 September 2001 (Google 2019). Broadly speaking, scholars have offered a variety of rich explanations as to why Islamic revivalist movements have expanded. Anthropological studies have, for example, focused on the individual stories of followers themselves, alluding to the fact that such movements can offer moral certainty within a rapidly modernising and urbanising society (Mahmood 2005; Deeb 2006). In contrast, political scientists look at cause and consequences, noting the ability of such movements to tap into popular grievances and mobilise resources through which they can influence political decisions (Hadiz 2015). Meanwhile, security analysts and foreign policy experts increasingly point to the sustained financial influence of states such as Saudi Arabia in promoting its own interpretations of Islam (Al-Shehabi 2008; Varagur 2020).

Taken together, these studies paint an insightful picture of a religious revivalism that can be personal in nature, but influenced by globalisation amid national economic and political insecurities. In exploring the dynamics of contemporary Salafism in Indonesia, this book largely agrees with this premise. Nevertheless, there remain a series of analytical gaps that remain unanswered, which this book seeks to engage with through an ethnography of conservative revivalism. In particular, I aim to examine the gaps between individual religious actions and the call for Islamic uniformity at the heart of conservative movements like Salafism. Indeed, if individuals are offered increased choice over which religious products they can buy and which preachers to watch, why have so many chosen strict socio-conservative Islamic values that stress homogeneity? This also leads to a second line of enquiry that is Indonesian specific and political in nature: Why has the 'conservative' turn successfully transformed political discourse and social attitudes, but as yet not led to a viable Islamic political platform?

Are we able to attribute this lack of political engagement to the fact we are living in what Bayat (2007) has described as a 'post-Islamist' age of Islamic activism? Or is the growth of these movements explained alternatively by economic incentives or individual rational choice? By themselves, these explanations fall short. As others before me have noted, any reduction of religious piety to a matter of rational choice or economic motivation ignores the involvement of well-off, educated communities, as well as the very personal sacrifices that individuals make to join a movement (Lehmann 2010). I aim to illustrate that there is a deeper logic at play here. Conservative Islamic activism is part of – not counter to – the increasing commodification we are seeing within Islam. The Salafis I refer to within this study promote themselves via concepts of class and social mobility that are popular amongst young and educated Indonesians – but always with piety as the point of departure. Far from seeing themselves as global religious agents somewhat detached from Indonesian life, they believe they are part of a religiously conservative moral vanguard – and have engaged in public debates through a variety of mediums to promote this very idea.

This infers that the attraction of Salafism is due not to its 'foreignness', but to its ability to leverage its global discourse to answer very local anxieties. Salafis may stress religious universalism and a strict adherence to religious practices, but activists have been notably astute in mediating between this strictness and concerns over the lifestyle choices of members, or the broader anxieties about being a modern Muslim in Indonesia. This moves us to the interlinked concern over the political dynamism of conservative revivalism, as it alludes to the fact that apprehensions over belonging to a nation-state identity remains important despite the global dimensions of Salafism. Salafis may challenge established religious norms, but the Indonesian nation remains the medium through which they interact with potential followers.

A cautionary note is required here, as I do not wish to oversimplify the connection between religion, democracy and the state by limiting our discussion to whether Salafis aim to capture state power or create an exclusive Islamist project. Instead, I draw from a broad range of political and anthropological works that define the state not just as a collection of structures and procedures, but also as a performative and discursive environment (e.g., Spencer 2007; Gledhill 2000). The structural dynamics of the state are important, but so too are the social relations, imaginaries and symbolic elements through which individuals come to understand themselves as religious and political subjects. To be sure, conservative Islamic activists must interact with state institutions every time they register a school or create a new religious foundation, and these interactions matter. But as I will outline in this book, religious activists also engage with the narratives and discourses that buttress what being a religiously pious Indonesian Muslim can mean in regard to rights, citizenship and access to political office.

These interactions have not led to a unified Islamist political project or emancipatory vision of an Islamic polity. In fact, Salafis themselves do not aim to create an explicit Islamic state in Indonesia, and Islamist politicians have uniformly failed to capture state institutions, gain a majority in parliament or even create a pan-Islamist agenda. Most Islamist parties fare poorly at the poll booth. Even the most well organised Islamist party, the Prosperous Justice Party (Partai Keadilan Sejahtera, PKS) has never managed to get over 9% of the national parliamentary vote. But at the same time, this has not led to a post-Islamist environment. Salafis may not be overly concerned with an Islamic state, but their social activism does have political consequences. Religious conservatives may deride democracy as an un-Islamic and man-made political system, but most are also acutely aware that greater democratic and civic space has been an underlying factor to their current success. Without a degree of tolerance from the state, preachers and educational establishments – like those mentioned in the opening vignette – would not have the space to reach out openly, influence public offices, or set political debates.

As conservative Islamic values percolate through society, they inform Indonesian social attitudes and local government decisions. Politicians of all affiliations see Islamic organisations as useful allies and vote winners, and appealing to the 'Islamic vote' has become a discernible political tactic. Michael Buehler, in his seminal work on Sharia law in Indonesia, observes that state elites often co-opt religious organisations as a means to garner cultural capital to boost their legitimacy, which drives a process of political Islamisation that is opportunistic rather than ideological at heart (Buehler 2016). Equally, some Islamic organisations and preachers have become adept at using their public platforms to offer their services as political mediums in exchange for political favour. The last 20 years has been characterised by the increased willingness and sophistication of conservative preachers to build alliances between politicians and religious scholars of different doctrinal loyalties. Often working on singular issues, these alliances have been at the forefront of growing anti-LGBTQ campaigns as well as demands to restrict religious minorities or charge Indonesians – both Muslims and non-Muslims – with blasphemy.

In short, the picture painted here is of a somewhat complex interplay between personal faith, political mobilisation, economics, and the institutions of the state. Conservative Islamic doctrines have moved themselves from the fringe to the centre of Indonesian public debates, which in turn has led to a qualitative shift in Indonesian political and religious tradition. This book offers an ethnographic examination as to how this is happening, not by focusing on elections, political offices or competition over state resources, but by looking at the activities of religious activists themselves. Through empirical research I dissect the discursive, historical and organisational patterns that have enabled conservative Islamic activism to grow amongst Indonesia's educated and urban classes, and the social, moral and pedagogical dynamics behind this growth. I offer an inductive account that explains how one strand of Islamic conservativism developed in 21st century Indonesia and has come to inflect a middle-class sensibility about what it means to be a modern Muslim citizen.

WHY SALAFISM?

As the opening vignette connotes, my primary focus concerns Salafism in Indonesia. I claim that a sustained Salafist social movement has capitalised on Indonesia's democratic transition to expand their *da'wa* (propagation) and advance a religious revivalism they have framed as both modern and aspirational. Salafis hold a rigid and literal interpretation of the Qur'an and Sunna, and closely follow a version of the Islamic sciences aligned to religious scholars, schools and donors in the Gulf and Saudi Arabia. But to understand Salafism, we must look beyond Western Asia and focus on the actions, discourses and perspective of Salafis in Indonesia, reflecting on how these shift over time and considering why a particular idea of religious identity can be both global as well as reliant on local histories of religious action. Salafis may have very real links to global Islamic networks, but they also flavour their proselytisation campaigns with Indonesian symbols and popular imagery, blurring the boundaries between religious propagation and appeals to Indonesian belonging.

Yet why focus on Salafism specifically? For one, it is arguably one of the most rapidly expanding forms of conservative Islamic activism not just in Indonesia but also across the world. Although the exact number of Salafis is difficult to come by, scholars have noted its growth in the UK (Inge 2017), the Netherlands (De Koning 2013), Malaysia (IPAC 2018), Yemen (Bonnefoy 2011) and Lebanon (Pall 2013), as well as Indonesia (Hasan 2006; 2010). A further reason to focus on Salafism is that despite increased public concern over its growth, frequent misunderstandings have contributed to Salafism's reputation as a controversial movement. In Indonesia it has been accused of following a strict and sometimes violent form of Islam that aims to erase centuries of local religious tradition. This is not without a degree of truth. Salafis certainly hold strict sectarian views that have fed into communal tensions and even, occasionally, militant religious violence in Indonesia. Indeed, from 2000–2002, Salafis played a leading role in sending several thousand young Muslims to fight in a sectarian conflict against Christian communities in Maluku.

For established Islamic organisations in Indonesia, Salafism has also presented an existential challenge to their authority. Nahdlatul Ulama have felt particularly aggrieved by the way Salafi scholars deride their own approach to Islamic scholarship, and have gone out of their way to paint Salafis as the vanguard of a broader effort to 'Arabise' Indonesian Islam (Van Bruinessen 2013a). The opening vignette alludes to a clearly visible tension between Salafism and 'local Islam'. Each new mosque, school, or social media platform that Salafi activities initiate increases the opportunity for this religious doctrine to reach a greater number of Indonesians – thus threatening more traditional Islamic authorities.

An ethnography of Salafism enables an untangling of this growth, while also moving us away from essentialist and often sensationalist political claims that Salafism is violent, is an arm of Saudi foreign policy, or even both.

Salafism is certainly strict, but careful study shows it also to be diverse and full of lively debates concerning how to be Salafi in modern society (e.g., Inge 2017; De Koning 2013). With this in mind, this book offers a grounded and reflexively informed approach that takes stock of the experiences and voices of young Salafis themselves. This by no means entails promoting a pro-Salafi counter-narrative against those who accuse it of being intolerant. Rather, it involves examining how Salafism evolves and how Salafis familiarise themselves with issues of faith and religious belonging within the context of 21st century Indonesia. Understanding why Salafism has proven so popular amongst particular Muslims, and what debates drive its expansion, necessarily enrich both our understanding of global Salafism, but also how Islamic activism influences Indonesian political discourse more broadly.

In following this line of enquiry, I draw upon extensive ethnographic fieldwork amongst Salafi activists in the city of Yogyakarta from 2011–2012 and follow-up research in 2016 and 2017. This research aimed to dissect the discursive, historical and organisational arrangements that have allowed Salafism to growth within this city. As I quickly came to understand, global religious references, educational institutions and financial support were important, but they did not define the movement. Rather, Salafis often framed their Islam as a particular understanding of *Indonesian* Islam, perpetuated as much by the discourses of national modernity and development as it is through a rejection to the immorality seen in wider society. This process was, moreover, lively and full of debate as Salafis often discussed how best to preach to new individuals, use modern technology, or even how to ensure they skirted the ire of overly zealous village security officials. It is this process of growth and debate which provides an important window into how Salafism is constructed as a movement.

As they seek to attract new members and shape society in accordance with their main theological and ethical tenets, Salafi activists come to operate in the spaces and ideological frameworks accessible to them. The fact that Salafis flavour their proselytisation campaigns with Indonesian symbols and popular imagery attests to this reality. As I argue throughout the book, this is one of the reasons *why* Salafism has been able to spread rapidly, but also why it is so controversial; its proponents support Indonesian values, but foreground an interpretation that emphasise a particular religious understanding of what it means to be Indonesian. This process is characterised by internal tensions as activists themselves are often left to decide how best to adapt seemingly 'universal' religious tenets to local understandings of authority, identity, action and faith.

A SOCIAL MOVEMENT APPROACH

To focus on the lively debates that inform Salafi activism, I adopt a social constructivist interpretation of Islam that takes account not just of religious doctrine but also of how religious doctrine is enacted in a particular socio-political context. Even though Salafis and other proponents of religious tradition believe Islam to be 'timeless' or universal, religion is treated here as a mutable social phenomenon. There are certainly numerous sociological aspects that join distant Islamic communities together, such as the Hajj, five daily prayers facing Mecca, and the requirement to fast throughout Ramadan. Yet as studies on cognitive development rightly emphasise, adherence to a specific religion lacks any singular cognitive meaning. Instead, it is subject to variation and change in relation to one's experience, age and situation (Heiphetz, Spelke, Harris & Banaji 2014).

'Locating' Salafism in Indonesia (or, more precisely, locating the actors and institutions that (re)create the representations and practices upon which any Salafi identity is based) requires a broad understanding of what can be encompassed within the concept of religious practice, belief and mobilisation. Accordingly, we must look beyond a textual reading of Salafi doctrine or an understanding of 'religion' as a predefined entity, instead seeing it as something that is alive in a particular time and place. It is fitting to approach Salafism as a social movement as it makes a sustained claim to a particular idea of how to live an Islamic lifestyle that can expand, adapt, and transform in relation to socio-political circumstance. However, given the broad range of social movement literature, I must briefly describe three elements that inform the approach taken with this book. While I emphasise that a social movement is a sustained effort to transform social reality, it is also contingent on complex agency, locality and a polycentric operational logic.

Agency

Although structural forces have a notable influence on religious mobilisation, my study emphasises the importance of local agency. Agency is complex, and religious doctrine is seldom interpreted without consideration of its surroundings and relationships to others. Adherents of a religious doctrine may be part of the religious in-group, but they also have other overlapping identities, affiliations and structural demands that influence how they make and remake themselves as religious agents. Individuals create a movement through interactions between each other, their religious principles and their environment. Inevitably, a doctrine's meaning and intent are altered through such interactions.[1]

In her seminal work on Islamic piety among women in Egypt, Saba Mahmood (2005) urges us to view faith through the prism of local agency. She argues that we must focus on the micro-practices of contemporary Islamic practice to understand its uniqueness and how individual piety is linked to an individual's search for an 'ethical' and modern subjectivity. Mahmood's work has inspired numerous scholarly studies that emphasise the need to see efforts of religious self-discipline as the defining feature in the formation of a religious subject. A similar concern with pious practices and lifestyles has informed rich works on Islamic revival in Pakistan (Iqtidar 2011), Lebanon (Deeb 2006), Egypt (Hirschkind 2009) and Malaysia (Frisk 2009). The observations of these scholars is relevant to this study as they provide a conceptual blueprint that urges us to foreground the local experiences of Salafi activists. The way one dresses, brushes one's teeth, grows one's facial hair, prays, performs *wudhu* (ritual washing before prayer) or greets others are all crucial to a religious subjectivity. Piety is a lived experience, through which the learning of micro-practices augments one's self-understanding of being pious and informs how one comes to think of one's place in the broader social community.

However, given my emphasis on social movements, piety and Islamic activism are not solely viewed as the inculcation of a particular ethic in this study. There remains a broader existential and outwardly focused plane, on which Muslims must navigate amongst themselves and the wider world in order to mobilise a particular Islamic identity. As this work will show, Salafi interlocutors saw their religious transformation as fragmented, personal and inter-subjectively constituted (Al-Mohammad 2010; Deleuze 2016). We must, accordingly, look beyond the internalisation of personal piety (what

---

1   An insightful elaboration on the complexities of agency is offered by Ronald Inden, whose 1990 work on India poses that while agents constitute part of a system, the system consists of overlapping entities as agents make and remake themselves and as they relate to one another through a 'scale of forms.'

Retsikas 2013 terms 'efforts of self-mastery') to the co-construction and lived experiences that define contemporary Salafism. We must, to paraphrase Al-Mohammad (2010), focus upon the social interdependencies and narratives that complicate how one creates, defines and maintains a (Salafi) lifestyle.

Locality

A social movement approach emphasises the localities in which Salafis operate. These spaces are where doctrines, to paraphrase Edward Said (2001), travel and undergo a process of transplantation, adapting to new contexts and facing challenges different from their point of origin). Localities do not dissolve in the face of globalising doctrines, but provide locations where ongoing forces of globalisation occur (Hepp 2009). They are, as Massey (1994: 139) reminds us, 'the spaces that define the everyday world of individuals, not merely spatially but also through a set of social interactions that create both coherence and difference'. Regardless of any self-proclaimed idea that Salafis comprise a 'universal' form of Islamic action, it is a social movement of religious renewal that evolves in conjunction with global and local developments.

For this reason, I refer to Salafism as a translocal rather than a global or transnational social movement. I am not the first to refer to Salafism as such, as Bonnefoy (2011) makes a similar point in his rich account of Salafism in Yemen. But our definition of translocality deserves further elaboration. Rather than seeing Salafism as somewhat decontextualised (global) or linked to national institutions or sponsors (transnational), I believe it is enriched through the agents involved in promoting Salafi doctrine, and the spaces, or localities, in which they do so.

In terms of scale, these localities include mosques, schools, businesses, radio stations, and religious villages that are connected by crisscrossing Salafi activists, donors and preachers. These venues act as spaces where doctrines and practices are learnt and enacted, but also through which activists themselves navigate the practical logistical and administrative requirements placed upon them by state officials. As much as Salafis may try, most of them do not isolate themselves in these enclaves. Importantly for our study, this includes Yogyakarta's numerous university campuses. Localities may thus be 'Salafi' in nature, but they are also spaces with a broader set of social interactions that encompass living and operating in Yogyakarta. They are places within which activists discuss concerns over Islam, including what it means in terms of being Salafi in contemporary Indonesia.

This concept of translocal builds upon a well-established scholastic tradition that uses the term to focus on how globalisation has led to a breakdown in the isomorphism of space, place and culture. For instance, scholars such as Gupta, Ferguson and Appadurai have shown how new electronic media and global migration have created new forms of public culture through which notions of state-based territoriality are dissolved or challenged (Gupta and Ferguson 1992; Appadurai 2003). My own formulation differs slightly, however, as I do not refer to the creation of diasporas or to the negation of the nation-state. Rather, I utilise the term translocal to refer to the role local spaces in Indonesia play in constructing an iteration of the global Salafi community. Analytically, I borrow from the work of Hepp, who refers to the translocal and local spaces where global resources are refracted through locally appropriated cultural codes and meaning. While Salafism may be global in imagination and doctrinal reach, the localities in which it operates provide reference points for ongoing globalisation processes, highlighting the increasing connectivity between different spaces all over the world (Hepp 2004 in Hecker 2010: 325–39).

In short, my reference to the translocal refers to the way Salafis (perhaps unwittingly) disembed Salafi doctrines from the context in which they were written, only to recombine them in the localities of Indonesia through their work with local activists. Translocal does not, in this sense, refer to the diminishing importance of the state or broader socio-political forces at play in Yogyakarta. Instead, it refers to the connectivity between global doctrine, the local mosque sermons and religious 'enclaves' within which Salafism spreads. These spaces are rife with political, cultural and religious tensions that reflect the struggles of adherents to understand, practice and adapt Salafism to their lives.

They are privy to what Tsing, in her intricate account of globalisation and environmentalism in Indonesia, has referred to as 'friction' (Tsing 2005). As Tsing describes, this friction alludes to the fact that the way global and local actors connect is often messy, as each can impinge on each other in the often contentious creation of place-based meanings. Global and local actors often hold different aims, but they can nonetheless come together to share resources and information (Tsing 2005). I seek to explore this translocal Salafist friction, which is as much constructive as it is destructive. I

16

acknowledge the global connections and universal claims behind Salafism, but also the fact that these are never enacted in the same way everywhere.

Polycentric Character

This book also builds upon a growing body of literature that investigates Islamic renewal using social movement theory (Bayat 2005, 2007; Wiktorowicz 2004). Salafism is a sustained collective effort that concerns itself primarily with personal religious renewal rather than collective political mobilisation. It aims to instil the virtues of Islamic 'purity' through the promotion of specific patterns of behaviour and lifestyles linked to a literal Islamic doctrine. In taking this line of enquiry, I should point out that I diverge from the branch of social movement theory concerned with contentious politics, resource mobilisation and political opportunity structures (e.g., Oberschall 1995; Tarrow 2012; Tarrow & Tilly 2009). Social scientists of this leaning define social movements as the result of intendedly rational behaviour by a collection of actors aiming to establish themselves in a political system or structure.

In my view, the aim of collective action does not lie primarily in shaping the nation-state, but in the construction of a specific identity and truth (Touraine 1992). Affiliated with what is referred to as 'new' social movement theory, the emphasis of this social movement school lies in how social agents aim to control the mode of learning, a particular culture, and how one comes to embody a specific lifestyle (and what this means).[2] This latter school has made valuable contributions to our understanding of the rise of the environmental lobby, anti-war movements, and LGBTQ rights activism around the world (Edwards 2014). Instead of reducing collective action to the sum of rational choices, the methodological demands of this school force associated scholars to deepen their understanding about how a particular truth is both constructed and acted upon.

With this in mind, the illuminating work of Lehmann and Siebzehner (2006) provides the most concrete starting point for the construction of

---

2   Melucci best developed this social movement approach. He postulates that that social movements are not always directly focused on the political system, and can be fluid, polycentric and culturally embedded in a specific context and time (Melucci, 1980, 1989, 1996). Social Movements are not necessarily concerned with direct political influence, but in the creation of collective solidarity (the formation of which is a political act in itself) that provides meaning to specific forms of living and 'seeing the world' (Melucci, 1996).

my own analytical lens. Their examination of Israel's Shas party illustrates how a contemporary religious social movement can spread an idea of religious belonging that overlaps with notions of private life, public action and political mobilisation. They argue that a movement of such a calibre does not necessarily have defined objectives or boundaries, but is a multi-layered and multi-directional effort sustained through a vast number of individuals who share a vague idea or set of identities that can shift in relation to lifestyle, age, social class and ethnicity (*Ibid.*: 30). In their estimation, religious social movements are not coherent hierarchical blocks, but rife with tension and disagreement, which – perhaps counter-intuitively – can greatly enrich the movement's characteristics.

Given the fragmented nature of Salafism, I take a similar approach and likewise aim to examine the horizontal connections among individual Salafi actors. Through sustained grassroots activism, Salafism challenges established Islamic practice and authority through a polycentric and networked pattern of action. It is best thought of, to borrow from the lexicon of Deleuze and Guattari (1983), as rhizomatic. It is a multiplicity, with parts of the network potentially connected to others through a logic of what they call *agencement* (arrangement), where actors popularise distinct concepts, become self-sufficient or articulate their doctrine by stressing various types of action (*Ibid.*). By referring to *agencement*, I recognise the importance of individual interpretation and practice in the transmission of Salafi principles and perpetuation of the movement. As I will explain, local Salafi actors have a degree of organisational and interpretative freedom, but yet continue to link with other Salafis across geographical distances through a shared idea of religious solidarity.

In short, Salafism is a movement that stresses agency and locality in an effort to transform lives through a network of social actors. The push and pull between tradition and reform, the ebb and flow of students coming and going from the city, as well as the tension between republican (nationalist) and Islamic ideas of solidarity, all inform ideas of what Salafism means in Yogyakarta. Salafis may argue that it embodies a 'universal' and 'timeless' religious truth, but the deeper meanings of religious association and action that drive engagement with the movement remain contextually relevant to the needs and anxieties of the populace.

A WORD ON METHODOLOGY

I undertook extensive ethnographic research in Yogyakarta from September 2011 to September 2012, with further fieldwork in 2016 and 2017. Both personal and professional motives inspired my search to understand the visible social changes that were occurring in Yogyakarta, a city that I had been intimately familiar with prior to my research. Having lived and worked in Indonesia for several years, I was aware of the growing space given to Islamic activists (particularly those with socio conservative values) during the presidency of Susilo Bambang Yudhoyono (2004–2014), and the effect this was having on ideas of tolerance and harmony in Indonesia. Church closures, attacks on religious minorities and the growing prominence of religious vigilantes were all part of the Indonesia I was living in at the time. It became important to me to understand the dynamics driving these currents in Indonesian society.

As a first step, I endeavoured to understand the impetus behind these trends, but not by using a legal framework or one concerned with political calculations, or even a human rights paradigm. Instead, my goal was to look at the deep cultural and social currents that were drawing local agents into Salafism, and how they came to be associated with religious ideas in the political economy of modern Indonesia. Salafism, both when I initially conceived of this project and today, has gained notoriety and is ideally suited to such a study. Simply stated, my aim was to engage with individual Salafis to better understand the interplay between local identities, religious resources and the social environment of Yogyakarta.

Connecting with Salafis was not easy; they are private and seek to separate themselves from non-Islamic society as much as possible. Being a non-Muslim exacerbated the challenge. Not only did I have to show my interlocutors that my interest in their movement was genuine, but I had to demonstrate that I was not motivated by a desire to 'disprove' or discredit their version of Islam. Salafis are acutely sensitive to negative accounts of their movement in academia, the media and the work of think tanks, and interlocutors frequently brought up examples of destructively misinformed works during our conversations.

In order to allay their fears, I adopted a position of 'methodological agnosticism' (King 1999; Woodward 2011) which did not aim to refute or disagree with the beliefs or lives of interlocutors. Nevertheless, this research was not without challenges and in our initial meetings, many interlocutors would talk about Islam in generic terms or attempt to convert

19

me, despite my insistence that my interest was academically driven. Several even suggested I convert in order to increase my access to the movement and strengthen my research. I politely refused on ethical grounds.

Although most informants were gracious, there was an initial suspicion concerning exactly what or whom my research was for (if not to better understand and so convert to Islam, then for what?). Incrementally, however, I was granted access to conduct my research by a network of Salafi activists in Yogyakarta who were on university campuses or part of educational outreach programmes in the city. Initially, this involved being allowed to attend religious lectures, including two weekly sessions, some spontaneous events, and some rural lectures. As I became a familiar face in the Salafi lecture scene, I was introduced to many enthusiastic activists who were keen to show me their *da'wa*, invite me to school events, and discuss religion into the early hours of the morning (much to the unease of my non-Salafi neighbours). Near the end of my ethnographic phase, I was invited to spend a month with individuals organising a series of mosque lectures and activities during the fasting month of Ramadan.

I complemented participant observation, my primary research tool, with 32 open interviews with activists from Islamic foundations in the city, as well as 26 interviews with individuals who lived in one of three Salafi enclaves (villages or boarding houses) in the city or its vicinity. I also collected approximately 100 religious magazines, books and 'bundles' (collections of magazine articles sold together and often focussing on one specific topic). These complemented my Islamic learning from lectures and helped me to formulate more intricate questions for participants. These works consisted of literature referring specifically to Islamic sciences (the majority of which were translations of works by Saudi and Yemeni *shaykh*) and more contemporary books written by Indonesian authors who wished to promote doctrinal lessons relating to child-rearing, gender anxieties, business and health. The use of these different but complementary methods gave me a more complete picture of Salafism. As my research progressed, I moved from a broad concern regarding individual expressions of Salafi faith and belonging to a more precise analysis of recognisable and inter-related systems of mobilisation and propagation.

I must provide a final two points on my methodology and the writing of my findings. Firstly, during my fieldwork I rarely came across those who had left the Salafi movement. They doubtlessly exist, and several interlocutors provided accounts of engaging, disengaging and re-engaging with Salafism. Yet while I acknowledge leaving the movement is an important topic that would greatly enrich our understanding of the movement, it lies beyond the scope of this project. Secondly, individuals shared their stories and often private experiences with me, and I remain indebted to the time, energy, patience and openness many interlocutors gave me. To protect people's privacy I have used pseudonyms for everyone throughout this work, with the exception of documented public Salafi figures or well-known foundations, schools or institutions. Further, I am aware that ethnographers create their objects of study as much as they 'discover' them. Interlocutors make guesses about what the researcher represents, which in turn influences how they choose to interact and what they often choose to omit or share.

Whilst at all points I attempt to be as accurate as possible, I am first and foremost a human and thus prone to error, subjectivity and mistakes despite my best efforts. Any misrepresentations – in terms of Salafi doctrine or the movement – are my own.

OUTLINE OF THE BOOK

Salafism is spreading in Indonesia in increasingly sophisticated and rhizomatic ways. Some strands of Salafism concentrate on rural life and shield themselves from daily political debate. However, these strands are complemented by a growing force of bold, charismatic, urban activists with middle-class aspirations. I am concerned almost exclusively with these latter activists and organise my description and analysis of them over the course of three sections, each with two chapters.

In the first section I look at the creation of the Salafi movement, and so chapter one begins with a description of what Salafism is, its global roots, and the emergence of Salafism during Suharto's New Order. Structural transformations during the New Order catalysed the growth of Salafism amongst Muslim students in Indonesia, enabling it to spread in Indonesia's rapidly expanding urban centres. During the Suharto era, a new wave of Islamic revivalism qualitatively altered how Islamic faith, authority and life choices were perceived. Salafism was a part of this transformation.

Building on this line of enquiry, the second chapter describes and analyses Salafism in Yogyakarta more directly. It begins with an examination of Salafism in democratic Indonesia, and the ruptures that characterised the movement. I look at how Salafis in Yogyakarta reacted to democracy in markedly divergent ways. On one side, the controversial preacher Jafar Umar Thalib mobilised his followers for direct political and violent action, sending approximately 7,000 combatants to the sectarian conflict that had engulfed Maluku in 1999–2000. In contrast, Salafis closer to the Yogyakartan preacher Abu Nida, who features more predominantly in my ethnography, focused exclusively on *da'wa* (propagation), opening new schools, foundations and welfare assistance initiatives across the archipelago.

The methods of this latter network have endured, and I offer a description of the actors, enclaves and forums that played a significant role in this expansion of Salafism. Agents took on a number of roles depending on their level of education and social position. They included preachers (*asatidz*, sing. *ustadz*), business and managerial professionals, and lay preachers (*da'i*). To make the ideal of an Islamic society more concrete, these actors created the impetus for adherents to live and operate in a number of religious sites. Creating an alternative notion of religious reality means the movement has actively expanded not just the number of those involved in Salafism, but also the number of spaces within which it can enforce a specific idea of a pure Islamic practice. The second chapter finishes with a description of the schools, villages and boarding houses that define Salafism.

Creating enclaves does not imply that Salafis define their social position as alien to Yogyakarta's social and political pressures. My empirical analysis discerned an acute ability amongst activists to organise, mobilise and project their religious values in relation to their surroundings. This is the focus on the second section of the book, which comprises chapters three and four. In chapter three I examine the religious lectures at the Yogyakartan university campus to demonstrate how the movement brings new members into the faith. Lectures encourage a specific form of intellectual and emotional engagement: individuals are urged not just to learn religious scripture but discover how to 'live' Islam. This idea is strengthened by the fact that the lecture is also an arena in which associational bonds are formed between *asatidz* and followers, and where Salafi micro-practices are inculcated and particular patterns of behaviour are learned. However, lectures can vary greatly depending on who is in attendance, and where and when they take place. The content of lectures is frequently tailored to the expected audience. The chapter explains that these forums not only bring individuals into the religious fold, but also reify social and class-based distinctions prevalent in broader Indonesian society.

The perception of Salafi mobilisation should not be viewed separately from the daily lives of other segments of the population. Amongst urban enthusiasts, *da'wa* is not alien to the growth of Islamic market services in Indonesia during the late 20th century and early 21st century. Chapter four extends our examination of propagational activities, although it takes us down a different path by analysing how urban agents promote their faith through new religious commodities, business endeavours, radio stations and online forums.

Salafi activism has come to include a range of goods and services such as books, magazines and social media platforms. A new class of moral entrepreneurs, many of whom are young IT graduates from elite Indonesian universities, mix ideas of modern aspiration and piety in ways that align with the trends of religious commodification and gentrification in Indonesia. The use of technology does more than facilitate access to religious material; it fundamentally alters the ways one can engage with Salafism. The creation of new commodities becomes a professional endeavour in its own right, allowing agents to create and influence patterns of religious expression and engage in full-time religious employment that links Islamic references with modern ideas of popular culture, social media and economic entrepreneurialism.

Both the production of religious goods and the organisation of Islamic lectures influence how Salafis come to define themselves as part of a social class of modern 'professional' Muslims, and this is the focus of the third and final section of the book. The fifth chapter elaborates on the ways activists promote their religious zeal as part of a modern subjectivity. I analyse three iterations through which urban Salafism is given modern social meaning in order to cultivate a religious identity. Whilst not wishing to detract from the deeply personal aspects of faith, the movement has promoted itself amongst students through notions of class, developmentalism and gender, all of which enact a particular lifestyle inherent to 21st century capitalist Indonesia. Activists predominantly drawn from secular universities have done much to imbue Salafi activism with concepts of Indonesian developmentalist modernity. Consequently, the notion of becoming a Muslim professional is as pervasive amongst urban activists as it is crucial not only to the movement's meaning, but also to a rendering of the idea of a Salafi community as one embedded in, rather than fighting against, modern Indonesian distinctions of class and citizenship.

The final chapter builds on this point by returning to the concept of Salafism as a social movement. Salafism is a movement that continuously evolves as a result of religious agents who work together and come to define (and dispute) the boundaries of religious action. As I explain, urban Salafis argue that their concept of religion and morality should be front and centre in social debates. They may have foregone direct political mobilisation, but, as it became easier to organise with like-minded conservative Muslims over the past decade, they have had marked success in increasing the resonance of their message. Moreover, urban Salafis have begun framing their movement as following in the footsteps of earlier reformist Islamic currents in Indonesia. This imbues their majoritarian view of Indonesian citizenship with a sense of purpose and legitimacy – much to the detriment of non-Sunni and non-Muslim religious minorities, whose rights are circumscribed by demands that the rights of the majority Sunni population be prioritised over all others.

This book urges us to think of Salafism not as a global phenomenon, but as a translocal movement reliant on Indonesian understandings of authority, identity, action and faith – which have all been transformed over the course of the state's existence. It has been able to expand in the 21st century because its substantial engagement with the socio-political environment has mediated local forms of mobilisation and religious understanding. This has happened as a result of a variety of new *da'wa* initiatives including sermons, social media ventures, business initiatives and even fashion. Yet far from being vehicles through which one merely inculcates a particular doctrine and practice, these activities have a wider social meaning. They are tailored to inform not just one's religious disposition but also to influence the way one thinks of oneself as part of a social class of modern 'professional' Muslims. The percolation of such Salafi narratives through the public sphere, combined with narratives of other Islamic movements, has led to Indonesia's current 'conservative turn' (Van Bruinessen 2013b). Salafi doctrine may be promoted as a universal religious truth, but as practiced in Yogyakarta, it remains contextually relevant to the needs and anxieties of city's urban population. It invokes a sense of religious belonging based on interpretations of Salafi doctrine that necessarily are entangled in local understandings of citizenship and public action.

THE CREATION OF A
SALAFI MOVEMENT

CHAPTER 1

A History of Salafism in Indonesia

'My nation shall disband into 73 different sects. All of them will be in the Hellfire except one.' They said, 'Who are they, O messenger of God?' He replied, '[They are those who follow] what I and my companions are upon [today].'[1]

I met Fawzan one evening after a religious lecture during the fasting month of Ramadan. In his 50s, Fawzan had thick glasses and a wispy, long beard. His two young children were in tow. He looked somewhat out of place at the lecture, not because of his clothes or demeanour but because he was older than most of the audience by at least 20 years. He nonetheless carried himself with an air of familiarity, greeting the preacher and younger attendees before making his excuses to depart. At the exit, we crossed paths and traded pleasantries, discussing the lecture and the potential traffic waiting for us on our separate ways home. The conversation soon turned to the progress of my fieldwork and preparations for the end of Ramadan.

During our discussion, we reflected on the development of Salafism in Yogyakarta and how it had changed in the three decades since its arrival in the city. Although he was too modest to say so, he was one of Indonesia's original Salafis, having joined the movement during the 1980s, when very few had heard of it. Fawzan currently worked at one of the religious schools set up by Abu Nida, Yogyakarta's founding Salafi preacher, and was a devout follower of the Salafi message. He was originally from East Java, but was not from a particularly religious background. As he described it, he came from an *abangan* upbringing – a term used to denote those who follow a syncretic form of faith. He previously assumed religious and Javanese traditions were almost one and the same and had been an avid practitioner of Javanese music. Upon finishing high school, Fawzan

---

1   Salafis often quote this Hadith. In full, Muhammad stated *'My nation shall disband into 73 different sects. All of them will be in the Hellfire except one. They said, "Who are they, O messenger of God?" He replied, "[They are those who follow] what I and my Companions are upon [today]."'* In another narration he replied, *'the Jama'a [group].'* In yet another, he replied, *'al-Sawaad al-A'zam (the greatest numbers, or the greatest darkness).'*

27

enrolled at Yogyakarta's Institut Seni Indonesia (Indonesian Institute for the Arts) when it had first opened its doors.

Fawzan described how he came to know about Salafism. As he told it, he had always felt uneasy with the way Islamic scholars were meant to be revered in his hometown, and also disappointment over how Javanese culture was affiliated with Suharto's New Order regime. Arriving in Yogyakarta, a city he believed to be at the heart of Javanese civilisation, he was shocked to witness the promiscuity of his fellow students. He recalled students drinking beer in his dormitory and staying up late into the evening. It was during this time that a roommate of his suggested he attend religious lectures, which is where he first began to follow Abu Nida. He claimed Abu Nida provided a different view of Islam than he was used to. Gone was the reverence to *kyai* (religious scholars) and emphasis on rote learning. Abu Nida charismatically spoke about Islam '*in this lifetime*,' and why one needed to embrace Islam to ensure one could atone for one's actions on judgement day. Abu Nida would answer questions directly, and it was his clarity that inspired Fawzan to deepen his involvement in the Salafi movement (Interview, Yogyakarta, 13 August 2012).

By 1988, Fawzan had attended a number of Islamic lectures, both Salafi and those linked with other Islamic groups active within university campuses. Having decided that Salafism is clearer, purer and less politically oriented than other religious currents, he committed himself fully to the movement. He undertook training to become a *murabbi* (religious guide). Soon after, he quit his studies of Javanese music (much to the disappointment of his parents) and began organising Salafi educational programmes. He recounted that Salafism in 2012 was different from Salafism in 1988; it had been smaller and more secretive, as fear of state repression and infiltration had haunted the movement. Nonetheless, the movement grew quickly and a considerable number of small cells were organised, many of which were charged with appealing to university and high school students. At the same time, as Salafism began to grow, other Islamic organisations became jealous of their success; the resulting conflicts ultimately forced Fawzan and his *murabbi* colleagues from the campus.

Fawzan may be older than most Salafis I encountered during my ethnography, but his explanation concerning his involvement in Salafism is similar to that of others I came to know. He had grown up in a more repressive period of Indonesian history than the present. But like many other interlocutors, he was from a semi-rural background, foreign to Yogyakarta, and of the first generation of his family to attend university. He was not particularly religious during his childhood, nor enthusiastic about the political corruption and exuberance of the New Order elite. His 'turn' towards Salafism had as much to do with a personal desire to better himself as it did from a social unease at the immorality he believed was plaguing Indonesian society. Salafism offered an idea of Islamic purity combined with a social image of a just and modern society, and this appealed to him.

Yet Fawzan's account also acknowledges the rupture his newfound religious beliefs had not just on his perceptions of Islam, but on how Islamic faith and Javanese culture fit together. His story may be personal, but the idea that local cultural traditions were somewhat at odds with Islam has a long history. This became a prominent feature of Dutch colonial policy, reiterated via anthropological accounts during the 1950s and '60s that prioritised the study of rich cultural and spiritual practices (see e.g., Benda 1958; Geertz 1960; Beatty 2009). These studies have had a lasting influence on the way Islam is perceived within Indonesia and the relationship between culture and religion. In fact, this concern with culture over religion informed postcolonial state policy, especially during Suharto's New Order (Bourchier 2014). It was only in the 1980s that anthropologists challenged the culture/religion taxonomy, observing that Islam, far from secondary to culture, is a set of beliefs and codes that transformed post-colonial society in its own right (Woodward 1989; Bowen 1993; Hefner 2000).

The greater affinity between religious and cultural practices stressed through these latter studies provides welcome reprieve. But we should take caution in concluding Indonesian Islam as somewhat exceptional or isolated from the rest of the Muslim world because of such cultural richness. Such a view has gained political currency as commentators and journalists alike point to Indonesian religious uniqueness, its propensity for tolerance and its 'smiling' nature (see e.g., Burhanudin & Djik 2013; Djik & Kaptein 2016). Indonesia's largest Muslim organisation, Nahdlatul Ulama, promotes the idea of *Islam Nusantara* (Archipelagic Islam) which they claim to have its own rich history, scholasticism and practice. Such an argument of exceptionalism does hold some truth; the history of Southeast Asian Muslim Sultanates, local religious saints and anti-colonial rebellion underscores a region of diverse and lively religious tradition. But emphasising this notion of exceptionalism runs the risk of obfuscating the way archipelagic

Southeast Asia has been connected to the wider Muslim world throughout its history. Islamic ideas have always flowed between Southeast Asia and the Middle East, informing anti-colonial rebellions such as the Padri War in Sumatra (1821–1837), as well as the reformist ideas of Ahmad Dahlan, a scholar who studied in Mecca and would establish Muhammadiyah, Indonesia's second-largest Islamic organisation.

The idea of an Indonesian Islam, separated from the wider ruptures of the Islamic world, is one of the reasons why Salafism – as an Islamic doctrine – is often framed as controversial. It is perceived as a foreign import that seeks to erase archipelagic Islam through a process that has controversially been referred to as 'Arabisation' (Van Bruinessen 2013a; Varagur 2020).[2] To its many Indonesian detractors, Salafism is used interchangeably (although incorrectly) with Wahhabism so as to equate it with the intolerant and conservative form of Islam typified by the dress and subjugation of women witnessed in Saudi Arabia. This is why scholars from the Nahdlatul Ulama have publicly campaigned against Salafism, seeing it as an existential and foreign threat both to their own form of Islam and to Indonesian society more broadly (NU Online 2012).

Adding to this stigma, there remains a tendency amongst policymakers to view Salafism through an overtly political or security-related lens, fo-cussing on its conservative tendencies or propensity for violence (see e.g., Fradkin 2008). What is often missing is a look at the deeper trajectories and anxieties that define the lives of Salafis like Fawzan. There are notable academic exceptions, however. For instance, Pall (2013) provides an ex-cellent examination of urban Salafism in Lebanon; Hasan (2006) delivers a definitive account of the rise of Laskar Jihad in Indonesia; Bonnefoy (2011) reports on Salafism in Yemen; and Inge (2017) takes an in-depth look at the daily struggles of young Salafi women in the UK. These works underscore the debates and differing geographical factors that have come to define Salafism, and I build on them throughout this book. While these au-thors point to a movement that emerged in each region in roughly the same decade (the 1980s) with similar links to global donors, scholars and Saudi educational institutions, they also point to an incredibly diverse movement filled with anxiety and individual concerns.

---

2   I take issue with this term, not only because it is inaccurate – as I outline through this book – but because it has racial undertones. Islam across the Arab world is in no way uniform – each of its strands has its own rich cultural history.

WHAT IS SALAFISM?

The first aim of this book is therefore to unravel and dissect Salafism, and we must start by examining what the term 'Salafism' actually means and where it comes from. In its most literal sense, Salafism takes its name from *as-Salaf,* 'those who came before us'. The *as-Salaf* are what Ibn Manzur describes as, 'the preceding group of people; those who have preceded you, from your forefathers and closest relatives, who are more advanced than you in age and virtue' (Ibn Manzur as quoted in Hassim 2010: 9). References to the *as-Salaf* pepper the works of Islam's earliest scholars, most notably al-Bukhari (810–870), Muslim (817–875) and Al-Awza'i (707–774), giving those who claim its usage a rich Islamic lineage (Hassim 2010). The label has also been used to describe particular groups of Muslims, such as the Ahl al-Hadith movement of the Abbasid caliphate (1261–1517), whose members were the first to be known as Salafi, a designation consistent with their efforts to purge Islam of non-Muslim accretions through the study of Hadith (Haykel 2009). Since then the name has been attributed to advocates, popularly referred to as the *Salafiyya,* of 19th-century reformist ideals first proposed by Muhammad Abduh, Jamal al-Din al-Afghani and Rashid Rida.

Use of the term 'Salaf' amongst contemporary Salafis is intended to denote allegiance to the ideas and energy of the 'original' Muslims. Salafis are specifically concerned with the first three generations of Muslims – the *Sahaba, Tabi'un* and *Tabi' al-Tabi'in* – who existed during the time of the first four Caliphs. Salafis argue that these generations are the original *Ahlus Sunna wal-Jama'ah* (people of the Sunna and Community), a phrase that signifies the correct following of the ways of the Prophet. Islam has, they argue, been corrupted since then by the introduction of *bid'a* (un-Islamic innovation) and the emulation of religious scholars through *taklid* (blind obedience to scholars). Much like the *Salafiyya* who came before them, Salafis believe in a need to re-open the doors of jurisprudence through *ijtihad* (independent reasoning) to re-engage with Islam through personal learning and introspection. Salafis subscribe neither to the Syafi'i *madhhab* (school of jurisprudence) that is popular amongst traditional religious scholars in Indonesia nor to the Hanbali *madhhab* revered by Wahhabist scholars. They are, like reformers before them, *post-madhhab.*

The similarities with 20th-century reformers end there. Whereas Abduh and Afghani urged Muslims to return to the original sources of Islamic science and re-orient religious faith in response to European modernity, colonialism and political thought, contemporary Salafis adhere to the Qur'an and Sunna (deeds, teachings and sayings of the Prophet) through the study of Hadith (sayings and doings of the Prophet and his companions). In following this *manhaj* (method), Salafis believe themselves to be the *al-firwa al-najiya* (saved sect) or *al-taifa al-mansura* (victorious group) (Meijer 2010: 41). In reference to their enlightened position, they cite a famous Hadith that foretells that the Muslim nation will split into 73 tribes, only one of which will follow the true path.

To uphold their 'saved' status, Salafis emphasise that Islam must guide all aspects of one's life, and one must separate 'good' and 'evil' or 'Islamic' and 'non-Islamic' in the world. They do so by emphasising strict textualism following the *athari aqida* (creed), and placing weight on the concept of *hisba* (the commanding of right and forbidding of wrong) as well as *al-wala' wa-l-bara'* (allegiance to Islam and renunciation of unbelievers). This latter concept is a prerequisite to becoming part of the saved Islamic group, reinforced through references to the work of the theologian Ibn Taymiyya. Ibn Taymiyya cautioned against imitating and following non-Muslims, and Salafis have integrated these writings into a coherent understanding of *al-wala' wa-l-bara* that divides the world into those who accept the word of God and those who reject it (Shavit 2014: 72).

A strict adherence to a timeless Islam should imply cohesion and clarity. But as I will show, this is hardly the case. Salafism is rife with divisions and differences about how the Salafi message should be propagated. There are those who engage in grassroots proselytisation (*da'wa*), direct political action, outright insurrection or a combination of all three. These divergences are captured by Wiktorowitz, who provides a typology of the broader forms of Salafism. He distinguishes among three trends: the *Salafiyya da'wiyya*, who engage with grassroots proselytisation; the *Salafiyya harakiyya*, who are openly political and aim to transform society through political activism; and *Salafiyya jihadiyya*, who, like Al Qaeda or Jemaah Islamiyah, catalyse social transformations with violence (Wiktorowicz 2006). Each of these, he argues, represents a different network of scholars, donors and actors, but all nonetheless share a similar vision that society must return to a pure and timeless Islam, based on a strict interpretation of the Islamic sciences.

Wiktorowitz's typology has become a benchmark for academics, journalists and policymakers concerned with Salafism, and not without reason.

My study is concerned with grassroots activism, and so examines those Wiktorowitz calls *Salafiyya da'wiyya*. Yet a note of caution is required before endorsing the Salafi types identified by Wiktorowitz. In her seminal study of Salafi women in the UK, Inge argues that this typology obscures as much as it illuminates (Inge 2017), making any analysis of Salafism dependent on its political manifestation. This encourages the assumption that purist *Salafiyya da'wiyya* are completely apolitical, which is inconsistent with Inge's own research that shows how subtle acts of praxis can have political consequences (Ibid.: 11). Echoing De Koning's research into Salafism in the Netherlands, Inge believes that acts such as wearing the *niqab* may not be meant as a political statement but can nevertheless become so when it is transformed into a public symbol (De Koning 2012).[3]

I agree with the belief that grassroots efforts to create a Muslim sub-jectivity can, over time, lead to subtle shifts in personal and communal behaviour that inevitably have political consequences. While Salafis pre-dominantly concerned with *da'wa* may not form political parties or en-courage outright violence, they do aim to alter the socio-political sphere through individual reform and communal activism by stressing the idea of *al-tasfiya wa-l-tarbiya* (purification and education) amongst Muslims. This is a sustained collective effort to transform society and social structures by constructing a specific identity and truth.

THE EMERGENCE OF CONTEMPORARY SALAFISM

One has only to examine the historical evolution of Salafism, both globally and locally, to understand how its social drive has political consequences. Salafism first emerged in Saudi Arabia during the 1960s and 1970s when the kingdom was undergoing socio-political transformations related to its grow-ing oil wealth. At the time, the kingdom was promoting itself as the protector of Islam by building new religious educational institutions and providing ref-uge to many Islamic scholars who faced persecution in other Middle Eastern

---

3 Wagemakers (2016) provides a more theological critique as he disputes Wiktorowitz's idea that all Salafis share a similar creed (*aqida*) but differ in their method (*manhaj*). He argues this to be incorrect, as not only does Wiktorowitz adopt a narrow definition of *manhaj* limited to the political sphere (and so unable to account for wider aspects of religious life attributable to one's *manhaj*), but he ignores that Salafis, all told, can differ on a number of creedal issues, such as the correct definition of faith (*Iman*) and nonbelief (*kufr*), as well as whether one can label another as a non-believer.

countries. These included Muhammad Qutb (brother of Sayyid Qutb), who became a religious lecturer in the kingdom after fleeing Egypt.

While boosting the credentials of the kingdom as a 'protector of Islam', the influx of scholars from around the globe – combined with an increase in the number of Saudi (and foreign) students studying Islamic sciences – created a pool of religiously and academically conscious individuals (Lacroix 2011). Not all of these academics espoused Islamic views in line with the religious discourse of the kingdom's Wahhabist religious elite, most of whom trace their roots to the Najd. Shaykh Muhammad al-Din al-Albani (1914–1999) was one such foreign scholar who began teaching at the Hadith department of the Islamic University of Madinah. Born in Albania in 1923 and raised in Damascus, al-Albani was a self-taught expert in Hadith studies. His early Islamic philosophy was influenced by the modernising tendencies of Muslim reformists Rashid Rida and Muhammad Abduh. He advocated egalitarianism and indifference to *shaykh* whose authority depended on their family or heritage, much to the ire of the Saudi religious elite.

Yet al-Albani's understanding of Islamic sciences was much stricter than either Abduh or Rida. In a manner similar to Muhammad al-Shawkani (d. 1834) (who also inspired the current Salafi movement as well as the South Asia-based Ahl e-Hadith), al-Albani took a more literal stance to issues of *aqida* (creed), following the *athari* creed popular in the Peninsula. Like al-Shawkani, he urged individuals not to blindly follow Islam or Hadith. To avoid perpetuating misinterpretations made by others, followers themselves must turn directly to these sources. For al-Albani, the most important aspect of Islamic scholasticism was the science of critique and fair evaluation (*'ilm al-jarh wa-l-ta'dil*) which assessed the morality and reliability of the transmitter (Lacroix 2011). He thus believed that one's religious mission began with untangling authentic (*sahih*) from weak (*da'if*) Hadith.

Al-Albani combined his expertise in Hadith with his ability to inspire students at the Islamic University of Madinah. Those who followed him became known as the Ahl al-Hadith (not unlike the scholars of the Abbasid era), and much to the displeasure of the Saudi Wahhabist elite, they began questioning the authenticity of Hadith previously assumed to be *sahih*. By implication, this was seen as questioning the authority of Saudi's religious scholars. As a consequence, al-Albani won few friends amongst the Wahhabist *shaykh*. In fact, he publicly stated Muhammad Bin Abd' al-Wahhab's (1703–1792) was not an expert in matters of Islamic jurisprudence; a move that brought him into direct conflict with the al-Wahhab family. After claiming that the face veil was not obligatory for women (as al-Wahhab had claimed), Wahhabi scholars ensured al-Albani's teaching visa was not renewed in 1963.

Nevertheless, by the time al-Albani was forced to leave, his ideas had spawned a following amongst students who would use the Islamic University of Madinah as a base for further religious activism. Moreover, despite the hostility levelled at al-Albani (and his followers) by Wahhabist scholars, there remained a degree of commonality between the two Islamic traditions due to their shared respect for al-Wahhab's concept of *tawhid* (monotheism and the absolute acceptance of the oneness of God and his attributes) and a strict socio-conservative approach to society and religion.[4] These similarities provided a base through which Salafis, from the late 1980s onwards, were able to benefit from an increase in religious funding from the Saudi Kingdom in order to promote their teachings around the world.

Al-Albani's ideas gained the most traction in the university's Hadith department, which became the nucleus for the first Salafi organisation, the Jama'ah Salafiyyah Muhtasiba (JSM), loosely translated as the Salafi community who practice the commanding of right and forbidding of wrong. The JSM was formed in the early 1970s with the approval of Shaykh 'Abd al-Aziz Bin Baz (who later became grand mufti of Saudi Arabia) and Shaykh Abu Bakr al-'Jaza'iri (who acted as its vice-guide), and established its centre at the Bayt al-Ikhwan (House of the Brothers) in Madinah. The JSM quickly expanded throughout the kingdom, opening branches in Mecca, Jeddah, Taif, Ha'il, Riyadh, Damman, Kuwait and other Gulf States. On the global level, its members formed links to the Ahl e-Hadith movement in Pakistan, as well as Egypt's Ansar al-Sunna al-Muhammadiya (Lacroix 2011).

The JSM had a short existence. By the end of 1977, the Saudi state was concerned that the JSM could transform into a political insurrection, not least due to the growing criticism of the kingdom by one of its members, Juhayman al-'Utaybi. They thus clamped down on the group, closed its branches, and arrested over 150 of its members and leading *shaykh*. These acts of suppression politicised the organisation's dissident members.

---

4   Salafis define *tawhid* as *tawhid al-rubuiyya* (the Oneness of lordship); *tawhid al-uluhiyya* (Oneness of Godship); and *tawhid al-asma' wa-l-sifat* (Oneness of names and attributes). It is worth noting that Salafi jihadists add one more form of tawhid that affects their methodology: *Tawhid al-hakimiyya* (Oneness of God's Sovereignty) (Haykel, 2009: 39).

Juhayman al-'Utaybi managed to escape arrest and muster a clandestine following that, on 20 November 1979, laid siege to the Grand Mosque in Mecca and proclaimed the return of the Mahdi. The siege, which lasted for two weeks and led to the death of more than 200 people, profoundly shocked the Saudi Kingdom and became the catalyst for even further restrictions against anyone remotely affiliated with the JSM. After the siege, al-Albani was a *persona non-grata* in the kingdom. Other JSM scholars were arrested and expelled, including Muqbil al-Wadi'i, who was incarcerated and then deported to his home country of Yemen.

The actions of Saudi authorities against the JSM and its leading thinkers marks a pivotal point in the development of Salafism – at least from a sociological standpoint. They ensured that Salafism would never have any particular centre and hence could not be viewed as a form of Saudisation. In the aftermath of the siege of Mecca, Salafism continued to grow in other countries, supported by institutions outside the Saudi Kingdom. Muqbil al-Wadi'i rejected any claim that Saudi Arabia had to religious legitimacy and he set up a number of religious institutions in Yemen. These institutions, known as the Dar al-Hadith, have since trained numerous Indonesian Salafis, including Jafar Umar Thalib, Muhammad As-Sewed and Luqman Ba'abduh (mentioned in a later section of this chapter and in the next).

Similarly, in Kuwait, Abd al-Rahman Abd al-Khaliq formed the Jama'iyyat Ihya' Al-Turath al-Islami (the Revival of Islamic Heritage Society) in 1981. Al-Khaliq had been a student at the Islamic University of Madinah and follower of al-Albani before being deported from Saudi Arabia after attacking shops displaying mannequins in the 1960s. His organisation would become a major funder of Salafi *da'wa* and schools around the world, including those linked to Indonesian scholar Abu Nida.

The fragmented expansion of Salafism into Kuwait, Yemen and other parts of the Gulf is one reason it has become a translocal and rhizomatic movement. Salafist organisation is not hierarchical. Instead, the movement relies on networks of associated actors who are loyal to a particular paradigm of religious thinking. The ability of Salafi advocates to expand the movement despite state repression demonstrates the strength of its sustained collective effort, although it has not been alone in this success; the world has witnessed a broader Islamic revival since the late 1960s (Mandaville 2007; Roy 2004). Salafism was able to grow because of these broader currents, but equally because the movement worked through an *agencement* (arrangement), where actors popularised distinctive concepts, became self-sufficient and articulated their doctrine in relation to local political developments (Deleuze & Guattari 1983: 2).

Despite the repression of Salafism in Saudi Arabia in the 1970s, the movement benefited from a rapprochement with the kingdom's authorities during the 1980s. This was in no small part due to the involvement of Saudi Arabia in the Afghan–Soviet war. During the conflict, Saudi Arabia financed militia groups to fight against the Soviets. One such group was the Jama'ah al-Dawa ila-l-Kita wa-l-Sunna (Group Preaching for the Qur'an and Sunna) of Jamil al-Rahman. Al-Rahman had studied with the Ahl-e-Hadith in Pakistan and was a follower of JSM scholars. He was troubled by the syncretic Islamic practices of the majority of Afghan fighters. This aligned with the *fatawa* (plural of *fatwa*) issued by Saudi Arabia's then-premier scholar, Shaykh 'Abd al-Aziz Bin Baz, who condemned the local practices of Afghan Muslims (Lacroix 2011). As the Afghan–Soviet conflict progressed, the Saudi regime – appropriately – became concerned about the war's political impact. However, Al-Rahman provided them with a group that was willing to follow the authority of Saudi-based scholars, which brought both the Jama'ah al-Dawa ila-l-Kita wa-l-Sunna and former members of the JSM back into favour.

Saudi Arabian fears that they could not control Islamic activism was not limited to the Afghan jihad. By allowing persecuted Islamic scholars from across the Middle East to teach in the kingdom in the 1960s and 1970s, they had inadvertently created an environment in which Muslim Brotherhood ideals mixed with the social conservativism of Wahhabist and Salafi practices. Known as the Sahwi (revival) movement, such scholars promoted a more puritan version of the Muslim Brotherhood, and became vocal proponents of religious, social and political reform in the kingdom.

Tension between the Saudi regime and the *sahwis* came to a head in the late 1980s and early 1990s. The flashpoint was the deployment of US troops on Saudi soil in response to the Iraqi invasion of Kuwait. As public opposition to the US troops mounted, the Saudi establishment clamped down on the *sahwi*, terminating their teaching contracts at universities and restricting their ability to deliver sermons in mosques. This directly benefitted Salafi scholars affiliated with Shaykh Muhammad Aman al-Jami, the head of the Hadith department at the Islamic University of Madinah – still a Salafist hotbed. Al-Jami and his followers emphasised the principle of *wali al-amr* (obedience to a ruler) as a Muslim obligation. Not only did this principle filter through to Salafi *da'wa* around the world, but by foregrounding its importance, al-Jami and his supporters were granted considerable favour by the Ministry of the Interior.

Rapprochement between Saudi authorities and Salafi intellectuals had global consequences. Through the International Islamic Relief Organisation, the Muslim World League, World Assembly of Muslim Youth, al-Haramain Foundation (officially disbanded in 2004), and branches of Saudi international educational institutions (including those in Indonesia), Salafis were able to fund and promote their *manhaj* globally. Yet as significant as this was for the movement, it did not bring Salafism under the control of Saudi Arabia. The continued existence of Salafi strands in Yemen, Kuwait, Jordan and the United Arab Emirates, as well as the Ansar al-Sunna al-Muhammadiya and Ahl e-Hadith, in Egypt and Pakistan respectively, ensured the movement lacked any one centre.

To complicate matters, at the end of the 20th century several of the most prominent Salafi scholars passed away.[5] Their deaths left the movement with no clear scholastic leaders, thus passing authority to a pool of revered, but less profound, scholars. Accordingly, there was, and remains, no central figure or institution that could dictate how Salafis across the world should act.

ISLAMIC REVIVAL IN NEW ORDER INDONESIA

Much like in Saudi Arabia, questions concerning Islamic authority and politics were very much alive in 20th-century Indonesia. During the late colonial period and early years of independence, trade unions, politicians and activists had attempted to use Islam as a unifying banner for the budding postcolonial polity. Islamic organisations such as the Muhammadiyah and Nahdlatul Ulama had been established to represent the diverse competing interests of the country's Muslims. Whereas Muhammadiyah drew from Muhammad Abduh's reformism, Nahdlatul Ulama represented the country's traditional establishment of religious *pesantren* (schools) and *kyai* (scholars). Adding to this picture was a lively push for an Islamic political project, driven by parties such as the Majelis Syuro Muslimin Indonesia (Council of Indonesian Muslim Associations, Masyumi), and the desire to

---

5   Notable among them were al-Albani, Muhammad al-Uthaymin (1929–2001), Muqbil bin Hadi al-Wadi'i (1933–2001) and the grand mufti, Abd al-Aziz Bin Baz (1910–1999).

enshrine Islam as the primary religion in the nation's constitution (Lukito 2012). While most advocates for an Islamist political project committed to pursue their goals peacefully, there was also a series of unsuccessful violent attempts to create a religious state, most notably through the Darul Islam (abode of Islam) rebellions in West Java, South Sulawesi, Kalimantan and Aceh during the 1940s–1960s.

The rich history of Islamic politics in the early years of independence has been well covered (e.g. Madinier 2015), and so I do not wish to repeat it in full here. But as the turbulent years of Indonesia's initial parliamentary democratic period (1949–1957) and President Sukarno's 'Guided Democracy'(1957–1966) gave way to the authoritarian regime of President Suharto's New Order (1967–1998), the opportunities for parliamentary Islamic politics or religious advocacy decreased dramatically. At the same time, the New Order regime oversaw rapid socio-economic development through years of steady growth, urbanisation and mass education.

The combination of political repression and economic development spurred a new wave of Islamic activism. Yet this generation of Indonesian Islamic activists no longer concerned themselves directly with politics, instead focusing their efforts on faith, authority, public philanthropy, education and religious services. This Islamic revivalism was deeply personal, and as Feely noted, penetrated further into social, cultural and even political life than it had in previous generations (Fealy 2008: 15).

This new generation of young Indonesian Muslims took advantage of emerging educational opportunities and technological advancements to tap into a broader global Islamic revivalism, communicating with like-minded persons around the world including with international Salafi scholars. The search for new ideas from abroad was exacerbated by Suharto's efforts to undermine the authority of established Islamic organisations and political parties. Despite the role Muslim militias had played in the anti-communist and anti-Chinese massacres of 1965–1967 that brought Suharto to power, official religious expression was curtailed by Suharto. The military who dominated the New Order elite, had spent more than ten years suppressing the Darul Islam (abode of Islam) uprisings (Dijk 1981; Juhannis 2006), and so were unwilling to share power with Islamic politicians and activists whose loyalty could not be guaranteed.

Grievances towards Suharto's regime had an ideological edge too. The New Order's understanding of national identity stressed notions of what

Bourchier (1998) has termed a conservative indigenism based on Javanese notions of communal assistance and *adat* (culture) rather than any archipelagic Muslim solidarity.[6] This did not mean that Islamic organisations ceased to exist; Suharto still used Islamic organisations to give his policies a nuance of religious legitimacy. However, the New Order – as part of a broader effort to 'depoliticise' a body politic – imposed tight restraints on Islamic activities, suspected communist sympathisers, ethnic Chinese, separatists, student activists, trade unionists and human rights lawyers. In this restrictive climate, the spectre of Islamic militancy played directly into state security narratives.[7]

Suharto's efforts to force all Islamic parties to adopt the national ideology of *Pancasila as their founding principle* became one of the most contentious issue for Islamic activists. Launched under the guise of national unity, this policy, known as the *asas tunggal* (founding principle) policy, caused huge concern amongst strict Muslims; most pointedly because they believed replacing Islam with *Pancasila* as the *raison d'être* of their organisation was un-Islamic. In 1984, for example, Muhammadiyah, Indonesia's largest Islamic reformist organisation, experienced intense internal disagreement about adopting *Pancasila* as its *asas tunggal*. In South Sulawesi, several Muhammadiyah activists broke away and formed what would become the Salafi activist group Wahdah Islamiyah. The Suharto policy also led to dissension amongst Islamic students in the Himpunan Mahasiswa Islam (HMI) (Islamic Student Organisation), a reformist student group with ties to former members of the Masyumi Islamic political party.[8] As a result, HMI split into two official factions, one of which refused to endorse the *asas tunggal*.

---

6   For example, see Djajadingrat-Nieuwenhuis 1987, Elmhirst 2000 and Pemberton 1994. It is noteworthy that the promotion of 'Javanese' values as essentially 'Indonesian', when combined with the government sponsored transmigration of Javanese to other parts of the country, only helped to ignite resentment of the dominance of Java (as a population and an idea) in the postcolonial state.

7   In 1977, for example, the government announced it had 'uncovered' links between the Islamic militant Komando Jihad (Jihad Command) and former Darul Islam families in West Java. In fact, unofficial connections between the group and sections of the Indonesian intelligence services had been well-documented, leading several to believe the sudden 'discovery' of the group was engineered to offset the popularity of the PPP in upcoming elections. See Mietzner 2009; Solahudin 2011.

8   Formed in 1947, the HMI maintained close links to Masyumi, playing a crucial role in the student protests during the mid-60s that helped lead to the downfall of Sukarno. However, its activism against Sukarno won it few favours from the new regime. This frustration became increasingly apparent in HMI thinking.

At the same time, the country was experiencing rapid economic development, increased access to education, rapid urbanisation and the introduction of new forms of technology (cassettes, TV and radio). From 1970 to 2010, the annual growth rate of the urban population was 4.2%, a figure higher than China (3.8%) and India (3.1%) (Samad 2012). Such mobility had an effect on Islamic authority, delinking many young Muslims from the practices of their parents or of religious activists from the early independence period. As these youth made their way into Indonesia's growing university education system, they were introduced to the religious study circles in them, which provided fertile ground for new religious responses to the political and economic climate.

There were two broad approaches that emerged from student religious circles in the 1970s and 1980s. On one side, a number of new intellectuals, such as Nurcholish Madjid, emerged to stress a new Islamic platform that has been referred to by Hefner as 'Civil Islam' (Hefner 2000). These scholars emphasised the need to reshape religious traditions into an inclusive project of social reform that would create a modern class of Muslim professionals not hostile to state ideology or to the pluralist nature of Indonesian society (Kersten 2015; Robinson 2008).

However, a rival position emerged that became associated with former Prime Minister Mohammad Natsir. Natsir believed the New Order had undermined the Islamic potential of the Indonesian *umma* (Muslim community) by foisting an anti-Islamic agenda on its population. Therefore, there was a need to theologically re-evaluate Islamic texts to spur collective action and a new religiously pious national identity amongst Muslims (Latif 2005: 391). These latter voices drew from a number of global religious doctrines, including Salafism, to make their case.

Scholars in both camps were responding to the same issues, yet it was the creation of *Dewan Dakwah Islamiyah Indonesia* (DDII) (Indonesian Islamic Propagation Council) in 1967 by Mohammad Natsir, which most directly catalysed the rise of globally oriented Islamic revivalism in Indonesia. Natsir saw the DDII as a move away from top-down politics to bottom-up social activities. As he jokingly stated, 'we are no longer conducting *da'wa* by means of politics but engaging in political activities by means of *da'wa*. The result will be the same' (Ihza 1995: 129). Having travelled extensively in the Middle East and South Asia during the 1950s, Natsir now used the links he had established abroad to transform the DDII into the predominant body through which Middle Eastern funds and scholarships flowed into Indonesia.

Natsir aimed to establish what he believed would be a young vanguard of activists. To that end, the DDII created the Islam Disiplin Ilmu (Islam as a Scientific Discipline) programme, which was established to train lecturers to speak in campus mosques at Indonesia's secular universities. This spawned a nationwide network of Lembaga Dakwah Kampus (LDKs) (Campus Propagation Boards) that spread to state universities throughout the country. Coinciding with the creation of LDKs, the DDII also funded the construction of a number of campus mosques that became centres where LDK activists could gather. These included the Salman Mosque at the Institut Teknologi Bandung (Bandung Institute of Technology), the Campus Mosque at Universitas Gadjah Madah (UGM) (Gadjah Madah University) in Yogyakarta, and the Arief Rahman Hakim Mosque at Universitas Indonesia (Indonesia University) in Jakarta. These mosques were surprisingly free from state surveillance, having circumvented suspicion by including the university rectors on their respective boards of trustees. The mosques were positioned as places where students could gather and discuss religion, life and society (Latif 2005).

DDII supplied the training and places where Islamic revival could occur, and they also provided scholarships to institutions in West and South Asia. As students who were trained in Islamic institutions abroad returned to Indonesia during the 1980s, they began using campus mosques to teach new-found religious ideals. They were fluent in Arabic and able to translate the array of Islamic literature they had become familiar with while overseas. For instance, the Muslim Brotherhood scholar Sayyid Qutb's *Ma'alim fi al-Tharsq* (Islamic Instruction) became compulsory reading for many campus activists. The idea of *ghazwul fikr* (war of ideas), which posited that Islamic civilisation was under threat from Western influence and ambitions, also became a popular lens through which to view modern political developments (Hooker & Fealy 2006). Such concepts were attributed to the Muslim Brotherhood and came to dominate the majority of campus LDKs in what became known as the Tarbiyah (education) movement (Bubalo et al. 2008).

The transmission of new Islamic doctrines undermined established forms of religious teaching in Indonesia. Where Nahdlatul Ulama and Muhammadiyah provided religious education through a vast network of *pesantren* and *madrasah*, the use of campus mosques offered another channel for the dispersion of religious information, often geared to those who had little previous engagement with Islamic scholasticism. Certainly, the mosque sermon had always been a pivotal medium through which to communicate with followers, but the campus movement began to use the Muslim Brotherhood *halaqah* (study circle) as their primary method of teaching. The *halaqah* is an informal gathering that stresses *tarbiyah*, personal morality, piety and the rejection of un-Islamic practices. It is normally led by senior students who act as *murabbi* (religious guides) (Van Bruinessen 2002: 133).

The *halaqah* was not a venue for explicit political indoctrination; rather, it focused on individual and moral self-improvement as the basis for any social betterment. Small *halaqah* were used to explain religious tenets using popular concepts and in that way appeal to students with contemporary lifestyles. This points to a qualitative shift amongst young urban Muslim students. As Latif (2005: 403) observes, compared to the 1960s or even the 1970s, by the 1980s university life 'revolved around the mosque and this intimacy caused the internalisation of an Islamic identity and Islamic mind-edness that was much deeper'. The effect of this shift is that Islam began to be seen as informing all aspects of public and private life, extending even to issues of marriage as student Islamic activists began to marry amongst themselves (Smith-Hefner 2005).

As this cadre of students left the campuses and moved on into the pro-fessional job market, Indonesia saw what Mahasin has termed the 'embour-geoisement of Muslim sons and daughters' (Hasbullah 2000: 15). Recent graduates mixed their pursuit of a religious identity with modern ideas of living, work and belonging in Indonesia. They created Muslim-oriented publications like the daily Republika, and established a variety of private elite Islamic schools and universities such as those linked to Nurcholish Madjid's Paramadina. A range of new Islamic products and clothing also began to emerge during this time, and it became more and more common to see women donning the *jilbab* (veil) in public.

By the 1980s, it was clear that Indonesia, like much of the Muslim world, was undergoing an Islamic revival that mixed notions of piety, class and modernism in ways not easily defined by the modernist Muhammadiyah / traditionalist Nahdlatul Ulama dichotomy that demarcated Islamic thought in the early independence period. Islamic authority was established, ques-tioned and consumed in ways that led to what Eickelman and Anderson

(2003: 13) call the 're-intellectualisation' of Islam. Piety and Islamic identity became congruent expressions of class identity. How one consumed specific commodities, watched particular preachers, or created new religious-inspired industries were considered avenues of religious expression.[9] For established Islamic organisations, the incursion of religion into new spheres of public activism posed a challenge. As a former head of Muhammadiyah explained, larger groups such as his own struggled to retain the appeal that had served them well for decades (Syamsuddin 1995).

This points to the enlargement of, to paraphrase the sociologist Manuel Castells, a knowledge economy – but with an Islamic flavour. As Castells notes, a knowledge economy arises when agents generate, process and apply knowledge-based information in a way that links global ideas of capitalist production and consumption with local methods of production, affiliation and action (Castells 2010). In Indonesia, one's Islam was increasingly expressed by which newspaper one read, which mosque one attended and even which motorbike bumper stickers one displayed (e.g., Hefner 1997; Lukens-Bull 2008; Muzakki 2008). Commodities, preachers and schools could be used to express and consume Islam in ways that identified one not just as pious, but as modern, educated and professional. These trends may have detached the idea of Islamic mobilisation from any explicitly political project, but they were nonetheless political, gradually percolating in public discourse through a visible surge in religious identity that continues to this day.

By the late 1980s and early '90s, the Muslim professional class began to successfully influenced legislative initiatives. They got the government to reverse the ban on headscarves in 1991 and pushed for the creation of an officially mandated *zakat* (tax and redistribution) body in 1993 (Effendy 2003: 113). An aging Suharto, increasingly criticised for the excessive corruption and nepotism of his regime, began to court Islamic intellectuals to prop up his rule. In 1991, he took a very public Hajj pilgrimage and allowed the Ikatan Cendekiawan Muslim Indonesia (ICMI) (Indonesian Association for Muslim Intellectuals) to be established. The ICMI was

---

9 Rudnyckyj's study of Islamic management training firms in Indonesia sheds light on how exactly this influences the external manifestations of Islamic faith and activism. He argues that the combination of market and faith produces a particular form of self that draws simultaneously from capitalist ideas of 'rational' behaviour and Islamic discourse to instil a specific idea of management (Rudnyckyj, 2009a, 2009b).

led by B.J. Habibie, the cabinet minister and Suharto affiliate who would replace Suharto as president in 1998.

This cooperative relationship between the Muslim professional class and the government created what Hefner (2000) calls a regimist Islam, used by Suharto to bolster the appeal of his rule. Indeed, many segments of the Islamic community welcomed Suharto's efforts of rapprochement during the 1990s, using the easing of the state's repression to openly propagate Islamism, build official schools and conduct public debate. Salafis in Yogyakarta – as we will see – benefitted tremendously from this trend, opening a number of officially recognised foundations and institutions.

As the New Order came under the scrutiny of pro-democracy actors during its final years, several Islamic groups came to Suharto's defence. This symbiotic relationship was reified through unofficial affiliations between members of the regime and conservative Islamic groups like the DDII and Prabowo Subianto, Suharto's son-in-law and head of the Indonesian military's Special Forces (Mietzner 2009).[10] However, Islamic expression had fundamentally shifted by the 1990s. It was not easy to convince or coerce all Muslim activists into supporting the New Order. Many campus-based Islamic activists were not swayed by short-term pragmatic political considerations and remained suspicious of Suharto's overtures. Indeed, religious authority had become ever more fragmented and difficult to control.

FOUNDATION OF SALAFISM IN
NEW ORDER YOGYAKARTA

The province of Yogyakarta was not exempt from the religious revivalist currents running through New Order Indonesia. Founded in 1755 after the division of Mataram into two competing kingdoms (the other half going to nearby Surakarta), Yogyakarta prides itself on its resistance to Dutch rule during the Java War (1825–1830) and the War of Independence (1945–1949). With a territory of 3,200km^2 and a population of approximately 3 million people, the Sultanate of Yogyakarta (known as the Sultanate of Ngajogjokarto Hadiningrat in Javanese) has played a pivotal role in the formation of the Indonesian state. Notably, the Sultan provided refuge for anti-Dutch forces during the War of Independence. As a result, the new republic

---

10 The linkages between Prabowo and Islamic intellectuals continue to this day, propping up his political ambitions in the twenty years since Suharto's resignation.

recognised the Sultanate as a *daerah istimewa* (special region) governed not by a provincial governor but by the Sultan directly. It is, consequently, an exception in Indonesia, as most pre-independence sultanates quickly faded in importance. To an extent, its special status protected Yogyakarta from the more coercive machinations of New Order governance, but the city remains a centre for cultural, nationalist and religious movements.

The sultanate is more than a system of government; it lies at the heart of a Yogyakartan identity. It co-exists alongside Indonesian ideas of nationalism and simultaneously maintains its own history, culture and authority (Woodward 2011). The Sultan's supporters believe it to be a protector of Javanese culture and religion, where the authority of the Sultan and his *kraton* (Sultan's court) mediate between the modernist tendencies of the republic and a respect for Javanese customs and language. [11] Local culture and spiritual practices – frequently referred to as *kejawaan* (Javaneseness) –influence the city's Islamic identity (Woodward 1989). Rich anthropological works attest to the overlap between Islam and cultural practices, such as the *slametan* (ritual meal) or *dukun* (spiritual healer) (Beatty 1999; Woodward 2011). Yet the sultanate also prides itself as a foundation on which an Indonesian civilisation was formed. Many early nationalist and reformist currents that shaped the Indonesian nation originated in Yogyakarta. These include the Islamic reformist Muhammadiyah and the cultural Taman Siswa.

Cutting across the spectrum of Islamic tradition, Yogyakarta is home to a large number of universities, including the prestigious Universitas Gadjah Madah (UGM) (Gadjah Madah University), Universitas Islam Negeri Sunan Kalijaga (Islamic State University of Sunan Kalijaga) and Universitas Negeri Yogyakarta (UNY) (Yogyakarta State University). A large proportion of the sultanate's population – especially in the city's north – are students drawn from across the archipelago and so not obvious followers of *kejawaan*. These students develop a bond with the city and its heritage while retaining their ties to their own regional and national identities. This results in unique student cultural and religious associations. Many of the city's universities are also home to campus mosques that have become

---

11 It was not unknown for Muslims to pray towards the Sultan's palace rather than Mecca until the early 20th century. This practice only began to die out after the protests of Ahmad Dahlan, the founder of the reformist Islamic organisation Muhammadiyah, who was originally a religious scholar in the Sultan's court.

spaces where new global ideas of Islamic identity have been inculcated and, as I argue, spread across the city and its people.

While Yogyakarta prides itself on its local identity of *kejawaan* and the Sultan, the city has also taken on a more modern outlook. Rapid urbanisation and a young student and migrant population have altered Yogyakarta in ways that have decreased the emphasis on social rank, Javanese language and traditional rituals (Guinness 2009). Students have transformed the north end of the city into an area of coffee shops, fashion outlets (*distro*), student accommodation and bookshops. Tapping into popular ideas of youth culture and patterns of economic consumption and aspiration, this contrasts with the spiritual and even artistic emphasis of the city's Javaneseness. Yogyakarta is thus not only an entity with its own identity but also a space where ideas of culture, religion and belonging are constantly being defined and redefined. It is, as Woodward reminds us, 'an array of hybridities in which pre-colonial, colonial and postcolonial Java and Indonesia all figure significantly'(Woodward 2011: 18).

The DDII provided the way for Salafism to make inroads into Yogyakarta. While not outright Salafi, the DDII was more than willing to work with global Salafi funders to facilitate the transfer of funds, ideas and individuals into Indonesia. In 1980, the DDII assisted in establishing an Arabic language centre in Jakarta that evolved into the Lembaga Ilmu Pengetahuan Islam dan Arab (LIPIA) (Institute for the Study of Islam and Arabic). The LIPIA is a branch of the Imam Muhammad ibn Saud University of Riyadh and, in its formative years, worked almost exclusively with the DDII to provide language training to activists who wished to study in Saudi Arabia (Hasan 2007). By 1984, it had become a major hub for the circulation of the works of several key Salafi and Wahhabist scholars. As LIPIA's alumni network expanded, it became a vital conduit through which Salafi ideas were translated and disseminated. Moreover, the first generation of Indonesian Salafi scholars, including Abu Nida, Yusuf Baisa, Ahmas Faiz Asifuddin and Aunur Rafiq Ghufron, received DDII-sponsored religious training both abroad and at LIPIA. These were the scholars who spearheaded the spread Salafism.

In Yogyakarta, Abu Nida (born Chamsaha Sofwan) made a concerted effort to preach the Salafi doctrine. Born in Gresik, East Java, in 1954, he was educated at a Nahdlatul Ulama educational institution before he moved to the Pesantren Karangasem, in Paciran, Lamongon, East Java at the age of

22. Pesantren Karangasem was participating in a DDII-sponsored initiative called *Transmigrasi Da'i* (transmigration preacher), the aim of which was to send students to remote areas of the archipelago to preach. Through this programme, Abu Nida spent two years in West Kalimantan – an area of deeply rooted indigenous beliefs and home to a number of competing Christian missionaries – where he successfully set up a mosque in his assigned village.

Having impressed DDII officials, Abu Nida received a scholarship to study Arabic at LIPIA before enrolling at the Imam Muhammad Ibn Saud University in Riyadh. While studying in Saudi Arabia, he was employed at the DDII coordination office in Riyadh (Hasan 2006). This work put him in direct contact with donors including the Kuwait-based Jama'iyyat Ihya' Al-Turath al-Islami, which would become Abu Nida's main sponsor several years later. After completing his studies, Abu Nida briefly joined Jamil al-Rahman's Jama'ah al-Dawa ila-l-Kita wa-l-Sunna to fight against the Soviets in Afghanistan in 1985, returning to Indonesia three months later. Again, it was the DDII who assisted him upon his return, and he briefly took up a teaching position at the Pesantren al-Mukmin in Solo. This *pesantren* was infamous for its linkages to Jemaah Islamiyah and the Bali bombers of 2002.

In 1986, Abu Nida moved to Yogyakarta where he was invited to teach at the newly established Pesantren Ibnul Qoyim by Saefullah Mahyuddin, its founder and head of DDII Yogyakarta. He did not teach there for long because staff became concerned about his opposition to the education of women – a view he later dropped when he started his own schools. Meanwhile, Saefullah, a lecturer at the UGM, introduced Abu Nida to the UGM's campus Lembaga Dakwah Kampus (LDK), known as the Jemaah Salahuddin. The Jemaah Salahuddin assisted Abu Nida in organising lectures at the university, which he quickly expanded to include several mosques in other nearby campuses. By 1988, Abu Nida had gained a sufficient following amongst students to organise a month-long religious instruction course, or *daurah*, where he trained several followers to become *murabbi*. These students were tasked with arranging smaller *halaqah*, where they taught university students.

SPLITS WITHIN LATE NEW ORDER SALAFISM

The alliance between Abu Nida and the Jemaah Salahuddin disintegrated by 1990, and Abu Nida and his followers were forced out of the UGM. Nonetheless, he had firmly established himself in the city, and was able to call upon a growing network of other Salafi preachers who were filtering into the city. Umar Budiharjo was an independent but like-minded scholar who had also attended Pesantren Karangasem. Like Abu Nida, Budiharjo had trained abroad, receiving a scholarship to study at the Islamic University of Madinah (graduating in 1985) before completing his masters at Islamabad University in 1987. In 1993, he opened Pesantren Asy-Syifa, a Muhammadiyah-affiliated school in Bantul. The school's curriculum followed a range of Salafi works and was Yogyakarta's first Salafi *pesantren* to educate the growing movement's adherents and their children. After Suharto's resignation, Budiharjo separated his school from Muhammadiyah and relocated it to the north of the city. He also opened two other schools and named them Pesantren Taruna al-Qur'an.

Adding to this expanding Salafi network was Abdul Afifi Wadud, who became a close ally of Abu Nida. Unlike Abu Nida and Umar Budiharjo, Wadud was a native of Yogyakarta and learnt about Salafism through self-study. His charismatic style made Wadud a popular figure amongst high school students in the north of the city. Many of my interlocutors credited Wadud with influencing their Salafi activism more than anyone else. Wadud also proved one could be pious yet economically savvy. He opened the first Salafi store in Yogyakarta in 1994, close to the UGM campus. It quickly became a hub for religious commodities and a source of employment for students wishing to subsidise their studies with part-time work (the store is described in greater detail in chapters 3 and 5). Indeed, if Abu Nida's *halaqah* and Umar Budiharjo's educational institutions provided two spaces where followers could converge to inculcate a specific religious outlook, Wadud's store offered an additional nodal point where activists could plan, assist each other and work together.

The creation of new religious schools, foundations and stores provided a religious environment where Salafis could develop their *da'wa* independently from the DDII, Jemaah Salahuddin and LIPIA. By the early 1990s Salafi scholars were able to circumvent the DDII and receive funding directly from international donors, although many still worked with the organisation. For his part, Abu Nida used connections made during his educational experience abroad to contact potential allies in the Arabian Peninsula. By 1993, Abu Nida significantly expanded his activities by establishing the Ma'had Tahfizhul Qur'an ('Ma'had' refers to an informal religious school) and, in the same year, created a Salafi village in Wirokerten, Bantul Regency (in the city's south) where his more avid followers could reside and study. In 1994 he formally founded the Yayasan Majelis at-Turots Al-Islamy (Majelis at-Turots al-Islamy Foundation, at-Turots) and, a year later built the Ma'had Jamilurrahman as-Salafy with the financial help of Saudi Shaykh Muhammad Ibn Muhammad Jabir Al-Madkhali.

No sooner had Salafis established themselves than the movement became fraught with internal conflict and division. Jafar Umar Thalib caused the most serious rift. He had come to Yogyakarta at Abu Nida's invitation and became known for his charisma, his hot-headedness and his vocal opposition to those he considered non-Salaf. Born in 1961 in Malang, he enrolled in LIPIA in 1983 but fell out with his teachers and never completed his degree. He was nonetheless able to obtain a scholarship to study at the Maududi Institute in Lahore, Pakistan, where he first became familiar with the Ahl e-Hadith movement. In 1987 he left Lahore to join the Afghan jihad, spending a brief spell with Abdul Rasul Sayyaf's Jama'ah-I Islami before linking up with Jamil al-Rahman's Jama'ah al-Dawa ila-l-Kita wa-l-Sunna.[12] Upon returning to Indonesia, Thalib took up a teaching position at Pesantren Al-Irsyad in Salatiga, yet left again in 1990. He then used the connections he had made in Afghanistan to go to Yemen to study under Muqbil ibn Hadi al-Wadi'i. Arriving in Yemen, Thalib became seriously ill and returned home after only three months. Nevertheless, his brief study with al-Wadi'i left a deep impression and strengthened both his connection to al-Wadi'i and his commitment to Salafi doctrine (Hasan 2006).

In 1993, newly established in Yogyakarta, Thalib publicly criticised Yusuf Baisa, the director of Pesantren al-Irsyad, his previous school. The rift between Thalib and Baisa emerged when Baisa allegedly stated that the Salafi *aqida* (creed) should be complemented by the organisational skills of the Muslim Brotherhood and wisdom of the Jemaah Tabligh movement. Though Thalib and Baisa initially made amends, Baisa continued to irritate Thalib by recommending readings the latter considered to have political

---

12 Abdul Rasul Sayyaf's Jama'ah-I Islami is worth mentioning. His group was linked to the Indonesian-inspired Salafi jihadist Jemaah Islamiyah. This demonstrates the overlap between different Salafi positions, at least in the 1970–80s.

leanings (ICG 2004: 13). At the heart of it was Baisa's alleged willingness to compromise the purity of the Salafi message, and Thalib quickly began to expand his criticism to anyone he perceived to be working with non-Salafi groups, such as the campus LDKs and DDII. This inevitably came to include Abu Nida, given his involvement with the DDII, thus dividing Yogyakartan Salafis into two camps.

Both camps remained loyal to Salafi scholars in the Arabian Peninsula. However, those closer to Thalib became affiliated almost exclusively to al-Wadi 'i's network of Yemeni schools, which questioned Saudi Arabia's pre-eminent position in the movement. Meanwhile, Abu Nida strengthened his linkages to the Kuwaiti Jama'iyyat Ihya' Al-Turath al-Islami foundation and the Saudi religious establishment (via the Saudi embassy in Jakarta). This gave the split a global dimension, especially when Thalib began sending his students to Yemen. This led commentators to dub his Salafi followers as the 'Yemeni network' (Hasan 2010; ICG 2004).

Salafism was thus divided into two groups who frequented different mosques, established their own schools and ran separate activities. Physical confrontations, although rare, also erupted, especially at mosques in the vicinity of UGM. It was more common, though, that each network would critique the other in their magazines and lectures. Thalib went out of his way to insult Baisa, Abu Nida and their supporters for abandoning what he believed to be Salafi purity. He labelled them Sururis after the scholar Muhammad ibn Surur al-Nayef Zayn al-'Abidin, who was living in exile in London as he had openly opposed the acceptance by many Saudi religious scholars of US troops on Saudi soil. Ibn Surur, seen as an overtly political scholar of Islam, was linked to the Sahwi movement in Saudi Arabia, and so the use of his name by Thalib was meant to denigrate 'deviant' non-Salafi leanings (ICG 2004).

CONTINUED FRAGMENTATION

The schism amongst Yogyakartan Salafis became increasingly intractable as each side escalated their rhetoric. It took on a global dimension not only because of the global references (such as Sururi) and the involvement of Middle Eastern scholars, but also because religious donors from Saudi Arabia and Kuwait were angered that Thalib had split the movement and so channelled their funds to Abu Nida's camp. Nationally, Abu Nida's network received support from many of the founding generation of Indonesian Salafis. This included Yazid bin Abdul Qadir Jawas, a former colleague of Thalib, who became and remained his most vocal critic until Thalib's death in 2019.

Nevertheless, Thalib's popularity continued to grow and his followers established several new schools in Yogyakarta, including the Ma'had Al-Anshar complex and Pesantren Difa'anis Sunnah (both led by instructors who had studied under al-Wadi'i in Yemen). As students graduated from Thalib's school, the Pesantren Ihya As-Sunnah, they set up their own schools across Java. Thalib's network came to include no less than 14 *pesantren* in Java, although Wahid (2006: 11) believes the real number to be in the hundreds.

This meant that, by the time Indonesia entered the democratic *reformasi* period in 1998, Salafism was firmly established but also deeply divided. This split, as the next chapter will show, led to a decentralised movement in which different Salafi networks sought to monopolise claims of being pure Salafi by de-legitimising rivals within the movement. There are no fewer than five opposing networks, yet these splits and differences should not lead us to conclude that Salafism has failed or lost its potency due to lack of internal cohesion. Regardless of how bitter the competition became between Thalib's followers and those linked to at-Turots, they both continued to draw from the same religious works and scholars, holding identical ideas of *aqida*, albeit differing slightly in their *manhaj* (method). Regardless of the number of networks, Salafism continued to grow across Indonesia.

From a social movement perspective, there is one final point to make. For a movement that claims strict adherence to a religious orthodoxy, disputes such as those mentioned previously allude to competition for leadership and materials. Yet they also emphasise an acute awareness of social and political issues. Scholars across the country inevitably had to answer to a variety of local political challenges as well as anxieties amongst their followers. As I will discuss, religious meaning is necessarily mediated through a blend of scripture and context. Campus lectures, schools, online media, religious villages and shops all provide a framework of intersecting environments which mutually reinforce the idea of a Salafi community. They also provide the movement with spaces for debates about how best to adapt and reform in light of emerging social pressures. It is to these spaces and the actors in them that I now turn.

CHAPTER 2

Twenty-First-Century Salafi Expansion: Opportunities, Actors and Spaces

'In January 1999 rioting in Ambon had started but by January 2000 it had yet to stop, and the government pretended it was incapable of dealing with the problem. In the end, after waiting one year, I could not be silent any longer and in January 2000 I made the Resolusi Jihad at a Tabligh Akbar in Yogyakarta ... in April 2000 I created the Laskar Jihad in Senayan, Jakarta and in May 2000, I left for Ambon and there we were in combat.'

—Jafar Umar Thalib, Interview, 22 November 2011

I n the spring of 2000, a little less than two years after President Suharto resigned amid mass protests, Jakarta's streets were again filled with demonstrators. These demonstrations were not the mosaic of student groups railing against economic turmoil, political repression and corruption that had taken to the streets two years prior. Instead, they consisted of bearded men wearing white Islamic robes – several of whom were brandishing swords. Led by the charismatic Islamic scholar Jafar Umar Thalib, these protestors were members of Indonesia's growing Salafi community, marching in solidarity with Muslims from Eastern Indonesia's Maluku province.[1] The year before, Maluku had become embroiled in a conflict that had taken a sectarian turn, pitting Muslims against their Christian neighbours. Thalib rallied his supporters to the defence of Muslims, and on 6 April he spoke to a gathering in Indonesia's national stadium. Attended by approximately 10,000 people, he declared the formation of the Laskar Jihad, a brigade that would enter the Maluku conflict on the side of Muslim communities.

This demonstration was part of a larger pattern of mobilisation amongst Indonesia's Salafi community that – as explained in the last chapter – had

---

1   The conflict erupted in 1999 after a fight at a bus terminal in the province's capital, Ambon, and quickly took on sectarian currents, pitting Muslim communities against their Christian neighbours. For more information, see ICG 2000.

been growing across Indonesia. The Laskar Jihad captured the national imagination at the time. The press debated the significance of Salafism, while volunteers collected donations at traffic lights and distributed free bulletins recalling the plight of Muslims and reminding the public of the Laskar Jihad (Hefner 1999). The weekly news magazine Tempo noted that Laskar Jihad was different from other Islamic groups, stating, 'the appearance of these soldiers is compelling: [wearing] long white robes and carrying samurai swords, swords or machetes' (Zulkifli et al. 2000: 24).

With the benefit of hindsight, we know that Laskar Jihad was short-lived, disbanding just over two years after it was formed, and represented only a minority of Indonesia's Salafi community. The brigade was nonetheless significant because it signalled a violent rupture in an otherwise peaceful grassroots movement predominantly concerned with education, welfare and proselytisation. Indeed, Laskar Jihad's influence lives on, not least for those affected by their involvement in the conflict in Maluku (Schulze 2017). It brought many young Muslim men – who joined Laskar Jihad with little awareness of Salafism – into the fold. Thalib's actions in Maluku, occurring as they did when Islamic militancy was becoming a concern both nationally (after Jemaah Islamiyah had conducted a series of church bombings at Christmas in 2000) and globally (in the aftermath of the 9/11 attacks), created an environment of suspicion towards Salafis that they have never been able to shake.

This chapter examines the dynamics and structural factors that have enabled the appeal of Salafism to grow and continue to resonate in Yogyakarta, despite such suspicions. While I maintain that the movement remains without a central, recognised hierarchy, Yogyakartan Salafis have create a particular understanding through which to promote their religious ideals. I will offer a brief account of the historical developments that have defined Salafism in the 21st century, and distinguish between those affiliated with Jafar Umar Thalib and Abu Nida, before focussing on the networks loosely affiliated with the at-Turots foundation. The at-Turots network has been far more versatile in the way it has adapted to post-Suharto Indonesia, mobilising followers, doctrines and resources through a specific arrangement of actors, structures and spaces. I offer an account of the composition of Salafism as well as a typology of actors and spaces that influence these actors. While actors and spaces cannot remain detached from the discursive and structural pressures present in the greater locale of Yogyakarta, they nonetheless fit together in a way that enables Salafis to promote a particular form of religious lifestyle – and this has allowed the movement to grow in 21st century Indonesia.

THE EARLY REFORMASI

Suharto's fall from power led to an unprecedented loosening of political restrictions, but also to a period of political instability. With his resignation, the logic that underpinned the coercive nature of the New Order collapsed (Siegel 2006) and this initially led to a steep rise in sectarian and ethnic conflict in Maluku (1999–2002), Poso (1998–2001) and Kalimantan (1999–2000) as well as an increased prominence of religious vigilantes and bombings. Much of this activity was, in some shape or form, interpreted as having religious significance tied to wider concerns over the position of Islam in the post-Suharto period (Sidel 2006).

Salafism was not detached from such anxieties, although their response differed greatly depending on whether or not they were allied to Jafar Umar Thalib. As the financial and political crises deepened, Thalib became a vocal opponent of democracy, believing that it would disrupt the growing Islamic forces that had so recently been encouraged by Suharto (Thalib 1998). This antagonistic position was solidified when Habibie, Suharto's immediate successor, began involving hard-line Muslim organisations to defend his presidency against the democratic movement. In this way, Thalib gained access to institutional actors and resources, which strengthened his resolve to mobilise politically (Hasan 2006).

In January 2000, three months after the Nahdlatul Ulama scholar and reformer Abdurrahman Wahid replaced Habibie as president, Jafar Umar Thalib mobilised his supporters for political action, taking care to situate his change of heart regarding politics squarely within the Salafi doctrine. Filling the Kridosono Sports Stadium in Yogyakarta, he established the Forum Komunikasi Ahlus Sunnah wal-Jama'ah (FKAWJ) (Forum for Followers of the Sunna and the Community of the Prophet), which concerned itself with ongoing violence in Maluku that had erupted in early 1999 between Christians and Muslims. The FKAWJ proclaimed a *Resolusi Jihad* (Jihad Resolution) which stated that it was obligatory for Muslims to be prepared for jihad against 'the enemies of Islam' (Hasan 2006). Thalib may have framed the conflict as an emotive call to defend

Muslims, but there were signs he had prepared for widespread mobilisation well before May 2000. While partaking in the Hajj in 1999, both he and his colleague Muhammad As-Sewed had obtained *fatawa* from leading Salafi scholars who agreed with his appeal for physical jihad in Maluku.[2]

Between 2000 and 2002, Thalib dispatched approximately 7,000 fighters to Maluku where, alongside other Islamic militias, they took up arms against the Christian population. As the FKAWJ and Laskar Jihad became more intimately involved in the conflict, their rationale for fighting evolved. If Thalib initially believed the government was unwilling to help Muslims, he later began to label the Christian militias they were fighting as separatist elements working against the state. Hasan (2006: 113) eloquently notes that the FKAWJ had begun to incorporate elements of national discourse into their pronouncements as a way to expand the resonance of their message. Together with DDII's Media Dakwah magazine and the Muslim Brotherhood publication Sabili, the Maluku conflict was by 2002 framed as a Christian led separatist campaign to undermine the integrity of the (Muslim) Indonesian nation. Laskar Jihad thus blended nationalist arguments of state unity with religious doctrine.

The combined appeal to Muslim solidarity and nationalism resonated with many young Muslim men. Mobile phones and the internet enabled FKAWJ offices in Java's cities to receive updates from those involved in the conflict. These were then compiled, edited, printed and distributed as monthly bulletins and daily information sheets handed out by volunteers at major urban traffic junctions across the country (Hefner 1999). This was an effective way to reach a much larger audience than the Salafi study circles from which the FKAWJ originated.

Despite the rapid deployment of thousands of volunteers, Laskar Jihad was unable to sustain itself for more than two years. Reluctantly, Thalib disbanded the group on the 3 October 2002, a week before the Bali Bombings,

---

2   This included Shaykh Rabi al-Madkhali, Shaykh Salih al-Suhaimi, Shaykh Wahid al-Jabiri, Shaykh Muhammad bin Hadi al-Madkhali, Shaykh Abdul Muhsin al-'Abbad and Shaykh Muqbil al-Wadi'i, all of whom agreed that waging jihad to defend Muslims was *fard al-ain* (an individual obligation), although with varying nuances. For instance, Al-Madkhali stressed that, should the government attempt to stop your waging of jihad, then you should not obey. Meanwhile, Rabi' bin Hadi al-Madkholi stated that jihad to help Muslims under attack for religious reasons was always obligatory (ICG, 2004). It is noteworthy that these shaykhs were approached again by Thalib's followers to disband Laskar Jihad.

after members voiced their concerns with Thalib's political posturing. They believed Thalib was using Laskar Jihad to further his own public persona. His frequent radio and television appearances solidified his image as a controversial but well-known Indonesian religious celebrity. His leading lieutenants, Muhammad As-Sewed and Luqman Ba'abduh thus returned to Saudi Arabia to consult the same *shaykh* who had previously supported Thalib. In response, this *shaykh* passed new rulings calling for the disbandment of Laskar Jihad. One, Shaykh Rabi bin Hadi al-Madkhali, voiced his disappointment at what he saw as Thalib's deviation, and belief he had created a Muslim Brotherhood-inspired – rather than a Salafi – jihad (ICG 2004).

After the demise of the FKAWJ, Thalib lost the limelight and much of his prestige in the Salafi community. Until his death in 2019, he continued to run a small religious school in north Yogyakarta and occasionally made public appearances – as when he called for the death of Jakarta governor Basuki Tjahaja Purnama in 2017 (Rogers 2017). Yet such pronouncements were almost always reactive and never led to the mass support he had prior to 2002. Nevertheless, Laskar Jihad's two-year recruitment and media blitz pushed activists loyal to its interpretation of Salafism into new areas in the archipelago, and so remnants of what was once the FKAWJ have continued to expand their remit ever since (Wahid 2006).

Once disbanded, FKAWJ members split into at least three factions, each following a different former member of the Laskar Jihad. These factions vigorously oppose one another and spend considerable time contesting each other's legitimacy (Sunarwoto 2016). One group follows Dzulqarmain, the former head of the FKAWJ's *fatwa* board. Dzulqarnain, who attended the Dar al-Hadith in Yemen, currently runs a school in Makassar. His followers are scattered around Indonesia, but they are most influential in South Sulawesi, where he was born.

Alongside the Dzulqarmain network is a competing Salafi strand led by Abu Turab al-Jawi. There is little information on this group. However, Abu Turab's split from the FKWAJ was the result of schisms at the Dar al-Hadith in Yemen following the death of its founder Muqbil al-Wadi'i. Whereas most former FKAWJ leaders believed the scholar Abd al-Rahman al-Adeni should lead the Dar al-Hadith, Abu Turab was closer to al-Rahman's rival, Yahya al-Hujuri (who ultimately gained control of the institution). The schism at the Dar al-Hadith thus reverberated within Indonesia, and only Abu Turab remained close to the new head.

The largest group formerly linked to the FKAWJ is the As-Syariah network, named informally after the popular magazine they produce. This network's most popular preachers are some of Thalib's key former lieutenants, including Muhammad As-Sewed and Luqman Ba'abduh. Ba'abduh has become the most prolific preacher in this network and runs a large Salafi school (Ma'had as-Salafy) in Jember, East Java. One of the As-Syariah network's centres is the Ma'had al-Anshar in Yogyakarta, currently led by Abdul Mu'thi, a former student of al-Wadi'i. Al-Anshar has trained numerous aspiring preachers through intense *mulazamah* or individual study under an Islamic mentor. Education relies on study circles that focus on learning specific religious texts under the guidance of tutors. Upon completing and memorising a given topic, the student receives *ijaza* (accreditation) and can move on to another work and/or teacher.

It was at the Ma'had al-Anshar that I met Ramli, who was then a 25-year-old student from Magelang, Central Java. Having originally undertaken religious studies in Bogor, he moved to al-Anshar in 2009 to be closer to his parents (Magelang is an hour's drive from Yogyakarta). He had heard of the school through magazines and word of mouth, and an *ustadz* in Bogor helped him to take up a position there. He believed his experience at al-Anshar was important to his quest to become a learned Muslim. It not only strengthened his religious knowledge but also gave him a community in which he could find a wife and start a family.

Ramli hoped to receive *ijaza* and augment his credibility as a legitimate teacher, but he also enjoyed living in what he perceived to be a pure Islamic community. While I discuss Islamic spaces in more detail below, it is noteworthy that Ma'had al-Anshar is in a Salafi dominated village founded by Ustadz Muhammad As-Sewed. It is home to approximately 300 followers who live in a village surrounded by rice fields and small farming communities, whose residents are easily distinguishable from Salafi residents due to the latter's strict dress code and social schedule (which revolves around prayer). Male residents of the Salafi village sport wispy beards, avoid *isbal* (trousers below the ankle) and wear *jalabiyaa* (robes). They spend their day conducting business between the hours of prayer. Some are involved in the sale of religious books, while others run herbal medicine stands, work as mosque caretakers or involve themselves in construction projects or farming.

It is a clean, simple and quiet village. Most houses are of modest decor, and few residents own cars. The only buildings that stand out in this humble environment are the mosque complex and the village's religious bookshop, Gema Ilmu (echo of knowledge). Both are plain and unadorned but well maintained and well resourced. Gema Ilmu employees, for example, have access to computers, and are able to use a company mini-van to shuttle between the store and other parts of the city to deliver books (which could also be ordered online). The well-tended appearance of these buildings attests to their importance and centrality in promoting the Salafi doctrine and the village to outsiders. Gema Ilmu staff hand out small religious books for free at local weddings and distribute flyers to clients to promote Salafism and invite them to the community's annual training session or *daurah* (Interview, Yogyakarta, 27 February 2012).

The bookstore and school play an important role in fostering the internal cohesion of the community, but the mosque is the key. The community comes together there for evening lectures and to discuss issues concerning the village, especially those that challenge the notion of religious purity. Sermons in the mosque emphasise that maintaining pious behaviour at all time is of utmost importance to save oneself from incorrect practices and to provide a religious environment for children.

Notably few residents have attended tertiary education, with most having completed high school in or around Yogyakarta. This is mainly due to their disdain for secular education, a belief found across all former FKAWJ networks. The lower levels of academic achievement are reflected in the career choices of the residents. One interlocutor who had lived in the complex for over ten years was a construction worker and freelance handyman (Interview, Yogyakarta, 27 February 2012). Another informant who ran a small bookstore subsidised his income by rearing goats (Interview, Yogyakarta, 27 February 2012).

Outside hours of prayer and religious lectures, the village felt empty as men busied themselves with a combination of study and work. The need to find multiple sources of income is not surprising given the larger-than-normal families and abstention from government-linked social development initiatives. It also meant that women worked from home to subsidise the family income. According to one interlocutor, the women would gather to bake cakes, sew clothes or prepare medicinal products to sell locally or on the Internet (Interview, Yogyakarta, 27 February 2012). Although stressing that a women's primary role is to look after the education and welfare of the family, women often got together in each other's houses during the day to study, assist one another with projects or just relax.

Ma'had al-Anshar and its surrounding community is an example of how the remnants of the FKAWJ have developed since 2002. Despite rivalries between different factions, these networks remain, and the influx of students to al-Anshar is testimony to the sustained appeal of this faction of Salafism. Yet the disagreements between former FKAWJ members attest to an inwardly focused obsession with defining purity that has hindered the movement's ability to form a cohesive whole, or to adequately adapt to shifts in Indonesia's socio-political climate.

Activists at the al-Anshar do not engage with government offices unless absolutely required (in cases of death, marriage or birth for example), and this has been consistent regardless of who holds power in Jakarta. The community has advocated for isolation, and the lack of large donors and the ongoing conflict in Yemen – where promising students used to go for study – has reinforced their disconnection from large swathes of Indonesian society. This is in stark contrast to Salafi networks that did not side with Jafar Umar Thalib during the Maluku conflict. It is to these networks I now turn my attention.

THE AT-TUROTS NETWORK

Although I was fortunate to have spent time with those previously affiliated with the FKAWJ, the bulk of my research involved activists that were on the receiving end of Thalib's hostility during the 1990s. Thalib's animosity to Abu Nida and those he claimed to be Sururi angered numerous large donor organisations in the Arabian Peninsula, who retaliated by diverting their funding away from him. In turn, his opponents used their superior financial resources to expand their *da'wa* (propagation) while simultaneously disputing the legitimacy of his FKAWJ.

Non-FKAWJ preachers such as Afifi Wadud, Umar Budiharjo and Abu Nida played on Thalib's political opportunism to bolster their own position as the true representatives of a pure Salafism. They promoted a politically quietist alternative, emphasising the need to remain outside any confrontational form of politics. For them, there was no contradiction in condemning democracy as a man-made entity that ran counter to Islam, while simultaneously remaining loyal to government leaders (provided they protected

Muslims) through the concept of *wali al-amr* (obedience to a ruler). Thalib, they argued, was unable to understand this and, as his actions in Maluku showed, was more interested in his own stature than in religious scripture.[3]

The strength of this argument was enhanced by its timing. It occurred just as the Al Qaeda-linked Jemaah Islamiyah were ramping up their bombing campaign in Indonesia. Indeed, the US-led War on Terror had implications for both religious funding bodies and Islamic political mobilisation. Abu Nida's biggest donor, the Kuwaiti Jama'iyyat Ihya' Al-Turath al-Islami, was added to the US Treasury Department's list of organisations funding terrorism. Despite US requests, however, the Kuwaiti government refused to close it down. This was mainly because the head of the Jama'iyyat Ihya' Al-Turath al-Islami had been replaced in the 1990s with Shaykh 'Abdullah Sebt, who was much closer to the Kuwaiti ruling family and less willing to fund political Islamic activism (Pall 2013).

While Kuwaiti support gave Jama'iyyat Ihya' Al-Turath al-Islami a new lease on life, it also meant the organisation came under near-total state control, and so funding was allocated to organisations who were not hostile to the Kuwaiti or their home (in this case, Indonesian) governments (Pall 2013). By not taking to the streets as Thalib did, those close to Abu Nida benefitted from these pressures and were able to use funds to create new foundations, schools and social services. Moreover, by not explicitly engaging with ongoing political debates, they were able to create a niche in the Islamic lecturing scene at a time when the FKAWJ, Muslim Brotherhood and militancy of Jemaah Islamiyah were increasingly visible. These Salafi preachers framed their doctrine as one for those who wished to learn about Islam but were overwhelmed by national political debates and the plethora of political actors claiming to represent Islam.

This message gained a moderate following on Yogyakarta's university campuses through groups such as the Yayasan Pendidikan Islam al-Atsary (YPIA, Al-Atsary Islamic education foundation), a Salafi student organisation formed in 2000, where I spent a significant amount of time. According to one of its founding members, the YPIA's roots lay in informal lectures organised by students who, having attended Salafi sermons during high

---

3   For example, his former colleague Yazid bin Abdul Qadir Jawas pointed to his inability to finish his studies at LIPIA, in Pakistan or in Yemen as proof that he was an antagonistic hot-headed figure, always confronting others rather than consulting doctrine. For more information, see Jawas 2004.

school, wished to continue such learning on campus (Interview, Yogyakarta, 28 March 2012). Building on concerns that Islam was increasingly in the public spotlight, the YPIA was a forum to connect with preachers who would promote a pure and de-politicised Islam, that was somewhat universal and outside the political climate (Interview, Yogyakarta, 28 March 2012; Interview, Yogyakarta, 24 April 2012).

Key to the formation of the YPIA was Afifi Abdul Wadud. Many of the YPIA's founding members had attended his sermons while at high school and they made an effort to invite him and his colleagues, also affiliated to the at-Turots, to their campus activities. Since its creation, the YPIA has expanded its activities and at present runs several educational programmes including informal lectures for potential converts/reverts in the student body. Arguably, it has become Yogyakarta's pre-eminent student Salafi foundation, and – as I show in the upcoming chapters – this has much to do with its members' ability to adapt to the post-Suharto climate. Yet it is not the only Salafi-inspired student foundation to emerge in Indonesia during the 2000s. Similar groups have become popular in Bogor (the Himpunan Ahlus Sunna Mahasiswa Islam, or HASMI), Makassar (Wahdah Islamiyah) and Bandung (the Yayasan An-Nuur Madinah).

University campus-based Salafi activism is complemented by the expansion of schools, mosques and foundations. In Yogyakarta, Umar Budiharjo relocated his Pesantren Asy-Syifa to the city's north and founded the Yayasan Taruna al-Qur'an (Taruna al-Qur'an Foundation). His school was renamed Pesantren Taruna al-Qur'an and became the centre of several religious businesses, publishing houses and a dormitory for university students. Budiharjo and his colleagues also founded two schools elsewhere in the city.

Similarly, Abu Nida's at-Turots foundation opened the Pesantren Islamic Centre Bin Baz (ICBB) in 2000 in Bantul. It is the biggest Salafi *pesantren* in Yogyakarta and includes a kindergarten, primary and high school. Catering to both boys and girls, the school – named after the late Saudi mufti – has become the administrative centre for the at-Turots foundation and is the hub of an extensive network of actors involved in social development projects, mosque construction and religious propagation. The at-Turots foundation also provides social assistance to local communities in Bantul and Gunung Kidul regencies, south of Yogyakarta proper.

This slow but steady expansion demonstrates that Salafism, far from being diminished in importance in post-Suharto Indonesia, has continued to grow and propagate its doctrine using innovative methods. They have worked with government bodies and through legally sanctioned entities. Schools, such as the ICBB and Pesantren Taruna al-Qur'an, abide by the standards and curriculum set by the Indonesian Ministry of Religious Affairs. Hasan believes that this alignment is due to pressure from the Indonesian government and general public who were suspicious of Salafi activism in light of Thalib's Laskar Jihad as well as the violence of Jemaah Islamiyah (Hasan 2010).

Yet working in cooperation and compliance with the government has paid off for the Salafi movement. By following a government-recognised educational curriculum, students from these institutions are able to attend Indonesian universities and are not limited to a future of religious study. In turn, this has enabled the schools to draw students from non-Salafi families in the surrounding area, often through locally targeted scholarships. The attraction of these schools is not their religious message, but their ability to offer a good education.

It was during the presidency of Susilo Bambang Yudhoyono (SBY) from 2004–2014 that Salafi enthusiasts solidified their expansion across the country. Whereas Megawati Sukarnoputri, SBY's predecessor, had resisted the will of Islamic forces, Yudhoyono's administration was characterised by a policy that not just supported the interests of religious conservatives, but shielded more violent elements from sanction and prosecution (Bush 2015).

Mietzner and Muhtadi (2018) note that during Yudhoyono's presidency, the government began to provide logistical support, funds and protection to the Majelis Ulama Indonesia (MUI) and its associates. Ma'ruf Amin, the current vice-president, served as head of the MUI's national Sharia Committee from 2004–2010 and was a member of Yudhoyono's Presidential Advisory Board from 2007–2014 (*Ibid.*). This enabled conservative Islamic groups, ranging from Salafi activists to vigilantes such as the Islamic Defenders Front, to build connections, access resources and gain sponsorship from Indonesia's educational, social and political institutions. Moreover, SBY's tenure became a time of increased attacks and heightened rhetoric against religious minorities (Harsono 2014). These attacks were often justified in the wake of *fatawa* passed by the MUI, such

63

as one against liberalism, secularism, and pluralism in 2005, and another against the Ahmadiyah religious community in 2008.

Yudhoyono's presidency affected the development of Salafism in three important ways. Firstly, as Mietzner and Muhtadi note, conservative Islamic values became more prevalent amongst university graduates. This suggests that between 2010–2016 the middle classes had shifted from being the most tolerant to one of the least tolerant groups in Indonesian society (Mietzner & Muhtadi 2018). For Salafis, this not only alludes to their success on university campuses, but also points to the conflation between Islam and urban professionalism that Salafis have adeptly capitalised on.

Secondly, the increased acceptance of anti-Shi'a rhetoric in public and political discourse gave Salafis a foothold to amplify their own message against promiscuity, pornography and immorality and gain a degree of legitimacy in public debate. In 2012, for instance, Abu Nida made a series of accusations against Shi'a Muslims at a *Tabligh Akbar* (great lecture) attended by government officials. This occurred only two months after a Shi'a community in Madura had been violently attacked, and the Minister of Religious Affairs Suryadharma Ali had publicly declared Shi'ism to be anti-Islam (Media Indonesia 2012). Salafis may not have involved themselves directly in violent acts, but their rhetoric nevertheless contributed to the growing acceptability of anti-Shi'ism in Indonesia (IPAC 2016).

Thirdly, by providing conservative Islamic groups with access to state institutions, the activism of such groups shifted towards a position of accommodation and collaboration with the state. It is notable that in Yogyakarta, Salafis linked to the at-Turots network began working with local government agencies to provide welfare to less-well-off communities, mobilise supporters to assist in public works projects, and to hold a series of conferences to denounce terrorism and radicalisation.

A key vehicle that allowed them to interact with state institutions was their use of the *yayasan* (foundation) legal structure, which has become the preferred mode of Salafi association in Indonesia. Salafi activists use this legal entity to manage schools, organise social activities, publish magazines (provided they do not antagonise state authorities), and create official channels to communicate with government bodies and receive funding for social welfare programmes.

Limited oversight and lack of transparency made the *yayasan* attractive to Salafis. During the New Order, *yayasan* were exempt from the controversial *asas tunggal* policy, as their activities were meant to relate to social, educational, humanitarian or religious charity and not politics. Further, the founder could vest decision-making in hand-picked trustees who could hold meetings behind closed doors (Aspinall 2005; 93). While many foundations served legitimate purposes, this ambiguity was convenient for groups that did not wish to be subject to state oversight, so many *yayasan* became vehicles for the political elite and the military to receive unofficial donations, launder money and make off-the-book profits (Antlov et al. 2006: Werve 2006).

The post-Suharto period has led to greater scrutiny over the financial dealings of *yayasan*, which are now subject to national audits (thanks to Criminal Corruption Law 31/1999) as well as greater transparency (due to amendments in the laws governing *yayasan* in 2001, 2004 and 2008). Yet the actual structure and *raison d'etre* of an individual *yayasan* retains a broad degree of institutional elasticity.

Many Salafis take advantage of this and the *yayasan* provides them a wide berth to engage in a variety of activities without having to subject themselves to intrusive government oversight. Moreover, the *yayasan* has increasingly dictated the modes through which Salafism operates, representing a structure through which actors can use a recognised institution to facilitate collective actions. The successful establishment of a *yayasan* has become a mark of success that solidifies an up-and-coming leader's reputation in his religious network. Forming a *yayasan* implies that one has solid financial, social and institutional links, often developed while working for other successful foundations. *Asatidz*, when setting up their own foundations, seldom sever relations with previous colleagues. They maintain these connections and keep each other informed of promising students or upcoming events and opportunities. As a consequence, activists are frequently affiliated with more than one foundation and can act as facilitators who participate in legally separate *yayasan* entities through unofficial, personal relationships.

Ustadz Abduh is an example of a person with overlapping connections. I met Abduh one evening at his home in Klanten, having been introduced to him by an interlocutor in Yogyakarta. Abduh was in his 30s and an active user of social media. He had been educated at the Islamic University of Madinah and, upon graduation, was recruited by Abu Nida to work at the at-Turots foundation. While at at-Turots, he began lecturing at the YPIA and publishing articles in the student-affiliated Salafi Pengusaha Muslim (Muslim Businessperson) magazine. He had recently moved to Klanten, Central Java (about 20 kilometres from Yogyakarta) where he had established his own foundation. With that foundation, he hoped to build a mosque and school. Yet he maintains contacts to Yogyakarta, not only by writing articles but also through a social media study group he set up while teaching in the city (Interview, Klanten, 4 April 2012).

RELIGIOUS AGENTS

Salafism operates in a loose, overlapping and rhizomatic manner. While many *yayasan* are linked to similar donors (such as the Jama'iyyat Ihya' Al-Turath al-Islami in Kuwait), or educational institutions (such as the Islamic University of Madinah), they remain institutionally and operationally independent from each other. Yet if we wish to fully understand the contemporary expansion of Salafism, our examination must include the role of Salafis themselves in perpetuating the movement.

Salafi activists play a number of roles. They can be preachers (*asatidz*), moral entrepreneurs or lay preachers (*da'i*) who conduct sermons. They can fund social activities or tap into wider trends of religious commodification. Such activists are certainly not the only people engaging with Salafi doctrine, but in post-Suharto Yogyakarta, they arguably play the largest role in driving Salafism forward. By describing this typology, I am not referring to the embodiment of predefined religious roles but to a set of activities that have developed in Yogyakarta. They are context-specific, mediated both by the religious tenets that guide Salafi faith and by the actions of actors in a given time and place. They provide an understanding of the logic that defines Salafi activism in Yogyakarta.

The Ustadz

The most important Salafi activists are *asatidz* (religious teachers – singular *ustadz* and *ustadzah* for females) whose combination of religious knowledge, charisma, access to donors, and links to religious institutions have sustained and expanded the movement. Plainly speaking, an *ustadz* is a transmitter of doctrine, often working in religious educational establishments, holding sermons throughout the city, writing articles in magazines, and providing personal advice to adherents. They can be both teachers and personal counsellors, advocating why one must follow scripture and how to so do in ways that align with one's social environment. *Asatidz* fit into the broader category of *mukmin* (pious) individuals, a concept crucial not only for Salafis but also for Muslims more generally.

The *ustadz* is not just a teacher but a role model of social and religious etiquette. Religious authority comes from one's knowledge not only of the Qur'an and Hadith but also of their interpretations by Middle Eastern scholars. An *ustadz* does not issue religious rulings (*fatawa*) but bases religious advice on the rulings of Arabian-based *shaykh* or the Saudi Arabian Majlis Hay'at kibar al-ulama (Council of the Committee of Senior Ulama). This distinguishes Salafism from other Islamic movements in Indonesia, and is a reason why Salafis are accused of being foreign to Indonesia. But this foreignness is a strength for followers as they believe it proves they are aligned with an unsullied Islam linked directly to the Arabian Peninsula.

The extent of the connection with Saudi Arabia is evident when examining the Salafi magazine As-Sunnah, published by the Yayasan Lajnah Istiqomah Surakarta (Surakarta Istiqomah Committee Foundation). Arguably one of the most popular Salafi magazines, As-Sunnah is distributed in Indonesian cities and migrant communities in Saudi Arabia. Out of ten issues published between October 2011 and September 2012, the magazine's question and answer section printed 44 questions, 29 of which were answered by direct reference to Saudi Arabian *shaykh*, predominantly 'Abd al-Aziz Bin Baz, Nasir al-Din al-Albani, Muhammad al-Uthaymin and Salih Fawzan al-Fawzan.[4] While such references create a corpus from which Salafis draw, the sheer volume of such *fatawa* still gives the Indonesian *ustadz* a level of flexibility as to which references they choose and why. *Fatawa* from multiple sources can be subtly contradictory, and selective interpretation occurs.

Yogyakarta is home to a number of *asatidz* who have obtained religious education in tertiary religious institutions. This does not imply personal tuition is no longer a way to pursue religious knowledge. Ustadz Afifi Wadud has, for example, received no official religious education despite

---

4 These editions of *As-Sunnah* were collected during my fieldwork. All are published by the Yayasan Lajnah Istiqomah Surakarta, Solo, Indonesia and included Year XV No. 6 (October 2011), 7 (November 2011), 8 (December 2011), 9 (January 2012), 10 (February 2012), 11 (March 2012), 12 (April 2012) and year XVI No. 1 (May 2012), 2 (June 2012), 3 (July–August 2012), 4 (September 2012). The year represents the Hijra Calendar, although the month of publication remains Gregorian.

being hugely influential. Yet for the majority of aspiring *asatidz* structured education is the surest way to establish one's reputation. The most coveted institution is the Islamic University of Madinah. It is currently led by Dr Hatim bin Hasan Al Murzuqi and consists of five faculties for religious study: Sharia, Da'wa and Ushuluddin, Qur'an, Hadith, and Arabic language, plus faculties of engineering and computer science. By 2018, 2,230 Indonesians had graduated from the university.[5]

A degree from the Islamic University of Madinah (or any other tertiary institution in Saudi Arabia for that matter) has become a mark of prestige for an *ustadz*. However, the number of scholars able to study abroad remains small. Many aspiring Salafis reverted to the faith while undergoing a secular university education, and so cannot speak Arabic with sufficient fluency to be able to study in Saudi Arabia. This suggests that the most prominent *asatidz* had previously studied at a religious high school or were part of a religious youth group prior to becoming involved in the movement.

This trend has begun to shift, however, due to the advent of online and Indonesian-based Salafi institutions which give those who come from non-religious backgrounds a better chance to gain religious qualifications and become a recognised *ustadz*. The Sekolah Tinggi Imam Ali bin Abi Tholib in Surabaya offers one such alternative. It is a government recognised tertiary educational facility, founded in 1996 and registered in 2008, that teaches approximately 180 students a year. It receives financial support from the Saudi embassy and many of its teaching staff are graduates from Madinah. It trains aspiring *asatidz* who, through intense Arabic classes, can find a way to continue their studies abroad.

Aspiring *asatidz* have also been turning to the online Al-Madinah International University (MEDIU) as an alternative to studying away from home. More affordable and accessible than other educational programmes, MEDIU offers part-time and full-time degree programmes up to the doctoral level in both Arabic and English. Originally founded in Madinah in 2004, the university relocated to Sha Alam Selangor, Malaysia, and received official accreditation from the Malaysian government in 2007. Financial backing and control of the curriculum remains in the hands of Saudi-based donors. All seven shareholders and five of the seven board members are Saudi nationals.

---

5   This information was obtained from the Islamic University of Madinah website: www.enwbe.iu.edu.sa accessed on 5 September 2018.

As such, the institution is an important local hub of *asatidz* knowledge and its significance cannot be overemphasised. Both the current coordinator of the at-Turots ICBB and the director of the YPIA were pursuing postgraduate study through MEDIU at the time of my original fieldwork in 2012 (Interview, Yogyakarta, 13 November 2011 & 24 April 2012).

The above-mentioned educational options are important for those wishing to become religious preachers. There are, however, other elements of equal importance. In order to gain acceptance and a following, an aspiring *asatidz* must engage actively with foundations, schools and mosques. Many foundations recruit young *asatidz*, offering them opportunities to hone their presentation skills. For example, the YPIA works in conjunction with several local mosques to provide young male preachers a platform to give 15-minute lectures after *dhuhur* (afternoon) prayers. Those who do well are invited to deliver longer lectures.

Another way an *ustadz* gains a following is by developing a particular niche of expertise. They can specialise in such topics as gender relations, business practices and online outreach, all of which appeal to the specific audience they want to reach. Ustadz Syahrul, a young *ustadz* linked to the YPIA, has become part of a drive to expand the virtual presence of Salafism through websites, mobile phone applications, and online TV and radio. Although he conducts sermons in mosques, Syahrul's dominant presence is online, where he either answers questions from a virtual audience or connects them to others who may be able to assist. As discussed in greater detail in Chapter 4, this has made him an important figure amongst young tech-savvy followers, not only in terms of religious education but also in providing several former IT students with contacts so they can conduct *da'wa* online.

The above briefly describes the role of an *ustadz*. While there are several recognised paths to increase one's standing, the different paths individuals take to becoming an *ustadz* cannot be ignored. For example, Arif was the head teacher at a Salafi school in the south of the city. He volunteered as an advisor to the YPIA and wrote numerous articles published on popular Salafi websites like Konsultasi Syariah (Sharia Consultation) and in the magazine Pengusaha Muslim. Born in 1980, he spent his childhood in Lampung, Sumatra, where his parents had relocated during the government transmigration programme. His family was originally from Yogyakarta and he returned to the city for his high school education; during his first year, he came across the Salafi magazine As-Sunnah.

Arif's interest in Islam grew as he continued his secondary education, although he attended few sermons, preferring to read magazines in his spare time. When Arif completed high school, he enrolled at the Universitas Islam Negeri Sunan Kalijaga (Islamic State University Sunan Kalijaga) to study Arabic. Studying at this university was rare for Salafi preachers given their hostility towards the apparently liberal and pro-Western Islamic orientation of this university.[6] He lived in a student hall managed by the Taruna al Qur'an and excelled in his studies. In his first year, Arif became part of the Salafi network by attending lectures and providing Arabic language tutoring to those in the YPIA.

Upon graduation, he wished to continue his studies in Saudi Arabia but, despite receiving references from his tutors, lacked the necessary connections or finances to do so. He thus undertook a master's in jurisprudence at the Universitas Muhammadiyah Surakarta (Muhammadiyah University of Surakarta) under the Salafi scholar Mu'inudinillah Basri. At that point, he had sufficient qualifications to teach and conduct sermons in mosques close to his home in north Yogyakarta. His main focus, however, is the students in the YPIA, the foundation that initially helped him learn about Salafism (Interview, Yogyakarta, 3 June 2012).

Arif's rise within the Yogyakarta-based movement is unique but demonstrates an alternate route for young, secularly educated students to become recognised *ustadz*. Certainly, this is not without its challenges. Arif was unable to get a scholarship to study abroad, despite his top marks at UIN Sunan Kalijaga. Yet the popularity of new tertiary institutions both in Indonesia and online have provided other avenues for enthusiasts to receive cheaper, more accessible and even part-time education at home. They do not have to travel abroad or rely on the patronage of more established *asatidz*. The YPIA's commitment to provide opportunities for aspiring *asatidz* to deliver brief sermons to hone their oratory skills, supports this trend.

This more accessible path to become an *ustadz* stature does not diminish the importance of Saudi Arabian or Yemeni training. However, it does demonstrate how the movement has developed ever more sophisticated

---

6   This university sponsored my field research and it quickly became apparent that many
     interlocutors believed it to be a bastion of liberal Islamic views.

and Indonesian-based institutions that give recruits the religious learning needed to advance their studies.

Moral Entrepreneurs

The spread of Salafi doctrine depends on more than *asatidz* as religious foundations provide a range of health, welfare, emergency relief and social empowerment programmes in local communities. *Asatidz* remain important to such endeavours, not least in socialising them to constituents and providing the religious authority needed to secure funding, but such work is largely performed by a group of organisers, instigators and managers that act as what Howard Becker has termed 'moral entrepreneurs' (as quoted in Bonnefoy 2011: 84).

I follow the work of Laurent Bonnefoy, who identifies the rise of moral entrepreneurs amongst Yemeni Salafis and uses the term to focus on an emerging array of preachers and individuals who wish to impose their idea of reform on society (*Ibid.*). My use is more specific. I use it to refer to those involved exclusively in the management of religious programmes or who are at the forefront of expanding the Islamic knowledge economy. Moral entrepreneurs, I argue, are at the heart of the process of commodification which has engulfed urban Salafism and Islam more broadly.

The advent of moral entrepreneurship is tied to broad social transformations amongst young Muslims and the growing popularity of expressing Islam through one's consumption and professional choices. Moral entrepreneurs are involved in framing religious meaning in a socially and economically congruent fashion. For instance in Yogyakarta, young Salafis sell religious clothing, prepare herbal medicines or offer halal services ranging from banking to marriage counselling. Most moral entrepreneurs are men between 20 and 40 years of age, although women have also created online ventures to sell clothing or religious products. A great number of these individuals have university degrees (overwhelmingly in sciences, business or IT) and increasingly work alongside *asatidz* in discovering new and more intricate ways to expand the movement. It is not surprising that the sale of merchandise – such as herbal medicine, DVDs, clothing and toiletries – has become a legitimate mode for religious professionals to make a living.

While I elaborate more extensively on the commodification of Salafi *da'wa* in Chapter 4, the ways these entrepreneurs strengthen the movement is important to our understanding of contemporary Salafism. A significant example of the entrepreneurial spirit can be seen amongst a group of former IT university students linked to the YPIA who founded the Yufid group in 2009. Yufid created a range of Salafi online websites, mobile phone applications, and an online marketplace for religious goods. While these products all help to promote religious ideals amongst young IT-savvy students, Yufid's expansion is both a result of, and a catalyst for, the engagement of young people who use technology to find religious resources. As their products reach new audiences, Yufid recruit recent graduates and even help them find employment in a pious environment that enables them to continue grow and propagate the faith.

Not all entrepreneurs are involved in economic ventures. Others manage Salafi foundations or schools. For example, Yudi, a former student from the Yogyakarta University of Technology, currently works as the secretary for a Salafi student foundation. Thirty-one years old, he runs the local office and sells herbal medicinal products from a store close to his home. Yudi explained that the management of religious activities has changed over the last decade, now relying predominantly on emails, text messages and database management (managing which preacher is where and when). Recent graduates have therefore become an important cog in coordinating funding, proselytisation and daily routines, because older *ustadz* are not as familiar with data management techniques, software and social media. Yudi explained that the foundation he works for holds regular meetings where new activities are proposed and planned, and old ones evaluated. *Asatidz* still provide religious oversight in these meetings, but managers give programme input (Interview, Yogyakarta, 3 November 2011). Consequently, those from a non-religious background can, through managerial roles, play a major part in organising foundations and religious programmes.

In short, Salafism has benefitted from the influx of enthusiasts whose technical knowhow enables religious doctrine to be aligned with contemporary lifestyle choices. They have become a group of propagators in their own right, strengthening the work of their peers by supporting and partaking in new economic or social media enterprises. One aspect of this expansion has been the growth of new religious magazines concerned with business (e.g., Pengusaha Muslim), health (e.g., Muslim Sehat, Healthy Muslim) and family issues (e.g., al-Mawaddah). This is not limited to men either, as women also publish magazines, sell products and provide advice for other Muslim women. Although Salafi men remain convinced that women should primarily take care of the household and family, the Internet and the proliferation of religious commodities have enabled women to work as managers and establish online ventures to sell products. Because looking after the household includes equipping it with religious products and commodities, they can increasingly tap into approved religious patterns of consumption to fulfil such obligations.

Da'i

If the *ustadz* and moral entrepreneurs expand the Salafi movement in urban environments, the spread into rural areas relies on the work of *da'i*. Derived from the Arabic term for one who invites people to the faith, to prayer or to Islamic life (Esposito 2003: 61), *da'i* are lay preachers who promote basic tenets without delving into the intricate details of the Islamic sciences. Trained by *asatidz* prior to being sent throughout the archipelago, *da'i* often have basic religious or even non-religious educational backgrounds. The majority of *da'i* I interviewed had attended a small rural *pesantren* in their youth or had only completed secondary or high school (equivalent to sixth form in UK), although several *da'i* have graduated from university. They also tend to come from more remote, rural backgrounds compared to their *asatidz* and moral entrepreneur colleagues.

Almost all religious foundations run *da'i* training programmes, which last for approximately three years. The at-Turots provides one such course, the I'dad ad-Du'at programme. They teach students how to correct religious *ibada* (religious practice) and *muamala* (social conduct), and stress the need to uphold correct *tawhid* (monotheism) and avoid *bid'a* (un-Islamic innovations) and *syirik* (idolatry). This is comparatively basic compared to the intellectualism of an *ustadz*, not least because many urban *asatidz* maintain a view that Indonesia's rural population is undereducated and subject to syncretic practices (Interview, Yogyakarta, 3 November 2011). Accordingly, *da'i* seek less to create astute holders of religious knowledge than to ensure that people uphold religious principles which forego the mysticism popularly associated with rural faith.

Trainee *da'i* usually live close to the *ma'had* (religious school) where they are enrolled. This live-in environment is important for several reasons. It provides students with an opportunity to witness and emulate the social etiquette of a pious community, which they can then take back to their target setting or home villages. It also allows *da'i* to tap into a wider network of *asatidz* and religious entrepreneurs who can later assist them, be it financially, logistically or with religious queries, once they graduate. By living in the vicinity of a school, trainee *da'i* are given the opportunity to find basic employment to fund their studies. It is not uncommon for shop assistants, IT administrators, primary school teachers and even labourers in Salafi communities to undergo *da'i* training.

Iman was a 24-year-old trainee from Sumbawa, studying to become a *da'i* at at-Turots. He was also an English teacher for young students at the local Salafi *ma'had*. Somewhat of a rarity amongst *da'i*, he has a university education. He stated that his religious knowledge, prior to enrolling, was basic and he was not particularly pious. He became interested in Salafism through magazines and began attending sermons at the suggestion of a friend. When Iman graduated from university, he enrolled in the *da'i* training programme and now states his life revolves around Islam. Upon completing his *da'i* studies, he hoped to return to Sumbawa and spread the message to his home community members, something he believes is obligatory for all proper Muslims (Interview, Yogyakarta, 29 February 2012). He will add to the 1,442 *da'i* that at-Turots claims to already have sent to villages around Java and other islands.

This brief description of *da'i*, *asatidz* and moral entrepreneurs shows the multiple actors and roles involved in developing and disseminating religious doctrine. While the relationships amongst actors are important, they are not necessarily cohesive. Actors push and pull Salafism in response to various pressures and concerns. Furthermore, despite the stress on the egalitarian nature of their Islamic message, the use of new technologies and the creation of religious roles inevitably remains interwoven with local ideas of social status and education. For example, a *da'i* working in a rural mosque stresses the importance of Salafi doctrine in markedly different ways than an *ustadz* addressing a crowd of university students. While students and those of an urban professional background become interested in aligning the movement with wider processes of commodification, their rural *da'i* colleagues promote an engagement with Salafism in a fundamentally different way – using local language and more basic religious tenets. I will look at the social significance of divergences among Salafi interpretations in the upcoming chapters. But first, I will continue an exploration of the dynamics of the movement by describing its use of spatial enclaves.

ENCLAVES AND RELIGIOUS SPACES

Salafi activism has a spatial dynamic which must be addressed if we are to understand how it has evolved in Yogyakarta. Religious spaces, or localities, assist in cultivating a Salafi disposition not just by promoting an ideal idea of space, but also by providing a place where adherence to patterns of be-haviour and prayer can be reinforced. The religious space is a fundamental building block in which a social ideal is first imagined.

Social ills derive from multiple sources that Salafis attempt to distance themselves from through the principle of *al-wala' wa-l-bara'* (allegiance to Islam and renunciation of unbelievers). Society, they believe, is corrupted by several elements including: the West who promote *hubbun dun-ya* (love of the earth) (Minhal 2011; Syamhudi 2012); Javanese traditions such as *Joyoboyo* (the Javanese zodiac) and *ziarah* (grave visits) that promote idol-atry (HASMI 2011; Jawas 2011); and corrupt Islamic practices tainted by political or liberal leanings (Saifullah 2011). Contemporary society, which they see plagued by political wrangling, demonstrations, corruption, *ikhtilath* (mixing of sexes), *taklid* (blind faith), improper *ibada* and the misuse of Islamic symbols become dangers that mark the deviation of the *umma* from the true path of the Prophet and companions.

To protect themselves from these issues, Salafi activists create enclaves that act as what Sivan calls a 'wall of virtue', where modes of dress, speech and voluntary social interaction are portrayed as characteristics of a pious world juxtaposed against the morally vacant spaces outside its boundaries (Sivan 1995: 17–18). Enclaves are characterised by intense social interaction, where time and space are heavily regulated group resources. Members are proud to be different, using forms of address (such as brother and sister) that they do not use with those outside the movement. Enclaves, furthermore, provide a degree of segregation between the non-Salafi and Salafi worlds as well as be-tween men and women. This is a fine balancing act because, although these spaces are important for strengthening a model of piety, they are not exempt from either government surveillance or the socio-political debates actors themselves bring into these spaces. They may offer what Lefebvre terms a representation of space in which a conceptualised idea of pious behaviour can be imagined and referred to (Lefebvre 1991: 39), but they are also networked spaces (Juris and Khasnabish 2013: 2–4) within which a particular cultural politics is negotiated, contested and debated.

Religious Villages

The principal enclave is the religious village – a space where individuals can both study and live. The focus of the village is to provide a place where Salafis can start a family and educate their children without fear the children will be influenced by secular forces. The largest enclave affiliated to the at-Turots network is a village in Wirokerten, Bantul, approximately five kilometres south of Yogyakarta. At its centre is Ma'had Jamilurrahman as-Salafy, a large school-mosque complex that is the heart of village life. Residents attend daily lectures, plan public events and conduct their prayers at the mosque. It is also a hub for a number of religious businesses, including publishing houses, and clothing and herbal medicine outlets, all located in the surrounding buildings. It was founded by Abu Nida in 1993 and, until 2000, was the administrative nucleus of the at-Turots foundation (after which its coordination offices moved to the ICBB). The village is home to approximately 300 people and is viewed as *the* residential area for many Salafi activists. It is separated from neighbouring villages by rice fields on all sides, with only two roads leading into the compound, one of which is a narrow dirt track winding through rice fields. Even with written directions, it is difficult to find the village.[7]

This physical separation is reinforced with religious and socio-economic markers. Those who live in the village dress differently and are often financially better situated than their non-Salafi neighbours. This recent development was noted by a researcher who has visited the village repeatedly since the 1990s. The village was initially of modest size and only grew in economic standing over the 2000s (Interview, Yogyakarta, 9 July 2012). There are now a number of large, well-built houses, simply decorated inside with ornamented Qur'anic verses as well as TVs and stereos – ostensibly used for religious purposes only.

The shifting demographics of the religious village are testimony to the greater access to funding amongst at-Turots members and their ability

---

7   The first time I attempted to enter the village I got lost repeatedly as this small road is
    extremely difficult to find.

to promote new Islamic business ventures. Many original members were preachers and religious enthusiasts who worked exclusively for at-Turots or within Salafi circles. However, residents now include a number of successful private-sector employees and entrepreneurs working in Islamic finance, IT and the bulk sale of Islamic goods. One interlocutor was part of this group and had lived in the area for almost ten years. He became interested in the movement while studying at UGM. Upon graduation at the age of 21, he married and moved to Wirokerten to expand his knowledge of Islam and live in a pious environment. When I met him, he was teaching young children at the Ma'had Jamilurrahman and working as a computer technician for the school and on a contract basis for other religious foundations (Interview, Yogyakarta, 29 February 2012). Like many residents, he is not Javanese but from another part of the country – Lombok in his case. The village's cultural diversity is mainly due to the *da'i* training programme, which attracts many from around the archipelago.

Compared to residents living close to the former FKAWJ Ma'had al-Anshar, women in Wirokerten are far more visible. While maintaining a distance from men, they are not prohibited from entering public spaces like shops (as they are in al-Anshar), their demeanour is more confident, and they have a far more active presence in businesses and religious schools than their al-Anshar counterparts. Additionally, not all women wear the full-face cover, citing a famous (but controversial) *fatwa* by Shaykh al-Albani that this was not a religious necessity. I believe this demonstrates a subtly different interpretation between these two Salafi networks.

Many Salafi continue to stress that the primary role of women is in the house and as maintainers of the family. But increasingly, women are active agents in a (segregated) women's sphere, running their own activities, becoming *asatidzah* (plural of *ustadzah*, female religious teachers) and entrepreneurs. Although not benefitting from the same opportunities as their male counterparts, these women teach and manage women-only sermons on university campuses to inculcate a specific idea of being a pious (Salafi) woman. The religious villages provide spaces where women can come together and create their own spheres, representing the transformational importance of the Salafi enclave. They are not alone here, as young teachers, students and businessmen also use the village as a mobilisational point in which to interact and work together to socialise particular ideas about Islam, find solutions to pressing matters, and create outreach programmes.

Schools

The village is but one type of space. It is complemented by mosques, schools and boarding houses that are all crucial centres within which Salafi faith and activism are enacted. In Yogyakarta, the largest school complex is the at-Turots foundation's Pesantren Islamic Centre Bin Baz (ICBB), established in 2000. Built on land donated by Yogyakarta's Sultan Hamengkubowono X, ICBB is located in Sitimulyo, Bantul, approximately 13 kilometres east of the city centre. Like Ma'had Jamilurrahman as-Salafy, it is in a rural setting of rice fields and small villages where several of its teachers live. Unlike the former village, it was designed specifically as a teaching and administrative facility (rather than a residential area) and contains several offices, large classrooms and playing fields.

The ICBB is home to approximately 300 students – both girls and boys – from kindergarten to high school. These include day students and boarders from across Indonesia, Malaysia, Singapore, Australia and Timor Leste. It is privately managed but follows a curriculum in line with requirements laid out by the Ministry of Religious Affairs. ICBB is more than just a school; it is the organisational hub of at-Turots. The foundation's main office is a large and busy complex that lies behind a water fountain and roundabout at the entrance to the ICBB complex. Radio Dakwah Bin Baz (Bin Baz Propagational Radio) is broadcast from here, and mosque construction programmes and *da'i* interventions are organised.

Given its size and central position in the at-Turots network, the school has attracted a number of independent religious businesses and entrepreneurs. The small road leading to the complex is lined with herbal medicine outlets, a religious bookstore and a travel agency that promotes trips to the Hejaz. As the school has continued to expand, at-Turots has built a housing compound next to it, promoting it as a pious and comfortable environment to raise one's family. The appeal of these houses is clearly aimed at a middle-class clientele. Each has a driveway for a car and a modern architectural layout with several bedrooms, a verandah and large windows. However, despite being promoted in magazines and through glossy brochures (on display at Islamic bookstores), at-Turots conceded that the foundation is having difficulty filling the units (Interview, Yogyakarta, 13 November 2011).

Umar Budiharjo's school is another example of a networked space in Yogyakartan Salafism. Compared to the ICBB, the Pesantren Taruna al-

Qur'an is modest in size. It is located in Lempong Sari, seven kilometres north of the city centre, and has about 200 male students in middle or high school. The school's origins are linked to the Pesantren Asy-Syifa founded by Umar Budiharjo in 1993. Like the ICBB, it is the centre of a religious foundation and so has a bustling central office with several shops, a clothing outlet, travel agency, catering company, small publishing business and university student dormitory within the vicinity. However, unlike the ICBB, which is surrounded by walls and a gate, the Pesantren Taruna al-Qur'an is not separated from the surrounding community. It is located on a busy through-road and many teachers live in nearby (non-Salafi) neighbourhoods. This means teachers, activists and students must engage with their non-Salafi neighbours (of which I was one) on a daily basis. As such, students at Taruna al-Qur'an are noticeably more at ease talking to both men and women who enter their shops or whom they encounter on the road.

Student Accommodation

As I have emphasised, the university is pivotal to the Salafi movement and its expansion across Indonesia. Much of this has to do with foundations such as the YPIA, reaching out to students through religious sermons and classes. I address the dynamics of these more thoroughly in upcoming chapters, noting here only that these foundations further engage students in the foundation by providing religious boarding houses. The YPIA runs 12 student halls including the Wisma Misfallah Tholabul 'Ilmi (MTI). All are run by a senior student *mudir* (head) who is responsible for the upkeep and activities of the *wisma*. Together with the YPIA secretariat, they organise student religious courses, and ensure all students are awake for morning prayers and partake in *da'wa*, most notably handing out the YPIA weekly bulletins at-Tauhid (for men) and Zuhairoh (for women) at mosques after Friday prayers. These dorms are segregated and contact between men and women is highly discouraged.

Wisma MTI is the largest of these halls. Home to approximately 20 male students between the ages of 18 and 30 years, the two-storey building is located in Pogung Raya, a neighbourhood next to UGM. Students have modest private rooms, sharing a kitchen and a communal space that doubles as the YPIA secretariat. The communal space is usually clean but chaotic, with books and magazines scattered on the floor or stacked in corners next to computer terminals that students use for their work (both academic and linked to the YPIA). The space is also used for formal foundation-based discussions, where guests are received and information about the YPIA activities is disseminated.

Every Wisma resident must enrol in a course of Islamic science and Arabic language, and all are obliged to study the Qur'an and Hadith from 5:30am every day. The dorm's *mudir* plays an important role in motivating and ensuring all members partake in such studies. Young *asatidz* also act as private counsellors, advising dormitory residents on personal matters of faith and student life. They can guide them to specific sermons or assist with employment opportunities if they are struggling financially. Many employees at nearby religious stores are young members of the YPIA, exposing these students to other Salafi networks in the city.

It is important to note that Salafis are not the only ones building boarding houses in the vicinity of the university campus. Privately run *asrama* and *kos,* which exclusively accommodate students, have been a part of Indonesian university life for a long time, and several of them have social and religious requirements for their residents. It is not uncommon for students from a particular ethnic background or religion to live together. As such, these boarding houses often serve as cultural and organisational hubs for students from a particular area.

Since the fall of Suharto, there has been a sharp rise in the prominence of Islam-oriented boarding houses. UGM, for example, has twelve YPIA-affiliated boarding houses as well as two large Wahdah Islamiyah boarding houses and numerous non-Salafi ones. All of these are located in the nearby neighbourhood of Pogung Raya which, as Banker has shown in her insightful work on the YPIA, has led residents to refer to the place as Kampung Hijrah, using the commonly used term *hijrah* to denote young Muslim revivalism (Banker 2019).

ENACTING SALAFI SPACE IN YOGYAKARTA

No description of space or the agents who occupy it would be complete without examining the social forces present in these schools, villages and boarding houses. They exist not in a vacuum, but alongside competing social, economic, cultural and political structures. They are part of what Massey calls localities: the spaces that define the everyday world of individuals not just spatially but also through a set of social interactions that can create both coherence and difference (Massey 1994: 139).

Salafi enclaves do not, as much as Salafis may claim to the contrary, represent perfect and timeless models of Islamic virtue. Instead, they are forums for the construction or representation of a Salafi ideal that must continually be negotiated and given meaning in relation to other representations of local belonging. The enclaves support the effort to segregate oneself from society, but they also become spaces where the difficulties involved in doing so are raised and discussed. For example, school administrators strive to create a pure Islamic environment, but by working with government offices, they must fly the Indonesian flag and interact with non-Salafi teachers. When actualising a particular image of religious society, activists must balance their ideals, the opportunities presented by government programmes, and the social demands of neighbouring communities.

Salafi villages and schools need to interact with community bodies on a deep and sustained level. An essential part of their geography is the *kampung* (or *desa* in Java) – the literal translation of which is village. But the *kampung* is more than this; it is the intersection of the broader narratives of national identity and state governance. Sullivan states that *kampungs* are 'communal vessels, shaped and directed by the machinery of state, containing a rich mix of social groupings joined together by a complex web of cooperative practices and relations, not by simple, raw, economic need' (Sullivan 1992: 120). It is both an urban and rural entity that forms a recognised government administrative unit linked to the offices known as Rukun Warga (Citizens Association) and Rukun Tetangga (Neighbourhood Association). Every 30–50 households are represented by an Rukun Tetangga head, who is responsible for registering all new arrivals in their constituency and organising meetings and communal activities such as the *ronda* (where male residents take turns guarding the village every night) and *gotong royong* (mutual assistance, where every member plays a role in social programmes to better the community).

The *kampung* plays a vital role in ideological perceptions of the community and its place in the nation. Sullivan explains that the image of the Javanese village and its apparent loyalty to the royal court was an often-used source of political legitimacy during the New Order (Sullivan 1992: 207). It acted as a bastion in the construction of what Bourchier (1998) refers to as a conservative indigenism that arose at the heart of New Order thinking. John Pemberton (1994: 10) suggests that Suharto's rhetoric promoted 'tradition in order to contain diversity and relegate it to the ineffectual level of local customs' where inter-societal harmony was managed by the court – in this case Suharto's political order.

The image of the *kampung* as a bastion of a timeless cultural heritage – but also of backwardness – is manifested throughout Indonesian society. Government development initiatives still use this language and focus on the *kampung* as the primary unit for development and social welfare. Ben White argues that the 2014 village law (Law No.6 2014) has only reified the myth that villages are islands of harmony, in which classless peasants work together through shared values of *gotong royong*, family and *rukun* (harmony) (White 2017).

The *kampung* and the government bureaucracy are physical and ideo-logical structures that overlap on Salafi sites and inform the activities of the agents who inhabit these spaces. Some actors, such as those at the former Thalib-affiliated al-Anshar, attempt to minimise their contact with the government. However, those in Wirokerten prefer to work with administrative offices, with one follower serving as the Rukun Tetangga representative for the village. They do this to allay suspicions about the village and its schools. A teacher at the ICBB mentioned that because Salafis were perceived (wrongly) as terrorists, at-Turots always informed both local government and security forces of their social activities as a show of transparency (Interview, Yogyakarta, 13 November 2011).

The *kampung* concept has more than just pragmatic implications. As Salafi-influenced university students graduate and move into enclaves, they engage with the *kampung* as both a physical and imaginary idea. As they do so, they become aware of the discrepancy between their notion of a pure religious village and the ideological construct of a *kampung* of indigenous values. There is also the socio-economic dimension. Not only do they envis-age their village as properly Islamic, but also as modern and forward-looking – with newly built houses, cars and visible wealth, compared to the humbler non-Salafi *kampung*s surrounding them. Salafi *kampung*s are perceived as islands of purity and modernity in areas of undeveloped rural life. This mobilises Salafis not only to guide their neighbours to a true Islam, but also to offer welfare, social programmes and educational scholarships. Indeed, in the aftermath of the Merapi volcanic eruption in 2010, Salafis were quick to establish the Merapi Islamic Centre for the relief, welfare and education of those affected by the eruption. Yet the premise of these interactions very rarely departs from predefined assumptions, socialised through government initiatives, as to what a *kampung* is (see Chapter 5).

The relative poverty of surrounding *kampungs* is also conflated with a notion that their Islam and social outlook is stuck in the timeless past. Salafi students frequently refer to the syncretic practices of rural Muslims, or those linked to NU, as *Islam Kampung* (Village Islam), an uncomplimentary term that refers to backward or non-modern ideas of belief. It is perhaps not surprising that those in Wirokerten or ICBB have frequently received an icy reception from non-Salafis in their localities. Salafis in these areas not only dress differently but, as they are often not from Java, do not speak Javanese. In turn, this leads locals to stress the foreignness of their Salafi neighbours. For instance, a local government official around ICBB denounced Salafis as being *sombong* (arrogant) because they chose not to participate in local *gotong royong* and seldom communicated with their neighbours on non-religious matters (Interview, Yogyakarta, 27 March 2012).

In a similar vein, Salafi actors residing in or active on Yogyakarta's university campuses must deal with a number of social concerns that can both inform and challenge the movement. Most visibly, the campus is a place where men and women mingle in classes and so, despite Salafi disapproval of such practices, students cannot completely segregate themselves from the non-religious patterns of behaviour that are common in student communities. Some lecturers even force Salafi women to take their veils off in class (Nisa 2012). While the choice of clothing and adherence to religious doctrine does signify one's loyalty to the movement, students must negotiate between their desire to uphold scriptural necessities and the reality of being young, socially mobile professionals. This process of negotiation transforms how Salafism is represented and enacted, and also informs the ways that students come to recognise their dual responsibilities to Indonesian society and to religion.

A NETWORKED MOVEMENT

By examining the type of actors and spaces through which Salafism operates, I have outlined a number of the dynamics behind contemporary Salafism's *modus operandi*. Specifically, I have described how Salafism has developed in post-Suharto Indonesia before analysing the structures, opportunities, spaces and actors through which it has done so. There is an important caveat here; the nature of my ethnographic endeavour implies that these methods may not be generalisable throughout Indonesia – what works in Yogyakarta does not necessarily work in other regions. In Aceh, for example, Salafis are far more covert because of organised local hostility, while in nearby Surakarta, Salafis have solidified their position by joining their branch of the Local Council of Ulema (MUI) (Majelis Ulama Indonesia). Nevertheless, the typology provided here does show the logic of *agencement* (arrangement). Different actors and spaces fit together to create a network of enclaves, schools and recognised scholars who represent the movement both collectively and independently from each other. Salafism is more than a collection of people and spaces. It holds to a set of messages that resonate throughout these spaces and gives the movement meaning.

This chapter has been relatively light with regard to doctrine and discourse, a condition I wish to remedy in the coming two-chapter section. Both chapters examine Salafi religious tenets – pertaining to creed, religious jurisprudence, and one's faith – and the contextual issues that inform how such tenets are promoted and applied. As I describe and analyse, tenets remain universally recognised across the movement (and were alluded to in the first chapter), but contextual ideas transform and adapt as they travel across the community. They can be communicated online or via magazines, books or radio. But most predominantly, they are transmitted via religious lectures that occur in the physical spaces of Yogyakarta's mosques.

In the next chapter, I turn to the mosque – a space that remains pivotal to Salafism. It is here that religious lectures are delivered, and these lectures are essential points of passage for all Salafis. Any examination of Salafism would be incomplete without exploring their role in constructing and mobilising a particular religious ideal. Indeed, they are the spaces where the link between doctrine and the broader concerns of activists are negotiated and given voice. Ideas of modern national progress and living a professional and socially mobile lifestyle are all discussed in mosques and have informed the movements growing middle-class perspective. It is to these processes, and the mosque sermon, that the book now turns.

RELIGIOUS PRACTICE
AND ACTIVISM

The Mosque (by Izabela Chaplin)

I'tikaf at the Al-Hasanah Mosque

Yogyakarta, August 2012

It was the fasting month of Ramadan, and many activists I had come to know over the past year had either gone home (as the month coincided with university holidays) or had committed to attending a series of Islamic events across the city. I was invited to attend lectures at Yogyakarta's al-Hasanah Mosque, a small compound located at the corner of a busy crossroads in the north end of the city. The al-Hasanah is a somewhat run-down and dusty complex, consisting of one main prayer room covered in stained carpet, and a labyrinth of backrooms that contain the offices of a religious radio station. The outside walls of the mosque are covered in a peeling layer of discoloured green paint and rusting barbed wire. The architectural design is more akin to the multi-layered, red-roofed mosques traditional to Java than to the Middle Eastern-inspired architecture preferred by Salafi activists.

The al-Hasanah has been a hotbed of Salafi activism since the early 2000s, and its daily activities were – when I was there – run by Ahmad. Ahmad was a tall, serious but animated individual in his early 40s, originally from Makassar,

South Sulawesi. He came to Yogyakarta in the mid-1990s to attend university. I came to know him through his work at the Salafi radio station based at al-Hasanah, and we had become friendly because we both lived in the vicinity of the Pesantren Taruna al-Qur'an.

During Ramadan, Ahmad worked hard to organise a series of lectures at the mosque – often six a day – going to great lengths and pulling many strings to fill an ambitious schedule. It wasn't uncommon to see him on the phone, reaching out to his formidable network to fill a slot when one preacher couldn't make it to an arranged lecture. At one point, he was able to recruit Abu Nida, whom Ahmad referred to as the grandfather of Yogyakartan Salafism, to fill a 45-minute slot with just 24 hours' notice.

The lectures covered numerous religious issues including tawhid (monotheism), aqida (creed), fiqh (jurisprudence), akhlak (morals), adab (culture), Qur'an and Hadith studies. This variety was important, as enthusiastic adherents are encouraged to attend lectures on all topics. It was, Ahmad told those in attendance, not just a month for fasting, but for religious study – when individuals should learn everything from Qur'anic verses to the proper way to pray, dress and relate to other Muslims, and even how to sleep, eat and enter buildings correctly. Islam, he insisted, covered everything.

The audience at Ahmad's lecture series were encouraged to dedicate the final ten days of Ramadan to living and studying in the mosque. This practice is known as i'tikaf, and its importance to Salafi enthusiasts is considerable. As one preacher told his audience during his sermon, people in contemporary society are often too busy to i'tikaf despite the fact it awarded the equivalent of 1,000 months of prayer. He wasn't alone in promoting i'tikaf. Several other lectures scheduled for the early days of Ramadan emphasised its value.

I was struck by how i'tikaf was positioned as equivalent to a numerical value of prayer, wiping out a number of sins, or worth a sum of hours of extra-religious study. Why were numbers so important in these proclamations? Were asatidz keen to use numbers because their audience was predominantly students – many of whom were enrolled in science or technical programmes? I never got an answer.

Ahmad invited me to stay at the mosque during the i'tikaf and I accepted his invitation. I joined about 15 other men who, with only a small bag of extra clothes, a towel and toiletries, committed to not leave the mosque for ten days and nights. We would spend our days studying (observing in my case), sleeping and participating in lectures. Ahmad was keen for me to see these acts of faith. He was particularly eager that I observe the Tahajjud prayer – an extra prayer conducted late at night/early in the morning – that he would lead during the i'tikaf.

One evening before the Tahajjud, I stayed up chatting with Ahmad, who extolled the purity of Salafism to me. Earlier he had seen me studying an Oxford University Press edition of the Qur'an, rather than the Indonesian version I often read from. He questioned what I was doing. When I explained that when I was tired, I preferred to read in English, he was quick to remonstrate me. After looking at the translation, he said the version I was reading could not be considered correct or proper because the original Arabic text did not appear next to the translated text. He stated that by failing to include the original Arabic text, sesat (deviant) Islamic interpretations could happen because the translation could not be verified.

Sensing I was going to interject, he quickly followed this up with a lengthy talk on the need to follow religion correctly even when it was difficult. This in turn led to a prolonged monologue about the personal efforts one must undertake to be considered a follower of the manhaj Salaf as-Salih. He brought up his previous love for heavy metal music. With almost conspiratorial excitement, he spoke about how he used to play guitar and how much he missed it. He had stopped playing when he realised it was causing him to take shortcuts with his faith. He felt guilty that when he heard one of his favourite rock songs playing in a car next to him at traffic lights, he still got excited. He warned me that it was in these ways Satan would influence someone and draw them away from correct social and religious practices.

Around 1:30 am, Ahmad excused himself from our conversation to wake those still asleep and prepare them for the night prayer. I was left to think about his comments and how they related to what I had witnessed during my stay at al-Hasanah. For certain, I saw individuals skip lectures they expected to be boring or uninspiring. I had even joined several students who invited me to 'hide' in one of the mosque's backrooms one Friday evening when Ahmad was looking for volunteers to prepare food before breaking fast. Moreover, I had witnessed (but not informed on) two individuals secretly leaving the mosque during i'tikaf to eat at a popular fried chicken venue across the street.

Nonetheless, at no point did I doubt the seriousness of those at the al-Hasanah Mosque with which they took their faith or their desire to conform to an Islam in line with the tenets of Salafism. Their faith, perfected through constant study, introspection and prayer, remained deeply private. The al-Hasanah was viewed as a bastion of religious piety in a world of social temptation and challenges.

This image was made vivid by the roar of cars and trucks from nearby roads juxtaposed with the peace and stillness of the mosque.

The Tahajjud was special though. It connected the al-Hasanah to other mosques in Yogyakarta and elsewhere around the globe. It was a node in the broad network of Salafi activism and religious revival. Ahmad was clear about this, stating the commitment of the i'tikaf singled out the al-Hasanah and underscored its involvement in a broader effort to be an example for Indonesians. Interlocutors at the al-Hasanah were also clear that they were part of something bigger, both in terms of being connected to a global umma (Muslim community), but also because they were at the forefront of a movement that was rejecting the ills of their immediate surroundings and the temptation it offered. They may individually fall short of the need to ignore aspects of the social world that might sully the purity of faith, but together they could succeed. In short, there was an underlying global connectivity on display, and an imagined religious solidarity that reinforced the deep nature of private piety, connecting individuals to each other and to the Muslim brotherhood.

CHAPTER 3

Informing Religious Practice: The Urban Lecture

alafi foundations and activists have been remarkably astute in the way they have promoted their religious message and adjusted it to the socio-political forces in their localities. This includes the proliferation of religious magazines, business enterprises, radio stations and commodities – which I address in the upcoming chapter. But arguably, the most important propagational activity is the religious lecture. The importance of these lectures derives not just from their promotion of Salafi practice, but also because they are arenas in which an audience can engage with preachers and each other to collectively participate in religious practices and discuss their significance for society. I thus offer an examina-

Figure 2. UGM Campus Mosque, Yogyakarta (photo by the author, April 2012)

tion of these lectures, the individuals who attend them, and the forms of interaction they encourage.

The importance of religious lectures as a form of activism cannot be overstated. Benedict Anderson (1991: 170) argues that historically, mosques have provided zones of freedom in Indonesia. They were anti-colonial activists' spaces in which to popularise and circulate ideas. Similarly, as discussed in the previous chapters, mosques gave students a place relatively free from the security apparatus of the New Order, and so became spaces in which alternative visions of society gained traction (Van Bruinessen 2002). Salafi lectures were no different. The most common form of gatherings are *kajian, ceramah* or *taklim* – each of which are small gatherings of students who discuss religious ideas. Since the 1980s, this has not changed. Then as now, mosque lectures are pivotal to Salafi expansion.

Democracy has enabled Salafis to hold religious forums openly. No longer working underground, preachers can freely link up one of their lectures to a series of works, radio shows or other activities. They can also tailor their lectures to different times of day, groups of individuals or social environments. In fact, one of the biggest transformations since the fall of Suharto has been the increased use of *kajian* – lectures tailored to university students and young professionals.

Lectures have become more sophisticated in format. These can be small intimate affairs dealing with specific religious works, substantial events organised around a particular theme (such as love or the family), *Tabligh Akbar* (Grand Lectures), weekly urban and rural lectures, or *daurah* (religious training programme) that last for several days. All of these are complemented by more intense learning – or *tarbiyah* initiatives – where a small number of students follow a particular curriculum.

Although interlocutors referred to lectures as either *kajian, ceramah* or *taklim* (both of which also mean religious lecture), organisers and teachers would frequently stick to *kajian,* and this was not without significance. The term derives from the root *kaji* (to teach) and literally means 'study'. It is frequently used in Indonesia to describe classes relating to topics as diverse as literature, culture and the social sciences. The noun has a secular connotation of intellectually oriented study.[1] *Kajian* has come to refer to

---

1   In comparison, the term *pengajian,* derived from the same root word, is used by Salafis to refer to predominantly rural and/or basic lectures. *Pengajian,* unlike *kajian,* holds historical

an urban-based lecture, specifically organised by university-affiliated Salafi foundations such as the YPIA.

Kajian are far more than spaces of religious edification. They are places in which doctrine and practices actively undergo a process of interpretative re-orientation. Preachers and followers openly engage with each other, religious texts and contextual realities to understand how to live Islam and engage with it both on a personal and communal level. Accordingly, they represent network spaces (Juris & Khasnabish 2013) where global Islamic resources are inculcated and also questioned in the context of broader cultural and political considerations. It is in these lectures that activists build a sense of religious belonging and the social bonds that sustain Salafism as a movement.

SALAFIS AND THE RELIGIOUS LECTURE

For Salafis, the lecture is the most commonly used method of *da'wa* (propagation) and remains at the heart of how the movement recruits and perpetuates itself. As a form of proselytisation, lectures are primarily concerned with bringing lax Muslims into the fold.[2] They rarely focus on non-Muslims (at least as subjects of conversion) and so underline how the movement (in Indonesia at least) is primarily one of reversion and renewal.

Salafi lectures vary greatly in design and form. As many foundations have taken advantage of the ability to work openly since the fall of Suharto, Salafi lectures have changed over time. Salafis affiliated to the at-Turots have, for instance, stopped using the *halaqah*, which was used during the 1980s and '90s. Now they organise open lectures, not least due to an uneasiness about whether the methods of the *halaqah* are linked to the Muslim Brotherhood, but also because they believe it encourages exclusivity rather than openness (ICG 2004). They have replaced *halaqah* with public religious study sessions that are tailored to different or perceived social *milieus*. These include the student/professional-focused *kajian*.

---

connotations to traditional forms of Islamic discussion and is widely used in reference to study under a Kyai (religious teacher). It thus differs in its descriptive nuance.

2   On this point, the Salafi scholar As-Suhaimi differentiates between *da'wa* aimed at Muslims and non-Muslims. With the former, one must stress the need for proper *ibada* and the requirement to avoid deviating from Islam. With the latter, one must begin by stressing the need for *tawhid* (monotheism). See As-Suhaimi 2007.

Lectures create emotive spaces where teachers or preachers appeal to individuals to follow Islam and to better themselves and society. *Asatidz* spend much time insisting that society is plagued with political wrangling, demonstrations, corruption, *ikhtilath* (mixing of sexes), *taklid* (blind faith), misuse of Islamic symbols, and *zinah* (illegitimate sexual relationships). The focus is on creating individuals who are *ikhlas* (sincere) and *mukmin* (pious) to counter these trends and to promote a particular solution that can be found through the personal embodiment and inculcation of Salafi principles and what Goffman refers to as micro-behaviours (Goffman 1972: 139). The argument for converting to Salafism (over another interpretation of Islam) may be unique in its discursive intricacies but, like many other reformist religious movements, it necessarily calls on actors to reflect on what Islam means in *this* world and one's actions within it.

Most of my interlocutors first encountered the movement at a lecture. It was an 'obligatory point of passage' through which almost all passed.[3] Individuals seldom joined the movement directly or immediately. It was more common for them to participate casually before moving on to more intense forms of engagement. Often one attended a lecture out of religious curiosity or was introduced by a friend or teacher. Interlocutors described their initial encounters with lectures as enjoyable. They 'made sense' and were 'egalitarian' in nature. The *asatidz* and organisers in charge were approachable and would not demand deference from the audience.

Yudi was an IT expert in his late 30s who founded the Salafi social media outlet Yufid, together with several friends (described in the upcoming chapter). He is from Central Java, but had lived in Yogyakarta since coming to the city as a young student in the early 2000s. Yudi recalled that he first learned about Salafism during his studies at the city's prestigious UGM. He stated: 'my friends often organised routine [Salafi] lectures on campus and afterwards I saw that there was one at my faculty and that's it! I tried it and easily joined. Afterwards I was interested' (Interview, Yogyakarta, 4 June 2012). However, more than chance brought Yudi to the Salafi lecture: he

---

3 This phrase 'obligatory point of passage' comes from the work of Michel Callon, who uses it in relation to actor–network theory to describe a point through which actors are forced to converge on a certain topic and/or purpose. My use of the phrase loosely aligns with this idea of passage, although I envisage it as a physical space where actors engage with each other rather than a potential group of actors or problems one must pass through in a given network. For more information, see Callon 1986.

was searching for a 'truth' beyond religion. Yudi stated he was hooked by Salafism because he:

> ... liked finding logic [in things] and it entered logic ... when I first arrived in Yogyakarta in the year 98–99, I also joined left-wing discussions (*diskusi kiri*). We talked about Das Kapital, Karl Marx and others. Now this also has logic. But afterward I met the organiser (*pembesar*) of the Salafi *kajian* and became sure in my heart, and afterward, that's it! Until this moment I have followed it like that.   – Interview, Yogyakarta, 4 June 2012

Yudi also noted that he liked that Salafism was different from his previous experiences with Islam. His father was the caretaker at a traditional Islamic *pesantren* affiliated with Nahdlatul Ulama, and so he grew up in a religious household. Yet he felt uncomfortable with the reverence given to the *kyai* in charge of the *pesantren*, and so had only casually been interested in Islam. By his own admission, he had not intended to become a pious individual during his studies. Nonetheless he was impressed by Salafism as, unlike the Islam he had grown up with, 'no figure was considered the ideologue ... who must be followed without question.' Instead, the Salafi lecture was led by an *ustadz* who was humble and not *sombong* (arrogant). They were more than a teacher. They were a counsellor and friend who stimulated those at their lectures to think of themselves as a community and part of the *jemaah* (religious community).

Yudi was not alone in noting the importance of the teacher in a religious journey. Salafi *ustadz* went out of their way to be seen as authoritative but approachable. Moreover, while each of those I met had a unique story to tell when it came to joining Salafism, there were marked similarities amongst them. Yudi's experience was typical of a male attendee at a university-oriented *kajian*. He was a nominal Muslim who was intelligent, enrolled in the sciences or technology, and not from a wealthy background. I observed that individuals from large urban centres such as Jakarta and Surabaya were under-represented in the Salafi movement. Most came from regions around provincial towns such as Solo, Semarang or Malang.

Lukman, another follower of Salafism, had a different pattern of engagement. This 23-year-old man with thick glasses had recently enrolled in a UGM master's programme in chemical engineering. When I met him during the month of Ramadan, Lukman had recently arrived in Yogyakarta from South Sumatra. Like Yudi, he was clearly intelligent: he planned to apply for a PhD scholarship to study in Germany that year. Unlike Yudi, Lukman had actively sought out Salafi lectures to use his time away from home to become a better Muslim. By his own account, his family was only nominally religious, and so his knowledge of Islam was self-taught and kept secret from his parents. As such, he saw his studies as a perfect time to increase his involvement in Islam. When we first met, he told me that 'many people think Yogyakarta is a city of intellectual learning ... they are right, but there is Islamic learning here, too' (Interview, Yogyakarta, 29 July 2012).

Lukman's drive to learn about religion was deeply personal. He could often be seen studying and he had sought out the lectures on his own. There was, however, an intrinsically social element to his motivation. He tacitly acknowledged that the mosque lectures were a perfect place to make new – and properly Islamic – friends. He lamented that his friends back home were 'not interested in religion or were attracted to political Islam' and often reluctant to practice Islam unless it was linked to political developments or protest.

Lukman knew no one when he first joined the *kajian* series, but he quickly befriended other similar-aged participants. He helped set up for the lectures or prepare the food at the end of the day when we would break fast. He would, I observed, partake in endless debates amongst his new-found co-religionists, and enthusiastically attend all lecture on offer. For him, as with others I came to know, lectures provided a place to learn and conform to a particular idea of religious ethic and practice, and so gain acceptance amongst peers. Yet they were inherently social spaces that – as I now aim to show – could quickly become fraught as questions about how to live a Salafi lifestyle ran up against real-world problems.

THE KAJIAN

For several months I attended a series of lectures given by Ustadz Solahuddin. It was by chance I met Solahuddin one afternoon while waiting to speak to administrative staff at the Pesantren Islamic Centre Bin Baz (ICBB), where he was a teacher of religious studies. As I waited in the school's reception building, Solahuddin approached me to see whether I needed assistance. He was a native of Yogyakarta and 29 years old at the time. Solahuddin was polite, quietly spoken and amiable. After a brief discussion concerning the objectives of my fieldwork, he impulsively invited me to observe his lecture that afternoon. I accepted, and we agreed to meet at the *musholla* (prayer hall) where he taught.

The significance of the lecture dawned on me later that afternoon when I met up with Solahuddin afterwards. He asked me whether I felt Islam made '*more sense than Christianity*' after what I had heard. I demurred from answering definitively and was unsettled that he may have mistaken my professional interest for something more personal. I repeated that my interest was of an academic nature. Solahuddin smiled and reassured me that he understood my intentions and was not trying to 'force me to convert (*paksa bermualaf*)'. But he did express his desire that I would receive *hidayah*, or a God-given desire to find the religious truth. Solahuddin told me that it was through a similar lecture forum that he had found his desire to study Islam. He went on to explain that it was during his university studies that he had begun to attend *kajian* and decided to dedicate his life to religion. He valued the lecture as both a popular and communal way to become familiar with Islam. It was a catalyst to one's drive to become *taqwa* (a fear and love for God) through personal introspection.

As I came to know Solahuddin over the next several months, I would often ask how he went from being a participant in a *kajian* to being an *ustadz*. He would describe the difficulties and perseverance necessary to become an *ustadz* and, perhaps more importantly, *mukmin* (pious). He mentioned that after attending *kajian* for several years, he wanted to deepen his religious knowledge. However, Solahuddin had no previous formal religious education and could not speak Arabic. As a result, he failed to get a scholarship to study in Saudi Arabia, which had become his goal upon graduating. Not to be deterred, he decided to marry his girlfriend (also an enthusiastic follower of Salafism who was studying in Bandung) and move to Yemen, where the couple lived for four years. There he was able to slowly pick up the language while being supported by his wife – who was fluent in Arabic and had found employment as a teacher. Once his Arabic was at a sufficient level, he studied at the Dar al-Hadith Institute (as described in the previous chapter, an important centre of Salafi learning originally founded by Muqbil al-Wadi'i) until 2010. He and his wife then returned to Yogyakarta and began teaching and lecturing on religious matters throughout the city.

Solahuddin's story demonstrates the tremendous personal effort that can go into religious learning, and the determination one must have to become a Salafi preacher. As my relationship with Solahuddin became more

97

intimate, he was keen to talk about a variety of political topics such as Islam in Europe and the civil war in Syria. But he maintained that the *kajian* and the forum it provided had given him the desire to follow Salafism in the first place. He stated that the interactive and egalitarian approach to learning led him to see Islam '*as it truly is*' (*Islam benar-benar*), and he hoped I too would begin to feel the same.

To better understand what Solahuddin meant when he talked about the egalitarian nature of the religious lecture, let me describe the dynamics of his own lecture series. I participated in the lectures on a weekly basis for four months. It was the first of several lecture series I attended during my fieldwork. Indeed, while I was fortunate enough to observe several *Tabligh Akbar* (Grand Lectures) and *pengajian* (rural lectures), my focus in this section deals exclusively with the more regular lectures referred to as *kajian*. The phrase *kajian* is used to describe religious activities predominantly in the university campus and amongst urban professionals. *Kajian* refers to the need to engage intellectually with religious science as part of a wider endeavour to holistically increase one's knowledge. The lectures are scheduled at times that accommodate university timetables and/or hours of regular employment, and encourage a particular type of *tafakur* (reflection) that fosters dialogue amongst attendees to discover how to live Islam.

The lectures are frequently compared to, and distinguished from, the rural lecture, or *pengajian,* which is seen as a basic Islamic lecture held by a *da'i* rather than an *ustadz*. The audience of a *pengajian* is assumed – often wrongfully – to lack the intellectual capacity of the professional and student groups of the *kajian*. As discussed in the previous chapter, perceptions of rural Muslims reflect a view within urban religious renewal movements – one where urban young professional Muslims represent a future-focused socially mobile Muslim class who will advance an Islamic modernity. Members of the *kajian* believe themselves to be an alternative to the backwardness and simplicity of their parent's generation, which was tainted with *bid'a* (un-Islamic innovations) and *taklid* (blind faith). The term *kajian* thus aligns with a general attitude that urban students can combine religion with professional employment, while rural communities are recipients of a combination of social development and basic religious training.

The *kajian* conducted by Solahuddin was organised on behalf of the student Islamic foundation, the YPIA. In 2019, the YPIA organised 46 weekly *kajian* across four university campuses in the city – up from the

28 weekly *kajian* offered in 2012. Complementing these *kajian*, which are managed directly by YPIA's secretariat, are a number of affiliated but unofficial *kajian* linked to the YPIA. These are instigated by YPIA boarding houses, *asatidz* or independent YPIA followers (rather than by the YPIA secretariat), many of whom endeavour to promote Salafism in their own academic department mosques or *musholla* (prayer rooms). In this way, enthusiastic followers assist in the spread of Salafism into new university departments or spaces. However, it is worth noting that the *asatidz* – who most students meet through the YPIA – retain control of the content of these unofficial *kajian*.

Solahuddin's *kajian* was in this latter category, as he was initially invited into the *musholla* by Azis, a third-year medical student. Azis had been in-volved in the YPIA since his first year at university and provided logistical assistance for the *kajian* – preparing post-lecture snacks as well as booking the space with the departmental *musholla* managerial board. He also assisted attendees, actively offering information to those who wanted to know more and/or wished to attend further YPIA lectures (Interview, Yogyakarta, 10 April 2012).

The *musholla* is a moderate size, two-storey building situated in the middle of the university's medical department complex. It is simple in design, and its ground floor is covered in green carpet with a large clock and small table located at the front. It is an open plan with no doors and a series of structural pillars. The public can see into the complex from the open green spaces adjacent to the *musholla*. Solahuddin's *kajian* were not very big, addressing 12 males and reportedly more females (although given strict gender segregation, I cannot confirm this). Women sat on the upper level of this two-storey structure and were only able to see the *ustadz* by peering over a small balcony railing. Male students were in their late teens and early twenties, and many had heard of the sermon through friends in the department. The lecture was scheduled for 4pm, when afternoon classes had finished.

Each *kajian* began with an initial greeting and introduction. Solahuddin would welcome participants and share information about upcoming reli-gious events. This would not take long and, after some further conversation to re-cap what the audience thought of the previous *kajian* (and any ques-tions as to its content), the lecture proper would begin. Solahuddin would sit cross-legged at the front with his textbook resting on a knee-high table upon which a microphone was placed. Male students sat in a semi-circle around the *ustadz* with Qur'an, notebooks and textbooks in hand.

The environment of the *kajian* was serious yet informal. Students turned up late, openly conferred with one another and checked their mobile phones. This did not detract from their interest in the topic, however. The *kajian* would last an hour and a half and cover a number of subjects outlined in a workbook given to attendees. By following the prescribed workbook, these lectures were part of a series titled *Nutrisi Hati* (Nutrition for the Heart) that were, with regards to Islamic sciences, fairly foundational. The aim was to instil a basic understanding and enthusiasm for Islam that, in the later sessions, would become a bridge to further *kajian* and activities.

In accordance with Salafi doctrine, the focus of the *kajian* was primarily on instilling correct faith – including *aqida* (creed) and *tawhid* (monotheism), and fighting *nafsu* (desire). Much of the emphasis was on personal *muhasabah* (introspection) and a need to follow true Islam by gaining proper *taqwa*. Yet Solahuddin was also quick to emphasise the importance of pure religious practice in the face of the perversions of society. By so doing, the values needed to become a pious Muslim were brought into sharp relief. Not only were they essential for religious salvation, but were part of a moral obligation to better one's social surroundings through Islamic principles. For example, when university students from across Indonesia became involved in demonstrations against a planned government fuel price hike in March 2012, Solahuddin argued that such worldly concerns only caused friction amongst the *umma* and distracted one's concentration from religious obligations. Similarly, in a separate *kajian* several weeks later, he reflection on the media frenzy around deaths linked to the *tomcat* (rove beetle), believing that while such deaths were unfortunate, one should turn to religion rather than gossiping and demanding a vaccine from the government.

These two examples are among the many reflections that characterised Solahuddin's lectures, used to portray an Indonesian society that did not properly respect Islamic principles. This extended to the university campus, which he saw as an environment that encouraged the mixing of the sexes and so distracted men from their studies and religious duty. This did not mean that the Indonesian government should be condemned, nor the campus avoided. They both provided the space and opportunity for people to engage freely with religion and receive an education. The problem lay with the people who chose not to follow religious tenets.

In another *kajian*, Solahuddin lamented on this issue. He spoke at length on the importance of prayer and why one should neither forget to pray nor pray too quickly. He stressed the need to get to the mosque 30 minutes before the Friday *khutbah* (sermon) began in order to relax and have time to reflect on one's relationship with God. This was not common practice in Indonesia, he continued, as the pressure of modern society forced people to speed through prayers in order to get back to work. Yet if one hurries through prayer, they will inevitably feel bored with religion and not have a proper understanding of *taqwa*. A hastened approach to prayers, he concluded, was like taking God for granted.

In his lectures, Solahuddin regularly reflected on Indonesia-specific tribulations like those mentioned above to highlight the lack of piety in society. But he did not shy away from connecting these local issues to global religious concerns. The conflict in Syria was mentioned as an example of the challenges faced by the *Ahlus Sunna wal-jama'ah* (people of the Sunna and Community) from so-called deviant forces. The conflict was portrayed as part of a wider Sunni versus Shi'i schism. This was relevant to Indonesians given it had its own Shi'a community. According to Solahuddin, the Syrian conflict underlined a problem with the Shi'a who, through Iran and Hezbollah, were backing both the Iraqi and Syrian governments as part of an attempt to encircle the holy cities of the Hejaz and eventually take control of them. The Shi'a were, he believed, not real Muslims but a group that caused division amongst the *umma*. Adherents needed to be vigilant of Shi'a infiltration into Indonesia and support their Sunni counterparts in Syria, who were under attack by the Assad regime and its allies (Interview, Yogyakarta 19 April 2012).

The concern with global issues was not, however, predominantly negative. For the most part, Solahuddin stressed the benefits of brotherhood with the global Muslim community and created a social imaginary of solidarity amongst pious Muslims around the world. He used his experience in Yemen (prior to the civil war) and Saudi Arabia as examples of model Islamic societies where people paid proper consideration to religion. He explained that Saudi Arabia was a place where people took time to respect religion and, as a consequence, Saudi society had achieved a higher moral standard. He recalled that when he was in the kingdom, he was always invited to the homes of strangers to eat after Friday sermons. This personal story was told in a tone of nostalgic reflection, a style that augmented its impact. In another *kajian*, Solahuddin reflected that a problem in Indonesia was a work week that followed Western tradition – holidays on Saturday and Sunday but not Friday. Turning to his audience, he asked rhetorically whether by working on Fridays, Indonesian Muslims truly respected their religion. He compared this common Indonesian practice to Saudi Arabia and Salafi schools across the province that closed for religious observance on Friday.[4]

This narrative of a perfect society that existed in parts of the Middle East juxtaposed with a corrupt Indonesia was not unique to Solahuddin's *kajian*. Over the course of my fieldwork, I noticed this to be a frequent part of the narrative in university-based lectures (although not in rural *pengajian*). It helped construct what Taylor and Gaonkar refer to as a social imaginary that promotes a specific way of understanding and mediating social and collective life (Gaonkar 2002). The fact many *asatidz* had studied in Yemen and Saudi Arabia provided a formidable tool through which to amplify the universal meaning of Salafism and its connection to some of Islam's most holy lands. Reflecting on this created the idea of an Islamic community which was both pure and modern and that, to paraphrase Taylor (2002: 106–07), would provide an understanding of one's situation and through which features one's world would become evident. It was also framed in a way that intended to resonate and align with the norms and concerns of the audience, tailored as it was to the student environment. It thus became a tool used to define the necessity of faith and provide a sense of perceived solidarity with other Muslims throughout the world.

The lecture was not solely an arena where Solahuddin expressed his concerns and religious knowledge; the forum actively encouraged participation. Such engagement was perhaps most evident during the question and answer sessions at the end of a *kajian*. Questions were written on pieces of paper and submitted to Solahuddin, who would then duly answer. Significantly, some questions were asked by women participants who, while unable to converse directly with the *ustadz*, would throw questions written on pieces

---

4   Examples were used to underline the reasons one should follow Islam correctly – an Islam that was inevitably linked to the global examples of piety and harmony. They were, however, detached from the very real events and complexities of religious practice in the Arabian Peninsula. From 2011 and 2012 relations between Saudi Arabia and Indonesia were tense due to the Indonesian government's objection to the execution of Indonesian maids by the Saudi government on what they saw as dubious charges. These executions led to a ban on Indonesian maids being sent to Saudi Arabia, as well as several demonstrations in Indonesia against the kingdom. Yet these events were never referred to in *kajian* and Saudi Arabia remained a convenient model of the proper emulation of the Prophet (and so a just religious society) could be actualised.

of paper over the balcony. I did not see this in any other *kajian* (and most likely only possible given the architectural design of the *musholla*).

A question asked more than once was whether one was allowed to study under the financial sponsorship of a parent who worked for a non-Islamic bank. In March 2012 when this was first asked, Solahuddin was non-committal in his answer. He stated that it was not allowed but could be permissible if a father who worked in such an industry did so with a good heart, because it was important to get an education. When the same question was asked a month later, however, Solahuddin first hesitated and then stated that he had consulted *fatawa* and concluded that it was forbidden. If a student were to truly abide by Islamic principles, they would need to find funding from other sources, although he conceded that one could continue studying while looking for such alternatives. I found both the conviction behind these answers and Solahuddin's explanations tepid. Nevertheless, his answers did demonstrate the need to negotiate between some of the harder points of doctrine and the realities of student life.

Solahuddin's goal was to impress on the audience that they were part of something more than a mere audience attending a lecture; they were agents on a mission to better society through their personal and collective efforts. Islam was both worldly and timeless, but also inherently modern and forward-looking. This message was strengthened by the bonds forged amongst *kajian* members, which Solahuddin actively encouraged. At the end of every session as water and snacks were served, men would sit and talk informally with Solahuddin about their lives or events on campus, frequently joking and comparing stories about their university experiences.

These informal points of engagement may have seemed casual, but they were – I came to understand – an integral part of the *kajian*. Solahuddin encouraged the audience to engage with one another. He stressed that they were a *Majelis* (council) that needed to work together to ensure they all adhered to religious practice. It is notable that over time, the men began to pray together prior to the *kajian*, in a style specific to Salafi doctrine.[5] Male attendees also began to adopt religious dress, facial hair and other Salafi markers. Several began expressing an interest in continuing to learn about Islam (Interview, Yogyakarta 19 April 2012). Collectively, they were thus beginning to con-

---

5   This style of prayer sees one touching feet with one's peers and follows the method outlined by Al-Albani. For additional information, see Al-Albani (2000).

nect with the movement that would shift the ways they approached society and religious practice. The interactive nature of the *kajian*, and the ability to converse intimately with the *ustadz* and with each other, was crucial to religious activism and the way Salafi doctrine was inculcated.

THE COMMUNAL NATURE OF THE KAJIAN

The communal nature of the *kajian* was evident during the different weekly lectures I was invited to participate in. These lectures provided spaces in which bonds between audience members and preacher were formed, creating moments of cultural and social tension through which global Islamic resources were translated and given substance. It was the horizontal relationships built in the lectures that gave religious doctrine social meaning.

While not wishing to generalise on the very personal nature of religious reversion (nor on the potentially multiple cognitive interpretations linked to ideas of faith), the lecture provided a space to accentuate particular values and socio-religious markers. The need to adhere to contextual demands led *asatidz* to align their *kajian* with local pressures. Lectures were organised predominantly on days off (such as Sundays) or at times that suited the schedule of the desired audience. Aside from providing content that reflected the potential anxieties of the audience, preachers notably omitted any criticism that could be seen to question the need for education or the desire to gain a better socio-economic station. The emphasis was on the moral deterioration of modern society and the need to increase one's religious faith to ensure a modern, progressive and economically secure future for all Muslims.

It was amongst *kajian* attendees themselves that the real importance of contextual considerations and what they meant for Salafism as a movement could be seen. These considerations can play an integral role in mobilising individuals for small-scale activities such as handing out leaflets. But they also form the basis by which micro-practices and religious tenets (or the desire to apply them) are learned, reified and given wider meaning through an *espirit de corps*.

Those attending Solahuddin's lectures altered the way they looked and expressed themselves. While the number of male participants dropped as the lecture series progressed, those that continued to attend would turn up early to discuss life, religion, study and their own activism. As they gained more confidence, they asked more questions, talked about trying to bring a friend to the lectures, and considered what other sermons or classes they should take when they returned to the campus the following semester.

This leads us to another point of analysis. The promotion of religious discourse in the *kajian* is geared less towards creating religious scholars than inculcating an embodied disposition through which one would attempt to turn oneself into a modern religious subject. I am not the first to argue this point in relation to Salafi reversion. Work amongst Salafi women in Indonesia led Nisa (2012) to draw similar conclusions. She states that a Salafi ethic goes beyond understanding religious scripture, as it requires one to consciously enact prescribed practices to govern one's conduct. Yet, it also became evident during my fieldwork that the interactive dynamics of the *kajian* can change the movement from within.

The *kajian* provides an opportunity for activists to contest and examine religious principles in ways pursuant to ideas of urban living or social mobility. While joining Salafism has elements of submission to both scripture and prescribed behaviour, the *kajian* is a forum where modern perspectives, methods of organising, identity and religious practices are debated. Agents consciously learn to carry themselves in specific ways, wear religious dress and scatter their speech with religious phrases. In these ways, they internalise their involvement in the movement and assume a common identity with others in the *kajian*. They also examine the implications of specific tenets by, for example, questioning the validity of practices in light of social constraints, or by finding religious justifications to delay the implementation of certain practices.

It is also notable that *asatidz* would talk about religious identity in terms that stressed both a modern and communal outlook. In order to entice individuals, *asatidz* could baulk at being too strict, and find compromises when it came to the most contentious issues, such as when Solahuddin demurred from providing a definitive answer about whether one could receive a scholarship from parent working at a non-Sharia bank. The audience was encouraged to participate in such debates and work together to reify the concept of the *Jemaah* from the inside. These often led to discussions about how they could become involved in *da'wa*. I frequently saw students in *kajian* devise plans about how best to hand out religious magazines or bulletins on the campus and in surrounding areas.

The *kajian* audience would work together to determine how they should conduct themselves in their immediate environment and how to ensure they adhered to a Salafi type. Frequently, they would correct each other, offer advice about how best to pray or where to go on campus to avoid mixing with the other sex, recommend boarding houses or mosques familiar with those in the movement, and even discuss which lecturers were more pious (an attribute they correlated with intelligence!). One of the most contentious debates amongst students concerned how to interact with a parent who, they feared, might have a hostile reaction to one's new Salafi faith. Lukman, who we met earlier, said that one reason he had waited until he left home to attend Islamic study groups was that he did not wish to tell his parents about his new-found piety. The more we discussed his parents, the more aware I became about his anxiety and unease. It was clear he was taking his newfound faith seriously, but found it difficult to bridge his changed life in Yogyakarta with the friendships and opinions of those in his home region of South Sumatra.

Lukman was not alone in his concerns. Others voiced similar anxieties, including Muhammad, a DJ at the Salafi radio station based at al-Hasanah Mosque whom I met whilst attending a *kajian* with Lukman. Muhammad was a shy graduate who had recently finished his studies at UGM, but had stayed on in the city to manage an Islamic boarding house. Originating from nearby Solo, he would often travel home for weekends, and he was visibly anxious about these trips to see his parents. For this reason Muhammad, unlike his co-religionists, was clean-shaven, as his father disapproved of Muhammad's Salafi faith, and so demanded he not grow a beard 'lest he look like the terrorists on TV.'

Muhammad had reluctantly obeyed his father, but was embarrassed by this compromise in the practice of his faith. His friends in the *kajian* and the boarding house suggested a solution: why not follow his father's demand for now but try to convince his father otherwise through *da'wa*? The Qur'an demands that parents be respected and, by following this tactic, he would not be diverging from the Salafi *manhaj* (method). Although not everyone agreed with this strategy, Muhammad was grateful for the support he had received. It was not an ideal solution, but he was consciously trying to live by Islam and even if his interpretation was imperfect, he had brought it to the community for consultation (Interview, Yogyakarta, 10 August 2012).

As anecdotal as this example may be, it demonstrates the subtle disagreements and compromises that create variations on what the finer points of Salafi praxis can mean to an individual in a given time and place. Reversion and the adoption of Salafi practices require a degree of self-refashioning.

They also involve deep social and personal negotiations as agents come to adapt religious doctrine to the context in which they live. The *asatidz* plays a significant role in catalysing this process by linking doctrine to the social landscape and perceived sensitivities of their audience. This is augmented by the social bonds forged amongst members as they come to think of themselves as the true Islamic community. Yet the intricate ways doctrine is applied to one's own social environment necessarily relies on actively engaging, questioning and altering one's behaviours in order to accept and be accepted by the movement – which is signalled by the religious lecture.

ADAPTING DA'WA TO THE LOCALE

It is noteworthy that religious norms often were mixed with social norms, and the boundaries of the two spheres were far from clear. Muhammad, for example, described his difficulties with his father as caused by his father's 'undeveloped' interpretation of Islam (*tafsir yang tidak canggih*). I will thus conclude this chapter by describing an event that clearly shows the communal nature of Salafi learning.

One evening during the latter half of Ramadan, Lukman and his colleague Arya visited my house on their way back from doing errands at a nearby *pesantren*. We talked at length about conduct towards non-Muslims. This conversation began as a reflection on a lecture we had attended that day. The preacher had stated that only true Muslims could be *ikhlas* (sincere). Lukman was quick to agree with this, stressing that while he was happy to have personal relations with non-Muslims, he could fully trust only those who shared a similar religious belief. Arya, sensing the unease this statement caused, qualified Lukman's comment by suggesting that it did not imply we could not all remain friends. It was rather that Muslims needed to be more aware of how they conducted themselves and who they trusted. What was important, he argued, was intent; I intended to learn (academically) about Islam and he intended to foreground Islam regardless of the temptations and challenges experienced along the way.

At the time, I was not entirely convinced by Arya's argument. It neither squared with what I had heard during lectures nor with what I had read in Salafi literature. Yet when taken into consideration with the interactive nature through which the Salaf and non-Salaf worlds are constituted, it made sense. Enforcing Salafi principles was not a clear-cut game, and could shift over time and in response to individual concerns. Whether or not to engage with a researcher such as myself, who – although not Salafi – was learning and participating in the movement, had no simple answer. Religious boundaries were as much about one's *niyya* (intentions) – and a recognition of one's *niyya* by one's peers – as they were about references to Salafi tenets. Local anxieties, Islamic discourses, power imbalances and peer pressures converged to define a Salafi ethic rife with contention and subject to constant reform.

The evocation of a Salafi subjectivity is not solely a project of internal self-transformation. It is tied to the creation of a communal ethic that defines how one navigates between Salafi doctrine, contemporary society and religious identity. Salafi scholars may be quick to describe their piety as pure and decontextualised. But closer examination of their lectures and activism enables us to see the communal debates and relationships at play within the movement. This alludes to an ethics of what Al-Mohammad (2010) defines as 'being-with', which emphasises the need to see selfhood as lying within a greater web of interdependencies and intercorporealities pertaining to human existence. Life becomes possible through and with other individuals as the enmeshment between beings indicates that 'not only that our existential coordinates are eccentric but so too are our ethical coordinates and responsibilities' (*Ibid.*: 441). Consequently, Salafi activists rarely rely on Salafi teachings alone. Instead, adherents rationalise choices through a web of social relationships that enable them to find solutions about how best to navigate the social world and display their intent to live a pious lifestyle to others.

As activists become more deeply involved in lectures, the social relationships developed there become the bedrock they build on when becoming involved in *da'wa*. *Da'wa* is key to any Salafi identity, and it can range from simple assistance in setting up lectures to establishing a range of Islamic commodities, websites, social media platforms or literary mediums. All of these spread the message of Islam and also provide diverse examples of how Salafis have become involved in wider processes of Islamic commodification in Indonesia. It is to these industries that I now turn, to show how Salafi *da'wa* has adapted to the locale of Yogyakarta.

108

CHAPTER 4

New Trajectories: Social Activism Beyond the Mosque

s Islam gains importance as a mobiliser for public action and association, it also informs the magazines one buys, where one lives, and which schools one's children attend. Not surprisingly, Salafi activism has become linked to such a drive within the public sphere, and market forces have come to alter the imaginative, performative and participative dimensions of the contemporary Salafi movement. This chapter examines the nuances of new *da'wa* (propagation) industries emerging amongst and promoted by Yogyakartan Salafis.

I am not the first to explore the significance of the growing visibility of Islamic symbols, commodities and economic industries in Indonesia or the broader Islamic world (Fauzia 2013; Latief 2013). Fischer (2008),

Figure 3. *As-Sunnah Magazine* (photo by the author, September 2013)

whose work is on Islamic consumption in Malaysia amongst middle-class Malays, shows how consumer practices give rise to new discursive meanings and fields through which Islam is practised and debated. Concerning Indonesia, Rudnyckyj's (2009a, 2009b) studies of Islamic management training firms show that a specific idea of Islamic engagement emerges from a combination of faith and market forces. These produce a particular form of self that draws simultaneously from capitalist ideas of 'rational' behaviour and Islamic discourse. What this implies is that religious fulfilment and specific patterns of consumption have become linked. As Turner (2009: 44) argues, 'life on earth is no longer merely a prelude to the consumption of happiness in the next world: the promise of consumerism is to have one's desires satisfied now.'

Consumer and economic practices, or indeed almost any interaction with market forces, can thus become imbued with religious significance and become a signifier of one's faith. Yet my use of 'market' connotes more than the actual physical commodities bought and sold. Instead it emphasises the patterns of behaviour and association promoted and transformed by these very activities. Islamic commodities inform the ways one creates markers through which co-religionists associate with each other, not just as Muslims but as Muslims belonging to a particular socio-economic stratum of society. As Fealy (2008) notes, the very process of picking and consuming goods become representational of how one defines both one's religious identity but also one's social and economic 'class consciousness'.

While I look more extensively at the discursive construction of a Muslim (or more accurately urban Salafi) class in the next chapter, it is notable here that the idea of a Muslim middle class – as a political and demographic category – has gained salient recognition across Indonesia. Indonesian Muslims symbolically use religious knowledge, mosque sermons and products to both engage with faith and publicly distinguish themselves from other religions and social classes (Hasan 2014; Muzakki 2008).

Islamic identity is enmeshed in a wider Islamic knowledge economy. By this I mean the process of agents generating, processing and applying knowledge-based information in a way that links global ideas of capitalist production and consumption with local methods of action (Castells 2010). Urban Muslims have increasingly come to think of themselves and their faith as congruent with a particular *milieu* or class by consuming specific products and even creating new industries of religious fashion (Hasan

2014; Jones 2007). Yet by doing so, they alter the very ways Islamic authority is established, questioned and imbibed. Islamic legitimacy becomes ever more dependent on the individuals who wish to engage with Islam rather than with someone whose authority is preordained via established religious authorities.

An eloquent examination of the growth of new *da'wa* industries amongst Indonesia's aspirational middle class is provided by Hoesterey (2012, 2015). His study of Abdullah Gymnastier (popularly referred to as Aa Gym) and the Movement to Build the Conscience of the Nation (Gema Nusa) underlines how new 'pop' preachers like Aa Gym have created a following amongst Indonesia's Muslim middle classes. This is not achieved through what Bayat (2002) terms 'joyless moralising', but by charismatically mixing issues of faith with pop psychology and notions of economic success (Hoesterey 2012). These pop preachers have recalibrated the prophetic tradition in order to promote an Islamic cosmopolitanism that aims to create a spiritual intelligence that complements one's intellectual and economic prowess (*Ibid.*). This adds to the commodified forms of Islamic expressions through which, as Fealy (2008: 16) argues, Muslims have come to selectively consume Islamic products from an ever-growing spiritual marketplace.

This does not mean that established preachers or organisations have become irrelevant. Rather, their authority has come to depend not just on their religious knowledge but also on their ability to appeal and relate to the life choices of their audiences. New Islamic social movements are a catalyst to these processes, directly appealing to younger generations of Muslims by re-inventing concepts of Islamic truth and praxis via charismatic preachers who communicate through the vernacular of slang, common language and contemporary examples of society. Salafis have used Salafi lectures and spaces to encourage individuals to use their social and professional skills to reach out to other like-minded Muslim via a range of mediums including social media, literature, the Internet and satellite TV.

We have thus seen the growth of new Salafi industries that directly appeal to educated urban Muslims. The proliferation of Salafi *da'wa* has come to include literature tailored to those concerned with living Islamic lifestyles, radio broadcasts on thematic social issues, websites and mobile phone apps for tech-savvy followers to access lectures or find religious content via Salafi-specific search engines, and a range of Islamic commodities

Figure 4. At-Tauhid Bulletin (photo by the author, September 2013)

sold predominantly by university students or recent graduates. In turn, this has transformed the movement and how one comes to understand how to live Islam as the formation of a religious selfhood increasingly intersects with the economic, social and political realms within which individuals live. Accordingly, this chapter will endeavour to explain the flourishing of these new forms of *da'wa* by describing how activists use their faith to interact with this aforementioned Islamic market.

Da'wa *Literature – Publications, Content and Distribution*

The advancement of Islamic virtues in print is an important part of contemporary Salafi *da'wa*. The popularity of this method can be traced back to the growing use of the printing press in the Dutch East Indies during the 19th century. The Islamic revival movements of the late colonial period promoted anti-colonial and Islamic revivalist sentiments in journals and cheap books. For instance, West Sumatran Islamic reformists of the *kaum muda* (young group) published a number of religious journals such as *Al-Imam* and *Al-Munir* – written in the Malay vernacular from which Indonesian is derived – on topics of religion and politics (Azra 1999). As literacy rates have increased in the latter half of the 20th century, it is unsurprising that this form of *da'wa* has become more popular. However, the topics, modes of distribution and scholastic affiliations have changed over time. They now include novellas, short stories and even Islamically inspired comic books.

Salafi foundations have contributed to the range of *da'wa* print publications. During the 1980s, the LIPIA printed crucial works by Saudi Arabian *shaykh* for distribution by the DDII (Hasan 2007: 89). By the 1990s Salafis had, according to the International Crisis Group, established more than 21 publishing houses of their own – a number that increased after B.J. Habibie lifted press restrictions in 1999 (ICG 2004: 12). The nature of Salafi literature has also changed over time. No longer curtailed by the New Order, there has been a considerable upsurge in both the quantity of Islamic publications and the range of topics that authors are able to address (Interview, Yogyakarta, 29 May 2012).

A significant portion of the contemporary Salafi-Islamic publication market is geared towards lifestyle choices, covering topics as varied as health, love, cooking and economics. Salafi publishers have both a national and local reach. For those with national ambitions – for whom publishing is a business unto itself – distribution frequently relies on networks of sellers who take orders at religious fairs, lectures and bookstores. In contrast, more locally oriented publishers often use their magazines or books to promote local aspiring preachers or as material to complement their own lectures or social outreach programmes.

Yogyakarta is home to several of these smaller distributors, including the YPIA's own Pustaka Muslim (Muslim Library) which circulates the weekly at-Tauhid bulletin. These bulletins are four pages long and often cover a single topic. They are distributed by activists outside mosques both on and off campus after Friday afternoon prayers. Although the exact number of bulletins distributed is hard to estimate, several interlocutors put the weekly print-run at over 200 copies (Interview, Yogyakarta, 3 August 2012). They are printed on cheap paper and aim to address timely social concerns that have received coverage in the popular media. The topic is determined through consultation between an *ustadz* and students, the latter of whom print and then distribute the bulletins across the city. Mosque sermons form a critical part of the bulletin circulation network. Participants at a *kajian* are frequently recruited to distribute at-Tauhid, and this is often their introduction to the broader web of *da'wa* activism. Lukman, whom we met in the previous chapter, was one such recruit. He volunteered to distribute at-Tauhid one Friday alongside his colleague Arya, who showed him how to use the bulletins to start conversations with individuals outside mosques.

At-Tauhid also provides students at the YPIA with a chance to test their own skills at Islamic writing. While each issue of at-Tauhid includes articles written by acknowledged preachers, there were also several students who contributed to the bulletin. An entire issue of at-Tauhid (No7.8) was dedicated to a critical essay by Habib, one such aspiring scholar and YPIA member. Habib was deeply concerned about the un-Islamic nature of Valentine's Day, a topic that has become an obsession for many conservative Muslims in Indonesia.[1] Habib argues that Valentine's Day needed to be condemned for corrupting Indonesian youth. Using language that is less concerned with religious tenets and more emotive and moralising in tone, he appeals to the anxiety that society was being corrupted by a foreign, Western culture. The piece urges readers to turn to Islam and use their skills to build an Islamic society. As Habib concludes, 'Do not let the intention of realising our love with our lovers, or not loving ourselves take place, as by immersing ourselves into the threat of Allah, we will receive a hard punishment because we are doing what is forbidden' (Habib 2012).

Bulletins provide a forum through which individuals could engage with *da'wa*, but they were complemented by numerous other publications. Notably, Yogyakartan Salafis publish a range of A6 size *buku saku* (pocketbooks) that offer simple summaries of important works concerning concepts of religious practice, *sholat* (prayer), *wudhu* and proper dress. While the title of a *buku saku* relate to actual works by prestigious scholars, the content is frequently in bullet point format with explanatory diagrams. For example, the *buku saku* version of *Sifat Shalat Nabi* (Ways of Prayer According to the Prophet) by Shaykh Nasir al-Din al-Albani is a mere 50 pages, while the full Indonesian language edition is over 250 pages.[2] These pocketbooks are predominantly aimed at rural audiences who, as has been explained, are deemed to have only a simple grasp of Islamic sciences. Despite being

---

1   Among other methods, religious conservatives hold annual demonstrations against Valentines Day, berating it as Christian, Jewish, secular or even just a 'sex holiday.' See Gade 2013, JakartaPost 2014a and Telegraph 2013.

2   I refer specifically to the translation published by Media Hidayah. See Al-Albani 2000.

written to rural Muslims, these pocketbooks are also popular amongst the clientele of urban bookstores, where the newest editions are commonly displayed on the store counter.

Another genre of books and magazines focuses on issues of religious life, economics, morality, the family, health and even cooking. As-Sunnah, a monthly magazine published in Solo, is arguably the most popular Salafi magazine amongst interlocutors, with a distribution of 20,000 copies a month. Every edition of As-Sunnah sports a glossy front cover, and its contents include featured articles often with coloured sketches and catchy titles, as well as a number of standardised sections and topical discussion pieces round out the content. Most issues promote a holistic approach to religion, covering aspects of lifestyle, politics, society and health. Topics range from dietary recommendations for children to herbal remedies for constipation (see e.g., As-Sunnah December 2011; July 2012). They also deal with more serious issues, such as orientalism, terrorism or corruption. The preacher Kholid Syamhudi wrote an extensive piece, arguing that Islamic practice in Indonesian society is plagued with the lies of orientalism which are used by the West to weaken the main tenets of Islam (Syamhudi 2012). He polemically argues that the practices of religious organisations such as Nahdlatul Ulama were incorrect, as they had been influenced by Western attempts to corrupt Islam.

These publications are not the only avenues through which life issues are addressed. A growing number of soft cover titles (a term used by publishers themselves to distinguish them from works of pure Islamic science) are also circulated. They often have catchy titles such as Abu Umar Basyier's Ada Apa Dengan Salafi? (What's up with Salafi?) (Basyier 2011a), an introductory work explaining basic Salafi principles through *bahasa gaul* (slang) and whose title references the hit teen movie Ada Apa Dengan Cinta? (What's Up With Love?). Another provocative title by Basyier is Indonesian Negeri Para Pendengki? (Is Indonesia a Country of Spiteful People?) (Basyier 2011b), a part of his Seri Obrolan Warung Kopi (Coffee Shop Conversation Series), which takes the form of a conversation between five fictional protagonists. In a narrative covering a range of political and social issues (such as corruption, education and poverty), the characters are convinced of the Salafi way by their wiser friend, who is portrayed as calm, friendly and helpful, using slang and everyday examples to underline the importance of religious principles.

All of the above-mentioned publications are sold by a growing network of publishing houses and Islamic bookstores across Indonesia. In Yogyakarta, the best-known store where these titles are available was founded by Ustadz Afifi Abdul Wadud in 1994. Strategically located next to the UGM campus, it has a large but modest layout, with green walls and shelves separating books into genres of strict religious learning (Hadith, *aqida*, and so on) and social knowledge (family, love and health).

I would often visit the store in the late afternoon, after observing a *kajian*. The atmosphere was usually friendly and filled with the sound of a religious sermon from either a radio or a religious DVD. Customers were expected to remove their shoes at the door and wear appropriate clothing. Opening hours revolved around daily prayers. Because they cater to a wider audience of Muslims, segregation between women and men was not enforced.

Hanif, originally from Central Java, managed the daily affairs of the store. He was aware of Salafism whilst a student at the nearby state university, but the preacher Wadud piqued his interest in the movement at a *kajian* he attended in the 1990s. Wadud offered him a job and he has worked there since, now in the role of manager. When I would visit the store, Hanif – if he was not out running errands – would describe his newest stock items. He would show me the latest perfumes or books that were on display. Our conversations frequently drifted to talk about how Salafism has developed in Yogyakarta. On one occasion, he reflected that the store was an example of the growing popularity of the Salafi *manhaj* (method). The shop had expanded from a small outlet for religious clothing in the 1990s into a store that sold not only the latest books and magazines, but also herbal medicines, perfumes and DVDs. It was – as he proclaimed and its logo attested to – a store that had nuances of the Middle East.

Although Hanif felt that the increased number of bookstores and publications confirmed the popularity of Salafism, I believe it is also an indication of a more qualitative expansion. It attests to the growing sophistication of Islamic literature distributed by activists. Salafis align themselves with the broader popularity of religious novels and lifestyle books. Indeed, Indonesia's book market has become saturated with a wide range of religious books, including Islamic 'romantic' and teen novels. Rokhman, in his work concerning the Forum Lingkar Pena and the author Galang Lufityanto elaborated on how an Indonesian Islamic teen genre mixes religious motifs with ideas of youthfulness, love and adventure (Rokhman 2011). Such ideas have also become 'mainstream', as happened with the religious love story and bestseller Ayat-Ayat Cinta (Letter of Love), which was turned into a hit movie in 2008. It was voted 'Favourite Book of the Year' in 2005 by Muslimah (Muslim Woman) magazine, narrowly defeating Harry Potter (Widodo 2008).

While Salafi literature does not include such fiction, they share bookshelves with such works in larger bookstores. As such, Salafis contribute to both the growing Islamic literature market as well as the popularity of new books by using catchy titles, slang or aesthetically pleasing covers.

RADIO

Complementing new religious books is the increasing use of radio to propagate religious messages. Salafi activists across Indonesia have been incredibly energetic when establishing such ventures, but they are hardly the first. For example, as early as 1967 anti-government preachers like Abdullah Sungkar and Abu Bakar Ba'asyir (the founders of Jemaah Islamiyah) had begun broadcasting through their Radio Dakwah Islamiyah Surakarta (The Islamic Proselytisation Radio of Surakarta), although this was shut down in 1975 for its hostility towards government policies (ICG 2002: 6–7). However, the previously mentioned lifting of government restrictions by Habibie, along with relatively lax government monitoring of the airwaves, has dramatically lowered the barriers to broadcasting religious content.

The significance of *da'wa* radio cannot be overestimated. It is one of the pre-eminent modes of religious dissemination in Indonesia. In a survey concerning public attitudes towards Islam, 42 per cent of the 1,500 respondents stated they received information concerning Islam via the radio. This figure was only exceeded by mosque loudspeakers (94%), recitations in public places (78%), TV (89%) and books (43%) (Hasan, Abubakar & Weck 2011: 32). Wahid (2006: 28) points out that an important feature of religious radio is that it offers a way for followers to listen to lectures without stepping into the mosque. This is especially important for reaching those who may have an interest in Salafism but do not yet feel comfortable publicly associating with the movement.

The most important Salafi radio station is RadioRodja in Bogor, West Java. Established in 2005 by Ustadz Badrusalam, a graduate of the Islamic University of Madinah, RadioRodja broadcasts lectures throughout West Java. After registering an AM frequency in 2007, it expanded its reach considerably, not least because it also owns several relaying frequencies in Bandung (West Java), Berau (East Kalimantan), Lampung (South Sumatra), Pontianak (West Kalimantan) and Tanjung Pinang (Riau). This is complemented by a cable TV station, which first aired in 2011 and claims to reach audiences in Australia, Europe, Saudi Arabia and the US. However, given the station broadcasts in the Indonesian language, it is unlikely these viewers extend beyond Indonesian/Malay speakers.

RadioRodja's programming includes pre-recorded and live lectures from notable preachers such as Yazid bin Abdul Qadir Jawas and the Madinah-based scholar Shaykh Abdurrozzaq Abdil Muasin al Abbad al-Badr. The topics vary greatly, but predominantly involve such topics as actualising Muslim morality (*aktualisasi akhlak Muslim*), the family (*kajian keluarga*), herbal medicine (*dialog kesehatan herbal*), jurisprudence in relation to the family (*fiqih keluarga*) and Arabic language lessons (*pelajaran bahasa Arab*).

Other religious radio stations include the smaller Yogyakarta-based RadioMuslim, which broadcasts from behind the Masjid al-Hasanah (al-Hasanah Mosque). RadioMuslim was established in 2008 by activists affiliated with the YPIA. Its connection to students is telling because, despite being officially independent from the YPIA, its target audience is young Muslims studying in high school or university. Initially limited to broadcasting over the Internet, it began broadcasting over FM frequencies after a local religious foundation financed the building of a radio tower in 2014.

RadioMuslim's scheduling includes weekly lectures recorded by *asatidz* in the YPIA network, such as Ustadz Afifi Abdul Wadud, and Kholid Syamhudi. They also broadcast lectures by several younger YPIA-linked preachers who wish to hone their skills and enhance their profiles. Frequently, these younger scholars are brought in to lecture on issues they and the RadioMuslim management believe are of concern to students, such as marriage, the stress of study, or the responsibilities of being an educated Muslim. The station also borrows pre-recorded content from RadioRodja such as lectures by Yazid bin Abdul Qadir Jawas and Shaykh Abdurrozzaq Abdil Muasin al Abbad al-Badr.

The day-to-day operation of RadioMuslim is the responsibility of its manager, Ahmad. Although not a religious scholar himself, Ahamd is a well-respected and liked by both students and *asatidz*. His interest in Salafism began when he was a teenager living in Jakarta. He started attending the sermons of Ustadz Hamzah Abbas, who appears on RadioRodja and to whom Ahmad attributes his initial interest in religion. He has lived in Yogyakarta since the late 1990s and it was during his time as a student in the city that he became involved in the movement, studying under the mentorship of Ustadz Afifi Abdul Wadud.

The majority of RadioMuslim technicians and DJs are recruited directly from the student body, although it is up to Ahmad to ensure the station's reputation remains intact, its funds are adequate and its programming adheres to Salafi principles. The content of RadioMuslim follows a structure similar to that of the previously examined *kajian*. It aims to evoke a set of ethical responses from listeners to entice them to engage with their personal faith and view society through the prism of religious doctrine. The station frequently mixes rhetorical narrations about social corruption with analogies concerning the life of the Prophet and its relevance to Indonesian Muslims.

While in no way a substitute for being physically present at lectures, RadioMuslim broadcasts live *kajian* and invites listeners to comment or ask questions by calling in or sending text messages. Because listeners are not physically present nor can radio programmers select who they broadcast to, women are able to listen to programmes and provide input that they would not be able to do otherwise given strict gender segregation in the physical space of a lecture. This has a significant impact on the nature of the questions asked.

I saw an example of this during a series of *kajian* held at the al-Hasanah Mosque that were broadcast live via RadioMuslim. In one lecture, an *ustadz* talked about *sakinah* (a term that literally means tranquillity but used to denote gender relations). The content of the *kajian* was tailored to a young, all-male audience, with the *ustadz* explaining that women were obliged to cook, raise children and provide sexual gratification in return for their husbands' protection. If they did not fulfil these roles, he stated that husbands were allowed to physically hit their wives, provided this was not done in anger. The use of corporal punishment, according to the *ustadz*, was necessary so that husbands would respect their wives and thus guarantee their rights.

I was comprehensibly uneasy and concerned with the preacher's line of thought, although those around me – predominantly young men in their early 20s – were avidly taking notes. Once the lecture was over, the DJ forwarded questions to the preacher that had been submitted by the radio audience. One was from a listener whose gender was unknown but believed to be a woman. She noted that the *ustadz* talked much about the rights of men over women but questioned whether this dependence aligned with the Islamic belief that men and women were equal. She asked why, in his opinion, women's rights were derived from the guarantees of their husbands rather than being derived from their own pious behaviour and love of Allah. Clearly caught off guard, the *ustadz* stumbled to respond. He prevaricated by suggesting that the caller was a woman and that women were indeed equal to men. He provided little further comment except to say that the Qur'an and Sunna protected everyone's rights, even declaring that they were *the* pre-eminent declaration of human rights, before quickly moving on to a question from another listener.[3]

The above example demonstrates the risks involved in radio broadcasts and the larger challenge of ensuring one's audience is not offended by a broadcast's content. Activists are acutely aware of this challenge, and for good reason. In 2011, Nahdlatul Ulama led a series of protests against the Salafi Idzatual al Khoir radio station in Ponorogo, East Java, after the station criticised local Islamic practices (Surya, October 2011). Claiming the radio station fuelled intolerance, activists were successful in getting the radio station to retract its criticism and promise to moderate its denunciation of local practices.

In Yogyakarta, Ahmad was keenly aware of the socio-political sensitivities involved in running a radio station. He recalled firing a DJ who between sets played the sound of a bomb blast. Although he did not believe the DJ's intentions were malicious, he feared the DJ's actions would be used by those opposed to Salafism to accuse them of having links to violent terrorist groups like Jemaah Islamiyah (Interview, Yogyakarta, 18 August 2012). For my part, I never witnessed any large protests or hostility towards RadioMuslim, although it was apparent that interacting with an audience beyond the mosque required a fine balance between local sensitivities and the desire for purity in the Salafi message. Despite these challenges, the use of radio demonstrates the power of modern technology to increase the reach of *da'wa*.

---

3   It is unknown why they DJ fielded this question, given it went against the flow of the lecture. Yet it is noteworthy that this occurred at a time when RadioMuslim's management was privately voicing their disillusionment with this Ustadz, who had recently been caught out for placing impossible demands on those conducting the call to prayer.

INTERNET VENTURES

Radio is quickly being eclipsed by social media and the Internet, both of which are having a transformative impact on religious propagation. Indonesian cities have become some of the most technologically saturated spaces in the world: there are currently 171 million Internet users in Indonesia, of which the highest density is in urban areas, with users between the ages of 15–34 (APJII 2019).

Social media apps, such as Facebook and Twitter, are remarkably popular. Forbes reports that Jakarta was the most active Twitter city in the world and Bandung, despite having a population of just 2.4 million, was the sixth (surpassing Paris and Los Angeles) (Lipman 2012). Further, it is Javanese urban centres like Yogyakarta that, according to the Indonesian Internet Service Provider Association, have the highest saturation of Internet usage, with an estimated 74 per cent of residents having frequent access to the Internet or social media (APJII 2019). This is not surprising given that the city is home to the largest concentration of students in any Indonesian city, a group that nationwide is the most online of any demographic (*Ibid.*). These students also benefit from the city's relatively good technology infrastructure (4G, broadband and access to WIFI) compared to the rest of the country.

With increased Internet availability, young Salafis have become adept at promoting the movement via a range of social media apps and websites. The combination of tech-savvy students and burgeoning demand for Islamic resources in Yogyakarta has provided new opportunities to discuss specific interpretations of Islam on a number of virtual interfaces. However, a note of caution is required. The Internet is not endowed with a coherent or specific meaning about what part it plays in the concept of *da'wa* and the *umma*. Amongst Salafis in Yogyakarta, it provides a platform on which activists can engage with each other and the broader community in ever more intricate ways, but it is not meant to replace or eclipse the importance of physical forms of mobilisation. Rather, as those who create websites believe, they are meant to facilitate and complement one's physical involvement in the movement (Interview, Yogyakarta, 4 June 2012). In addition, one's intimacy with this environment depends on one's professional capabilities (an ability to design websites or read content in a specific language), one's social position (ability to own or access a computer, or even consider this as an important part of one's daily life), as well as geographical location (urban environments are more densely saturated with Internet technology).

Blogs have become a popular way for preachers to socialise and build on their activities and *kajian*. For example, Solahuddin, whose *kajian* was examined in the previous chapter, runs a website with his wife (a fellow religious scholar). Organised into several easy-to-navigate sections, content relates to various themes including *fiqh praktis* (practical jurisprudence), *fitnah zaman* (sedition of the times), *inspirasi* (inspiration), *curhat* (*curahan hati*, or outpourings from the heart), *sakinah* (tranquillity) and *shalihah* (women who protect their piety). While one of many Salafi-inclined blogs, Solahuddin's site is unique in that it deals with issues of *sakinah* and *shalihah* – relations between men and women, and the piety of women. He co-writes these sections with his wife, and they include posts such as how women can shop in public without causing *fitnah* (sedition). Much like his physical lectures, the content of the blog is aimed at young adults concerned not just with their faith but with notions of social mobility and aspiration. He and his wife use the website to reach out to students wishing to learn about marriage or seeking counselling or assistance in finding a suitable partner.

It is amongst students that online *da'wa* has truly gained a foothold, and the Yufid group is at the vanguard of Indonesia's Salafi cyber activists. Occupying a two-storey converted house in a residential area just off Kaliurang Road in the north end of the city, Yufid's large and busy office is filled with computers and young men sporting wispy beards and religious clothing (including t-shirts with religious motifs on them). The office is simple in design. There are a few religious posters on the wall, but it is otherwise bare. Its open-concept layout with hot-desks and communal meeting rooms epitomises the new flexible workspace of late capitalism. This is perhaps unsurprising as Yufid was formed in 2009 by young IT graduates who wanted to work together to promote the Salafi movement they had become familiar with through student-oriented *kajian*.

Receiving start-up capital from a religious philanthropist, Yufid's first project was yufid.com, a search engine that provides potential followers with access to approved Salafi sources. Yufid.com operates a customised Google search platform that includes an ever-increasing database of virtual sources whose Salafi-ness has been confirmed by Yufid's network of employees and associated *asatidz*. Additions to this site can be made by users via the site's submission process or, more commonly, they are entered manually by Yufid employees based on their own searches. Despite the group's evident IT skills, there are no shortcuts to verifying content and staff have spent years compiling the catalogue of resources. They began by creating a list of the most prominent (and familiar) *asatidz*, foundations and magazines, and then asked these sources for further recommendations. This care ensured the credibility of the site. As one original Yufid member stated: 'If we do not know who [an author is], we then reference from his students or from another Ustadz who already knows him' (Interview, Yogyakarta, 4 June 2012).

The Yufid search engine is interesting in a further regard. It provides the clearest entry point for understanding the networked nature of the Salafi movement. Starting from a small number of *asatidz* and foundations immediately linked to the YPIA and thus familiar to its founders, it has expanded outward by examining the linkages between these individuals and groups with other Salafis in Indonesia. It then examined the links between these latter Salafis, and so on. Who is included in the search engine is worth noting. For example, the publications and websites of scholars linked to the remnants of Thalib's FKAWJ are not listed on yufid.com. Neither are the publications and websites of the Salafi organisation Wahdah Islamiyah, despite Wahdah Islamiyah being the largest Salafi group in the country – but also the most politically engaged. As Wahdah Islamiyah are not part of the at-Turots network, they were not included in Yufid's search engine.

Since launching the search engine, Yufid has extended its online portfolio to include a further 14 websites and 15 mobile phone or iPad apps that can be downloaded from iTunes or Google Play. It reportedly has had 4.4 million visits to its sites and has 900,000 combined Twitter and Facebook followers who visit not only yufid.com, but also an online Islamic encyclopaedia with a Salafi slant and an educational website that provides lecture videos about Arabic, mathematics and physics. This last site targets young Muslims who want to succeed academically.

Most Yufid products are intermeshed with the idea of facilitating Islamic learning for an aspiring class of tech-savvy professional youth. They have made a series of e-Qur'ans with electronic Hadith references, Arabic language apps and the Tanya Ustadz (Ask a Preacher) programme, all available for download on iPhone, iPad and Android devices. Tanya Ustadz is an interactive and free programme that allows users to anonymously post questions to a discussion board of *asatidz*, who then respond on the app's public interface. Questions are not limited to those of a purely religious nature but also include those related to socio-political or personal issues. For instance, one reader asked about a non-Muslim in his office who was donating *zakat* (tax and redistribution) and wondered whether, given his lack of Islamic faith, this was allowed. One of Yufid's on-call *asatidz* answered almost immediately that *zakat* from *kafir* (non-believers) was not to be received (Baits 2014). While Tanya Ustadz is not intended to replace physical contact amongst religionists, it shows how people can engage with the movement both instantly and anonymously. It has enabled potential followers to seek religious advice and guidance about issues that they may otherwise ignore or would not be confident to ask in person.

According to Yufid, the growth of their religious social media does not follow any pre-conceived strategy or plan, but relies on the resources available at a given time and the input of employees who constantly monitor the wider religious debates and fashions in society. As one founder put it, 'we are not an organisation, but suddenly can move ourselves to a certain flow ... this is called a community' (Interview, Yogyakarta, 4 June 2012). This alludes to the ability of the group's members to rapidly work together in order to pool resources, respond to their own ideas and the perceived need of their audience. More than any long-term plan, this defines how Yufid operates.

The group's ability to expand is influenced by several further factors. For one, the group consists of IT specialists and not religious experts. They must therefore build linkages to Islamic scholars who would be willing to help them with religious content and oversight (such as with Tanya Ustadz). Many such relationships rely on Yufid's association to the student Salafi movement, but are in no way pre-ordained. *Asatidz* can often be too busy or simply uninterested in assisting the group. Those who are willing tend to be in their late 20s or early 30s, share an interest in the potential of Internet *da'wa*, and are linked predominantly to propagational initiatives that target urban professionals rather than rural communities.

Yufid's direction is also influenced by other considerations. The group uses tools such as Google Analytics (because 65% of their traffic comes from Google searches) and iTunes Store to monitor downloads and comments about their products. Based on this data, they amend and tailor their message, adapt their sites to specific search criteria and build new applications. For example, although the group originally focused on an

Indonesian student audience, they noticed that many of their apps – especially those aimed at teaching Arabic and Islamic principles to children – had been downloaded in Saudi Arabia, France, the UK, Germany and the US. Several of the downloaders requested applications in English and, as a result, a number of multilingual platforms were developed. This includes the MuslimDua application, which is now available in Arabic, English and Indonesian to teach children the different religious statements one is meant to make over the course of a day.

Yufid has also recently launched two English language sites to reach the huge English-speaking audience – although the majority of their content is Google-translated from Indonesian articles and so suffers from poor grammar and other mistakes. The less-than-perfect text content does not detract from the visual appeal and informative layout of these English sites nor, more importantly, from the broad success of Yufid.

The IT expertise of Yufid has enabled them to adapt to an increased demand for online applications and this consequently alters the form of da'wa in several significant ways. As Yufid's foray into English language da'wa demonstrates, the target audience is global. It is not based on distinctions between acknowledged followers, lax Muslims, or even non-Muslims; categories that would influence the content of da'wa in physical proselytisation missions. Instead, they target digital natives and adapt their activities to suit this group.

This does not mean da'wa is de-territorialised, however, as Yufid builds on ideas of being a modern, educated and socially mobile Muslim in ways specific to their Yogyakartan environment. Their idea of a digital native is meshed with their own patterns of online and offline behaviour. Moreover, local young preachers use social media ventures to increase their following in a geographically and socially situated setting. Having said this, such online ventures do nonetheless imply that da'wa increasingly can be influenced by both a local and global audience that engages with sites not solely as recipients but as consumers who provide feedback about how a project aligns with their own needs and concerns. It is thus characteristic of the new forms of commodified religious engagement that are becoming ever more popular in Indonesian urban centres.

COMMODITIES, MODERNITY AND DA'WA

The proliferation of diverse *da'wa* industries signifies how living an Islamic lifestyle informs how one promotes one's faith – mixing associative, economic and consumptive patterns of behaviour. These new *da'wa* industries provide ever more intricate ways for moral entrepreneurs to promote their faith, turning *da'wa* into a professional occupation in its own right. Not concerned with direct political affiliation, this generation of religious enthusiasts use their faith to promote an Islamic ethic tied to the challenges of modern living. This is much deeper than pragmatic political considerations as it aims to transform public debate and space. We must remember that while the dual processes of commodification and religious reversion drive – and are driven by – an expanding market for religious goods and lifestyles, the rise of such social-economic industries can alter the meaning of Islamic practice and *da'wa* itself. The fact that actions encapsulated under the term have shifted in line with the social transformations of 21st century consumer-driven capitalism should therefore be of little surprise.

Salafis stress that their *da'wa* must remain grounded in religious principles to ensure they do not veer into *bid'a* (un-Islamic innovation). The Salafi scholar Fawwaz bin Hulail bin Rabah As-Suhaimi (2007) has set a guiding framework for the concept of *da'wa*. He believes one can engage with local customs via *wasa'il adiyah* (normalities in a given area) and *wasa'il ta'abbudiyah* (methods of practice), although one must scrutinise whether these local normalities are not *haram* (forbidden) in the first place. Referring briefly to mediums through which *da'wa* can be conducted, he builds on the principle of *wasilah* (approaching Allah), believing one can engage with media tools that are commonplace (*biasa*) in society (explicitly mentioning radio and loudspeakers), provided they are not used in any form for activities considered *haram* (*Ibid.*). While this gives some guidance about the religious considerations required when planning *da'wa*, his analysis remains limited in explaining just how it should be enacted in relation to the growing Islamic economy; not least if groups like Yufid are setting new precedents rather than responding to what is already *biasa*.

There is thus a degree of vagueness concerning the limits of *da'wa*, and this is manifested in open disputes amongst activists. For example, individuals from the Ma'had Al-Anshar, the Salafi *pesantren* previously affiliated to Jafar Umar Thalib, vehemently disagreed with the use of TV for *da'wa*.

They argued that the Yemeni scholar Shaykh Muqbil al-Wadi'i believed it was forbidden and that the use of TV by RadioRodja and the Salafi organisation Wahdah Islamiyah meant they were promoting *bid'a* and thus were not truly Salaf. Ma'had Al-Anshar members also took issue with the growth of student *da'wa* groups such as Yufid and RadioMuslim. Their feeling was that these groups spent too much time talking about thematic issues rather than religion. In support of their rigid interpretation, one interlocutor who sold books at the Gema Ilmu bookstore (attached to Ma'had al-Anshar) stated that the sale of Islamic books could not be considered *da'wa* as it was, first and foremost, a form of *nafkah* (livelihood) (Interview, Yogyakarta, 27 February 2012). Despite the obvious benefits to readers, the sale of consumer products could not be considered as *da'wa* given the dangers of using religion for profit.

These differences of opinion demonstrate the divergent interpretations about how one may engage with one's surroundings, and how different religious networks vary in their interpretation of Salafism and normalities in a given area. It also underscores an obsession with micro-practices that can then be used to discredit one's Salafi rivals (and thus fragment the movement further). Nevertheless, the younger generation's use of social media has altered the aim of propagation as well as the visible markers through which one's piety is expressed. It is worth noting that this does not mean new forms of *da'wa* inspire a shallow form of religious engagement. Indeed, many of these new *da'wa* pioneers were deeply involved in their religion and often made social and personal sacrifices for their faith. Further, one had to be recognised as pious by others in the movement and so, while one could search content via Tanya Ustadz, this does not in itself make one an acknowledged Salafi. Piety or *mukmin* is as much a personal mark of inward piety as it is an external signifier bestowed on one by the wider Salafi community. Without this social acceptance, it remains difficult to become a legitimate agent of *da'wa*.

Despite a continued need to be physically engaged with one's network though, campus-based male activists have nonetheless developed a new set of *da'wa* industries that distinguish them from older Salafi agents. They wear t-shirts with catchy Islamic logos, and carry book bags and computers covered with badges and stickers promoting specific religious products or brands. Returning to our rhizomatic analogy, this highlights how Salafis have grafted themselves onto debates concerning what a progressive and modern Islamic community should look like and, by supporting industries that sell a range of new commodities, have altered the way urban activists represent themselves to wider society. They still draw from scriptural references, but the increased popularity of religious commodities and market forces enable them to enact a modern and economically astute form of religiosity, interweaving faith with the wider economic forces that influence aspects of religious identity in Indonesia.

A COMMODIFIED SALAFISM?

Throughout this chapter, I have examined the ways Salafi activists promote the movement as well as how they align it to the growth of an Islamic economy. *Da'wa* is an ever more professional venture run by a class of moral entrepreneurs. They broaden and deepen the movement's repertoire of activities that can be used to engage with constituents and tailor religion to their needs. The use of the Internet, radio, literature and fashion all suggest how skilled activists frame *da'wa* to issues of lifestyle, commodification and prospects of social mobility. But by so doing, they have blurred the lines between what is strictly religious and the wider socio-political forces present within Indonesian localities. Piety is not only presented as a pure form of Islam, but also – via slang, pocketbooks and informal literature – is frequently seen as a necessity for a stable, economically viable, successful and modern society. This renders it as something dependent and inter-linked with uniquely Indonesian narratives of faith and identity.

Yufid and RadioMuslim signify this trend by tailoring the Salafi message to an urban, upwardly mobile professional class that not only benefits from access to social media but is supposed to be a viable agent of modernity. This is not surprising, given those behind these ventures are either students or former students who have come to think of themselves as a progressive modern Muslims. I will expand on this point in the next chapter, where I elaborate how the actions and perceptions of urban agents frame Salafism not only as religious doctrine but as part of an inherently modern subjectivity.

ISLAM AND THE POLITICAL IMAGINATION

Religious Study (by Izabela Chaplin)

The Political Activist

Yogyakarta, September 2016

I met Hasto at a cafeteria close to his university's electrical engineering department. It was 2016 and we hadn't seen each other for four years. A lot had changed since then. Hasto had graduated, was married with two young children, and had spent several years teaching at an Islamic boarding school in Central Kalimantan. He had recently returned to Yogyakarta to enrol in a PhD programme.

As we sat down to drink tea, he recalled the evening five years earlier, two days before Idul Adha, when we first met. At that time, I had arranged to interview a young religious student who'd had notable success selling Islamic herbal medicines at a small Salafi boarding house in the centre of the city. My interviewee was late and Hasto let me in. What began as a polite conversation while I waited for my scheduled interview quickly turned into something more significant. Hasto was intrigued by my project and offered to show me what Islam meant to him and the local community, believing there was a need to correct Western lies and accusations against Islam. He invited me to return to celebrate Idul Adha, as he would be participating in the prayers and festivities at a nearby mosque.

Over the course of Idul Adha, he showed me around the mosque and introduced me to others. Together, we assisted in distributing freshly slaughtered meat to locals. This led to a more prolonged relationship and, over the course of the year, we met frequently to discuss religion. Yet as I prepared to leave Yogyakarta in 2012 and Hasto was finishing his degree, our contact diminished to the occasional message or email.

In 2016, when we realised that we would both be back in the city again, we immediately made plans to meet. We picked a cafeteria close to his university department. It was a relatively quiet setting with small groups of students gathered around large plastic tables, presumably talking about upcoming projects or relaxing after class. The cafeteria was part of a well-designed campus of academic buildings with large trees lining the avenues down which students and motorbikes flowed. It was an oasis of peace compared to the bustle of the surrounding city, and the trees provided a welcome relief from the midday heat.

Hasto looked older and thinner than I remembered him. As we talked, he mentioned he had often been sick while living in Central Kalimantan and had returned to Yogyakarta for both his health and that of his family. He now had two young children and a wife who depended on him. He also wished to be closer to his parents, and Kalimantan was too remote and difficult to get to from his hometown in East Java.

I sensed that Hasto had found his life in Kalimantan neither easy nor enjoyable. He had always, I remembered, been interested in pursuing further education. It became clear that he had gone to Kalimantan because he felt duty-bound to teach others about Islam, and so had volunteered for the position after he'd graduated. The school was a familiar location in the Salafi network he had come to know. These networks often sent promising students to spend several years in remote parts of the country, where they had time to reflect on religion, focus on da'wa and start a family. It had not been particularly easy, as the majority of people he collaborated with neither spoke Javanese nor had a similar background to him.

Not surprisingly, Hasto was happy to be back in Yogyakarta doing something he thought was promising for his and his family's future. He aspired to work as a researcher at the university and – as had been the case several years before – this interest in academia provided a common ground for our otherwise divergent lives. It also meant that he could resume being involved in the da'wa he'd been part of during his years as a student; he felt more at home back on campus.

In passing, he mentioned that another benefit of being back in the city was that it was closer to Jakarta and he could observe the opposition to Basuki Tjahaja Purnama (better known as Ahok), the former Jakarta governor, even if he didn't actually join the growing Islamic campaign against Ahok. This comment, occurring in mid-September 2016, struck me as odd. It was clear that Ahok would run for governor, and slowly it was emerging that his most likely opponents would be Anies Baswedan (the current governor) and Agus Yudhoyono. But the ethnic Chinese, Christian Ahok had not yet been accused of blasphemy, which was the alleged cause of the mass demonstrations that occurred later that year. I was interested in what Hasto was referring to and when asked, he replied: 'Ahok is corrupt, he made money from buying land from a hospital and he uses the police to silence Muslims in Jakarta.'[1]

I had previously heard murmurs against Ahok, but these were often from leaders or prominent preachers with vested political interests in Jakartan politics. I knew that they were trying to find a Muslim alternative to Ahok but were increasingly frustrated with the lack of support or interest. But this was the first time I had heard this sentiment from an activist in Yogyakarta. Seeing that I was interested, Hasto continued to explain what was happening. In a hushed but excited tone, he mentioned a Twitter campaign called #selamatkanibukota (save the capital city), which was part of a larger campaign. They – meaning conservative Muslims – had meant to march on 18 September 2016 from the country's national Istiqlal Mosque in Jakarta (the largest mosque in Southeast Asia) to the anti-corruption commission, where they would demand that Ahok be investigated.

However, the march had not gone as planned. According to Hasto, Ahok had made sure the police didn't provide the necessary permits to allow the march. Instead, activists were forced to stay in the Istiqlal Mosque. Yet even this had its challenges. The mosque caretaker, Hasto claimed, had been worried about the mosque – a national symbol – being used for political purposes, and so the rally could only go ahead after assurances that those involved were not going to campaign for any particular candidate in the mosque.

I was unable to verify whether the caretaker had actually been opposed to the march, but I did confirm that the #selamatkanibukota hashtag had been making the rounds. Moreover, I noticed that several prominent Salafis, including one preacher in Yogyakarta, were directly involved in organising the campaign and had made their way to Jakarta to part take in the events.

---

1   Hasto was referring to the 2014 purchase of land from Sumber Waras hospital by the Jakarta government. The land price was too high, and so the corruption committee was looking into the case. It was one of two corruption cases to emerge against Ahok in the lead-up to the election, the other concerning alleged kickbacks in the Jakarta Bay land reclamation project.

The campaign against Ahok had clearly caught the attention of many Salafi, and this wasn't limited to Jakarta and Yogyakarta. In 2016, I was living in South Sulawesi where I knew another Salafi activist named Hanafi. He had publicly stated that Jakarta was a majority Muslim city and that Muslims, via the concept of al-wala' wa-l-bara' *(allegiance to Islam and renunciation of unbelievers), needed to ensure they were not tainted by the rule of Christians and Jews. Like the thwarted march, this campaign was not initially very successful. I discussed this with Hasto and he agreed that any anti-Ahok campaign 'was with its challenges', yet he was optimistic. It would be an uphill battle to say the least, but he had confidence that good Muslim candidates would be put forward to oppose Ahok, and a broader campaign would build on the momentum from the mosque gathering. He explained that the demonstrators had prepared a nine-point proclamation that would be circulated to mosques across Jakarta to ensure Muslims would not vote for Ahok. Point four of this proclamation explicitly calls 'upon the Muslim umma to hold tightly to their religion and only choose a Muslim candidate, and know it is forbidden to choose a non-Muslim or not vote.'[2]*

With the benefit of hindsight, it is clear that Hasto was describing the beginnings of a successful mobilisation against Ahok. But at the time, the plan sounded far-fetched. Ahok had a clear lead in the polls, accusations of corruption were largely unproven, and the mosque gathering at Istiqlal received only passing media coverage. It took a doctored video of Ahok allegedly insulting the Qur'an, and a clear political campaign – with money from vested political interests – to mobilise a successful, Islamically influenced challenge against him.

Even before all of this came to pass, however, Hasto seemed convinced that the campaign was something big, stating that it was the first time he could remember Muslims coming together with a unified voice. As we spoke more about Ahok's gubernatorial election chances, Hasto said he believed 'Muslims were finally working together.' I asked what he meant, and he stated that the meeting at Istiqlal had brought together numerous individuals, including members of the Islamic Defenders Front, Muhammadiyah, Council of Young Intellectual Ulama of Indonesia (MIUMI) and Wahdah Islamiyah, who had all agreed on the need to stand up for the people. This agreement, he believed, showed their willingness to work together and look past their previous differences.

---

2 Translated from '*Diserukan kepada umat Islam untuk berpegang teguh kepada agamanya dengan hanya memilih calon Muslim dan haram memilih non-Muslim dan haram golput.*'

I was amazed that he supported an action that included the Islamic Defenders Front (Front Pembela Islam, FPI), a vigilante group known for attacking brothels, places serving alcohol, and even multi-faith demonstrations. Their antics had previously earned them the ire of Salafis in Yogyakarta, including Hasto. In 2012, he had remarked to me that he believed they were the extreme right, lamenting that they gave Islam a bad name. 'Times have changed,' he said, as Muslims were being oppressed by the Indonesian Democratic Party of Struggle, the ruling party of President Joko Widodo. They supported secularism and so Muslims needed to come together against them. He opined that while the FPI and Salafis may have different methods, they were all good Muslims.

The support of Hasto and his colleagues for the campaign, as well as their willingness to collaborate with the FPI, was a departure from the apolitical position I had known of him and Salafism in 2012. There was a newfound confidence and urgency to ensure the political field was, as they saw it, of benefit to Muslim interests. Filled with ideas of creating a nationalist Islamic and inherently modern state, concepts such as al-wala' wa-l-bara' *were being redefined to allow Salafis to work with other Muslims like the FPI in a campaign against non-Muslim rule.*

*As we paid for our tea and made plans to meet again, I asked Hasto whether, in his eyes, a non-Muslim should ever be governor. 'Maybe in [Hindu] Bali,' he replied, 'but not in Java, Sulawesi or Sumatra ... the people wouldn't stand for it.' 'We' he concluded, meaning conservative Muslims, 'need a government that is pro-umma and pro-community (*masyarakat*).' I couldn't help but feel that amongst Salafi activists, the* umma *and national community were becoming indistinguishable.*

CHAPTER 5

Becoming Indonesian? A Modern Salafi Subjectivity

This book has so far dealt with the history of Salafism, how activists operate within Indonesia, the spatial niches Salafis create, and the communal dynamics through which individuals are brought into the religious fold. In so doing, I have endeavoured to show that Salafism is far more context-specific and privy to local influence and personal anxieties than it may first seem. This does not render the global dynamics of the movement defunct. Instead, while the challenges of creating a 'pure' religious code may cause deep cleavages and disagreements amongst Salafis themselves, local contextual necessities have catalysed a rhizomatic form of affiliation through which the movement has come to thrive amongst diverse communities. Individuals are not mere converts but active agents who, if they commit to the doctrine, inculcate and transform Salafism to create a particular understanding of religious life, authority and selfhood.

In this chapter, I explore the social narratives through which agents locate the significance of Salafism in their lives, proposing that the wider social impetus of religious personhood remains grounded in the debates and ideas of religious action pertinent to contemporary Indonesia. As I noted in previous chapters, activists embody and practise their faith in contextually sensitive ways, forming an Islamic subjectivity that is both communal and private in nature. Heiphetz et al. (2014) explain that what religion and faith may entail is not absolute but subject to variation, and so can differ in relation to one's experience, age and situation.

Anthropologists have also noted the difficulty of discerning what absolute belief can be, pointing out the necessary vagueness required when studying issues of faith, piety, custom and religion. Sperber, for instance, observes a number of concepts used by anthropologists under the label of belief (including taboo and totanism) (Sperber 1996: 16). This point has been taken up by Van Leeuwen (2014), who suggests that religious credence lacks any single cognitive governance and can lead to a number of perceived normative orientations both susceptible to free elaboration and vulnerable to special authority. He argues that we often focus on the difference in content of religious doctrines without considering the multiple attitudes that can exist within the rubric of faith itself.

For this reason, my goal is not to discover an absolute or universal definition of Salafi faith, but rather to examine the complex representations through which individuals come to share a communal identity. These may differ in their nuances but nevertheless contribute to an overarching religious solidarity that sustains the idea of a coherent Salafism. I may not be able to develop a one-size-fits-all explanation of what Salafism is and why it appeals to individuals around the globe, but this is precisely the point. Personal belief can differ from individual to individual, and understandings of Salafism necessarily transform as they pass from actor to actor. Yet despite Salafism coming to encapsulate a series of deeply personal – but potentially multiple – representations, there remains, as Sperber (1996: 83) points out, a 'degree of resemblance between the communicator's and the audience's thoughts' through which both real and imagined solidarity is formed. My aim here is to study the transformation of such meanings and why some representations are diffused by individuals and others are not (Sperber 1985).

Much cross-Salafi solidarity is linked to the social bonds activists create amongst themselves in sermons, schools and boarding houses. The frequent visits from prestigious global *shaykh*, the ability to use similar funding streams from abroad, the shared aesthetic markers recognised through dress and prayer, and a common religious language that distinguishes them from other Muslims – all provide visible traits that allow Salafis to recognise themselves as Salafis. This is most apparent with the concept of *al-wala' wa-l-bara'* (allegiance to Islam and renunciation of unbelievers) and *hisba* (the commanding of right and forbidding of wrong), which Salafis enact as verbal tools intended to govern social behaviour and define who belongs and who does not. *Al-wala' wa-l-bara'*, a central element of the Salafi creed, is intended to act as a barrier that protects Salafism from being diluted through interactions with non-Islamic concepts. In Indonesia, it has led to a range of Salafi literature that cautions against local Islamic tradition and Javanese mysticism such as the *ramalan Joyoboyo* (Javanese zodiac), alternative medicines, spells, *ziarah* (grave visits) and visiting the *dukun* (spiritual healer) – all of which are labelled *syirik* (idolatry) and, as such, contravene the unity of Allah (HASMI 2011).

138

Not surprisingly, close attention is paid by activists to the micro-practices through which one can define oneself as part of the movement and forge a degree of solidarity with one's co-religionists. These bonds, in turn, add a personal and real-world dimension to the scriptural boundaries illuminated in Salafi doctrine. As became evident during my fieldwork, Salafis define principles less through scholastic reasoning than through the prism of how one must come to live Islam in the modern world. *Al-wala' wa-l-bara'* and similar religious principles may create imagined boundaries through which Salafis promote an idea of good and bad, but they are more mutable than any face-value reading of them might suggest. Indeed, there are few explanations as to what *al-wala' wa-l-bara* actually means when it comes to engaging with non-Salafi educational institutes, Sharia businesses or religious consumerism (for example).

Our focus must thus turn to the ambiguity and anxiety involved in reconciling Islamic orthodoxies with contemporary social dilemmas. How one comes to demarcate the ethical boundaries of Salafi selfhood is necessarily linked to the bonds one forged with one's co-religionists in a specific environment. Developments and transformations can occur incrementally, reproduced through numerous iterations influenced by intra-Salafi debate and the horizontal, networked and interdependent nature that define Salafi spaces.

In Yogyakarta, Salafism has become heavily embedded in the campus experience of activists, especially in science-based faculties. This has been crucial to interweaving Salafism within contemporary debates concerning class, nationalism and citizenship that circulate around Indonesia. Salafism now recognises itself as modern, progressive and forward-looking, as well as timeless and literal. This image is far from coherent. It has emerged through numerous cognitive iterations, all of which inform locally relevant understandings of a Muslim subjectivity, but differ in their focus and effect. In this chapter, I look at three of these modern iterations: the concept of being middle class, the underdevelopment of the rural village, and the perception of womanhood. In so doing, I will highlight how Salafism has become increasingly sophisticated in the construction of an Islamic ideal – an ideal that is both sacred and achievable through real-world social and personal transformations.

WHO BECOMES A SALAFI?

I have so far shied away from providing a definitive typology of who joins the Salafi movement, as adherents come from a variety of backgrounds and join for different reasons. However, it was obvious that the majority of university-based interlocutors came from moderate (but not poor) rural or semi-rural (within a 16-kilometre radius of a major city) areas and were the first generation of their family to attend university. Although the YPIA and similar Salafi foundations organise lectures at a number of universities and faculties, most lectures take place close to medical or science facilities. The Mardliyyah Mosque, where Abu Nida began lecturing in 1985, was close to the medical facility. Further, the majority of my interlocutors had, or were undertaking, studies in medicine, physics, IT, chemistry or pharmacy. Only a few were involved in the social sciences and humanities, and even fewer in Islamic studies. In fact, Salafism is virtually absent at the State Islamic University Sunan Kalijaga, where I myself was affiliated during my fieldwork.

Many factors are involved in the saturation of Salafism in scientific faculties. One is the derision of *ilmu social* (social knowledge) by *asatidz*, and their caution against an interest in the study of secular Western theories that place man, and not God, at the centre of the world. In contrast, preachers were quick to praise the benefits of scientific knowledge, which factored into who was attracted to the movement and who was not. Yet the recruitment of individuals from predominantly science-based departments necessarily meant Salafism was expanding in institutions that were not only science-based, but bastions of what Barker (2005) terms Indonesian developmentalist modernity.

In his account of Palapa, the Indonesian domestic satellite system, Barker explains that a particular form of modernity spread across Indonesian science faculties during the New Order. As he notes, Palapa was viewed as a proud engineering achievement and a feat of Indonesian progress (*Ibid.*). Launched in 1976, Palapa was one of a broader series of industrial 'lighthouse' projects intended to create a particular perception of Indonesian national culture (*Ibid.*). The projects symbolised the development of the nation, and scientific faculties were at the forefront of promoting such technology. These institutions were also centres of a powerful developmentalist discourse that served New Order political ambitions and, as they took hold, mapped out an image of national progress distinct from what had gone before.

The role Indonesia's engineers and scientists play in mediating between technology and society is not unique. Studies have examined the importance of techno-political discourses in colonial ideology (Schulte-Nordholt 2011), nation-building projects (Anderson 1991; Hill & Lian 2013; Leslie & Kargon 2006), as well as contemporary debates concerning progress and development in Southeast Asia more broadly (Morris 2000). Indonesia is no different in this regard. During the New Order, Suharto referred to himself as Bapak Pembangunan (the father of development and the ideology of modern developmentalism was as much part of New Order political culture as was the threat of violence (Anderson 2001; Siegel 1998) of the use of Javanese tradition (Pemberton 1994; Sullivan 1992).

As such, newly opened infrastructure projects or scientific achievements were accompanied by elaborate ceremonies that provided a grounded experience through which Indonesians could share in the perception that the nation was being developed. The power of this discourse has diminished in the decades since Palapa was launched (Barker 2005), and especially after the end of Suharto's New Order. Nonetheless it continues to percolate within university science departments and government ministries. In fact, through a combination of student community service programmes such as the Kuliah Kerja Nyata (Student Study Service, KKN) and the current government's continued focus on infrastructure development, developmentalism remains influential.[1]

The ideological nuances of this developmentalist modernity inevitably overlap with Salafi ideas of a perfect Islamic society. On one side is a backward and undeveloped Indonesia, rife with tradition and superstition, and on the other is a modern, forward-looking and egalitarian (Salafi) Islam. An example of this modernism was on display during several lecture series I attended, including a Kajian Akbar (large kajian) at Yogyakarta State University (Universitas Negeri Yogyakarta). The event was an informal gathering attended by approximately 20 men from a Salafi boarding

---

1   Since 1973, Indonesian university students have been expected to assist local less-fortunate communities through the KKN, a course requirement which sees them volunteer to improve the lives of other Indonesians. Although much of this work is of genuine benefit to all involved, the concept of KKN has strengthened developmentalist notions amongst the student population.

house. It was hosted by a student of mechanical engineering, who – after welcoming the audience – asked their names and then demonstrated his intellectual prowess by reiterating each name to show he had memorised them. The idea was to underscore the type of Muslim the boarding house created: one who was disciplined, intelligent and good at his studies.

After displaying his memory skills, the student introduced Ustadz Rahman, who gave the main talk. Aside from serving as an *ustadz*, Rahman was a lecturer in the mechanical engineering and had received his doctorate in Japan. He frequently used popular scientific images to explain why one needed to return to Islam. For example, he stated that discovering the proper *aqida* (creed) held a similar significance in one's life as discovering how to produce electricity had for Thomas Edison – useful to the public and also to one's private intellectual and spiritual growth. He stated that living in an Islamic boarding house created good Muslims specifically through classes relating to *aqida, manhaj* (method), *fiqh* (jurisprudence), *ibada* (religious practice), Hadith, Arabic and *mental dan akhlak* (mental strength and morals). It was part of a wider mission to fashion Muslims who, according to Rahman, held several specific characteristics: clean *aqida*, true *ibada*, robust morality, intellectualism, the ability to fight their desires, good at keeping time and meeting deadlines, independent, disciplined in their tasks and useful to others.

The above example was not an isolated instance but part of a broader narrative through which many campus-based *asatidz* and other moral entrepreneurs emphasised the harmonising nature of piety with modern scientific or business education (of a capitalist bend). Tapping into the concerns of how to negotiate the stresses of modern urban life, agents have come to use notions of developmentalist modernity to add a social dimension to their claim to represent a fair and 'saved' society.

The prevalence of Salafism in science-based faculties provides a unique dimension to the expansion of Salafism. It enables individuals to see themselves as pioneers in industry and mechanical innovation, while also laying the personal moral groundwork for their pious and incorruptible future. Yet even this image included three cognitive iterations that stressed ideas of being middle class, engaging with underdeveloped rural communities, or how to obtain perfect gender relations. They were different from each other, but often overlapped as individuals debated with each other to create a wholistic understanding of what it means to be Salafi in modern Indonesia.

142

ITERATION ONE: A MIDDLE-CLASS CONSCIOUSNESS

The rise of a middle class in Indonesia and across Asia over the past three decades has received significant attention from social scientists (Ansori 2009; Latief 2013) and development institutions (ADB 2010; Samad 2012). With specific reference to Indonesia, the Asian Development Bank has noted that a middle class has grown from 25 to 43 per cent of the population from 1999–2009 (ADB 2010: 11). While this growth can be attributed in part to a redefinition of middle class to anyone earning more than US$2 a day (just over the poverty line), it nevertheless underlines the expansion not just of a perceived middle class, but to what Van Klinken and Berenschot refer to as a broader class consciousness that drives ideas of political and economic engagement. They claim class is not just a question of income, but also a political concept that explains the differences between social behaviours over matters of the common good (of one's class) (Van Klinken & Berenschot 2014).

Scholars before me have already pointed out that how class consciousness informs Islamic revivalism (eg., Hasan 2014; Fischer 2008; Iqtidar 2011). In Indonesia, Brenner (1996) eloquently describes the growth of such sensibilities amongst female Muslim university students in 1990s Indonesia. These women expressed a notion of Islamic identity that simultaneously rejected the Western elitist culture of the political classes and the backwardness of their parents' generation. Believing themselves to be the model of a new Muslim modernity, they developed a sense of Muslimhood through which they demonstrated their religious identity and traversed the demands of being a modern yet pious individual.

In a similar fashion, Salafi activists have used concepts of modern living to portray their religion as part of a professional socially mobile class consciousness. They use terminology and images that promote specific economic patterns of behaviour aimed to define them as part of a modern Muslim middle class. Religious practices are mixed with specific notions of class-based consumption, an imaginary that they are striving for a pious modern future, and an emphasis on secular study as an avenue to aspiration and success. All of these have been framed as dependent on one's (correct) piety and attributable to being a member of the saved Islamic group.

The notion of a modern Salafi subjectivity linked to the emergence of a new middle class complements the idea of developmentalist modernity.

It positions Salafis at the forefront of a generation of university-educated indigenous creators (as opposed to recipients of development aid). They are both capitalists and philanthropists who are using their expertise to engage in the Islamic knowledge economy through the creation of religious commodities. The Salafi magazine Pengusaha Muslim (Muslim Businessperson) is a case in point. It bridges between religion and capitalist practices by reflecting on notions of aspirational piety and religious consumption. It is run by the Yayasan Bina Pengusaha Muslim (YBPM) (Muslim Businessmen Foundation), whose office is tellingly located in the same building as Yufid. The two independent groups are closely connected, and several founding members of Yufid are also active in YBPM.

The YBPM started in 2005 as a Yahoo Group. It was a forum for like-minded young activists who wished to promote simple and clear Islamic business practices (and support each other in doing so) (Interview, Yogyakarta, 4 June 2012). The YBPM believes itself to be the heart of Islamic business. It created the Komunitas Pengusaha Muslim Indonesia (Indonesian Community of Muslim Businessmen), which began holding public *kajian* concerning business and the Sharia in 2010 and launched the magazine soon afterwards.

The emphasis for YBPM and Pengusaha Muslim does not lie explicitly with the promotion of a Salafi doctrine. As one editor explained, its target audience is broader than those already familiar with Salafism. They want to reach those who 'have yet to know about the method of the Salaf as-Salih' in order to increase the economic prosperity of Indonesian Muslims (Interview, Yogyakarta, 4 June 2012). While all principles in the magazine are Salafi, fostering this business ethic is meant to tie into popular demands for a viable Islamic economy amongst Indonesian Muslims collectively. Pengusaha Muslim's aim, in its simplest form, is to promote economic practices that align with Sharia to ensure that Muslims can take advantage of market forces amongst Indonesia's professional urban classes. It warns that one's economic engagement with Islam should not be misguided by the popular commercialisation of the celebration of Idul Fitri (the end of the fasting month of Ramadan), or by Islamic clothes on display at large commercial stores (the sale of which allegedly benefits savvy Christian businesspeople). Instead, one must be thoughtful and strategic, buying only from authenticated Islamic vendors (Badri 2012).

144

By promoting religion as complementary to contemporary market forces, Pengusaha Muslim and the YBPM are transforming the ways of Salafism in ways that are as rich in economic wisdom as in theology – and whose drivers are not just *asatidz* but intellectuals, professionals and successful businessmen. Entrepreneurs like those affiliated with Yufid exemplify this trend. However, this concept cannot be decoupled from the environment in which such ideas take form – the university campuses where Salafis create and sell an array of commodities that mix popular imagery and religious quotations. Nowhere has this been more visible than through the production and sale of Salafi-inspired t-shirts, commonly referred to as *distro* apparel (which derives from the word *distribusi* or distribution).

As a concept, *distro* originated from the underground punk music scene in Bandung in 1993. It enabled youth to design and sell wares through collectively owned outlets that doubled as forums where music and political issues could be discussed. By 2003 *distro* had exploded into the mainstream, and student designers – often from well-off backgrounds and benefitting from better technology than their punk forerunners – were able to replicate and reconstruct global labels. They frequently rearrange the logos of multinational companies to include catchy phrases or humorous alterations. By 2006 there were over 200 *distro* brands in Bandung alone and the trend has spread to other urban centres including Yogyakarta (Uttu 2006).

Student Salafi activists have created their own religious *distro*s. Predominantly sold on the YPIA website or Yufid's online shop, this is a means of income to subsidise one's studies. Like their non-religious counterparts these *distros* showcase innovative commodities that aim to capture the youth market by mixing popular iconography and catchphrases. For example, Yufid produced t-shirts with a sketch of a plane, train and car with the tagline *Apapun Cara Mudiknya Sholat Jalan Terus* (Whichever way you go home, keep on praying) that they sold prior to the annual migration as people returned to their villages for Idul Fitri 1433 (August 2012). Similarly, several YPIA-linked students formed the Kaos Oblong label and sell t-shirts with tag lines such as *Jenggot Yes, Isbal No!* (Beard Yes, Long Trousers No!). Kaos Oblong also produce t-shirts promoting the Muslim. or.id website via a graphic logo stating '*Visit Muslim.or.id*' in a similar design as the Indonesian government's tourist campaign of *Visit Indonesia*.

According to interlocutors, the rationale behind these ventures is to endorse and expand the popularity of their services rather than create a new form of *da'wa* (propagation). Nonetheless, it reflects a growing entrepreneurial spirit amongst aspiring religionists (Interview, Yogyakarta, 4 June 2012). These student activists have, through the production and sale of products, shifted the perceived relationship between piety and economic success. For these agents, Islamic business becomes an extension of good piety and morality. The wearing of these products – as a young pious university student involved in *da'wa* and religious business – shows that Salafi adherents are modern, educated and innovative, cutting a specific image that combines Salafi dress and student ideals of fashion.

This creates an interesting position for *da'wa* in contemporary Indonesia. Not only are commodities a form of proselytisation, but the actual process of creating and sustaining an Islamic business can also become a way to advance Islamic principles. By emphasising select aspects of their faith, these commodities can reflect having 'made it' in the contemporary capitalist market. Whilst in no way detracting from the deeply personal nature of individual belief, religious industries promote an idea of religious identity that is part of a modern response not just to social corruption, but also intellectual stagnation and lack of development. Significantly however, this implies that far from being an emancipatory movement geared towards the social empowerment of all of Indonesia's Muslims (as Salafis occasionally claim), individuals deploy ideas of modern lifestyle, commodification and class, all inherent in capitalist Indonesia and the socio-economic inequalities within it. Islamic activism may call for a return to a form of living based on the ways of the Prophet and his companions, but activists remain embedded in a perception of society based on class distinctions, unwilling to separate their vision of an Islamic past from the influences that define contemporary urban living. This becomes even clearer in the way urban activists perceive rural Javanese communities.

ITERATION TWO: THE UNDERDEVELOPED KAMPUNG

Amongst urban and campus-based activists, the idea that Salafism is a modern, forward-looking ethical identity is reified through references to, and comparisons with, the perceived underdevelopment of Indonesia's rural communities. These *kampung* (village) communities are seen as simultaneously pre-modern and beholden to an Islam riddled with superstition – issues that are framed as two sides of the same coin. Salafi *asatidz* never tired

146

of proclaiming that bad religious practice led to a breakdown in *muamala* (social cohesion), and in turn caused disunity in the *umma* and the fall of Islam's place in the world. For urban activists, this narrative holds developmentalist implications because *muamala* necessarily came to include one's ability to develop as much as it did to a 'correct' religious outlook.

In Chapter 2, I touched on this narrative and now wish to return to consider Salafism and rural communities. The expansion of Salafism into rural villages is not without controversy as villagers are not always enthusiastic about accepting Salafi tenets they believe to be 'un-Javanese' and not in line with their customs. As one *ustadz* stated in relation to his village-based *da'wa*:

> We frequently face hindrances but, Alhamdulillah, these are overcome with the help of Allah. Sometimes our *jemaah* is attacked by residents because they do not want to receive a new understanding ... if this is the case, they are not appropriate and all they have to do is ask (us) and, lets discuss it together.   (Interview, Yogyakarta, 11 November 2012)

The *ustadz* made it clear that there was a difference between what he considered appropriate behaviour and the inappropriate reactions he observed in the village. However, despite such challenges, many urban-based *asatidz* have assisted *da'i* in slowly expanding their network into rural communities.

A pivotal part of this relates to the *pengajian* (rural religious study) which is advertised through rural religious radio stations, mosque noticeboards and welfare programmes. I attended one such *pengajian* series organised by one Salafi *yayasan* at a mosque a 90-minute from Yogyakarta. Located in a small farming village, this mosque lies on the slopes of Merapi volcano. It's complex also houses a Salafi foundation that runs a *da'i* training facility and radio station. The mosque, built in an architectural style more akin to the Middle East than rural Java, was constructed in 2009 and looks out of place with the small villages, rice and strawberry fields surrounding it.

The *pengajian* have become increasingly popular since they began in 2009. Salafis active at the mosque stated that while they may never have felt outright hostility from their neighbours, relations were initially reserved. According to one individual:

> [T]o begin with, there indeed wasn't much respect. But as time passed the response of the community became better. Maybe this is because we differ in our understanding [of Islam], compared to them.
>
>   (Interview, Magelang, 15 April 2012)

147

By the time I first attended in 2012, these *pengajian* had become well known within the local community. Villagers referred to the Salafi activists, the majority of whom came from the cities of Solo and Yogyakarta after graduating from university, as 'good Muslims' given their involvement in local affairs. They emphasised the extent to which the group had provided local villagers with assistance after the eruption of Merapi volcano in 2010 (Interview, Magelang, 15 July 2012).

The *pengajian* attracted approximately 100 men (and an unknown number of women) who came dressed not in Salafi-esque clothing but a mixture of *sarongs* and *songkok* (a black traditional hat). They packed into the mosque's moderately large hall every Sunday morning to hear the lecture. It was not only a religious service but also a social gathering. Many attendees came 15 minutes prior to the lecture to meet friends and talk amongst themselves. The actual *pengajian* would then be given by a guest lecturer, almost always someone from the nearby Salafi *pesantren*. The *ustadz* would sit in front of his audience at a full-size table and give an hour and a half talk of a broad thematic nature – 'educating children' or 'corruption' – drawing parallels to the life and experiences of the Prophet Muhammad. The male audience would sit scattered on the mosque floor or outside, while women were be located behind a screen on the right side of the mosque.

This *ustadz's* style was light-hearted, mild and polite, and his criticism of contemporary society was always subtle. He seldom delved into world politics, preferring to talk about welfare, behaviour and social justice. In a lecture given just before Ramadan, he asked the audience to 'moralise' one's religious practice (*mengikhlaskan ibada*) to assist in building an ethical society. A big part of this was, he stressed, not to be arrogant, even towards those who wish you ill, and accept that everything was in the hands of God. Sensitive to the composition of his audience, he occasionally switched from Indonesian to Javanese, most notably when he wished to find a catch phrase that could summarise a particular issue he was reflecting on. In these cases, he would stop and ask the audience whether this was the right phrase, although this felt rhetorical rather than a genuine attempt to garner their input. He would also sprinkle his lecture with references from the Qur'an and Hadith and quickly tie these to a solution to a local issue. On one occasion, he stated that modern trading practices were not Islamic because they created inequality and jealously. If one changed one's economic practices to those prescribed to by Islam, local trade would become more equally distributed, benefits would be linked to merit, and exploitation would end. Similarly, he stressed that modern society was too promiscuous, as youth could freely consume alcohol and disrespect their parents – an issue one local informant later stated was of concern amongst parents in the region.

The answer to all issues, the *ustadz* would explain, lay with correct *muamala* and *ibada*. Yet the nuances of this message differed from the urban *kajian*. Rather than pushing the audience to think of themselves as a 'saved' group or promoting further learning, the stress in this rural *pengajian* was on good morality and practices that emulated the Prophet and his companions. Instead of engaging the audience in explicit religious discussion, he stressed how Islam, as a value system, can promote a series of norms and habits of positive social benefit to the community. Virtues such as patience, justice and forgiveness were key to the creation of a better off and fairer society. It is notable that the promotion of these simplified concepts was also rarely open to public questioning, as would be the case with during a *kajian*. When asked why this is so, a number of informants replied that rural communities, only having a simple education and living in an environment steeped in *bid'a* (un-Islamic innovations), were often stuck in their ways and not fully able to grasp the significance of religious sciences (Interviews, Yogyakarta, 3 November 2011 and 28 March 2012). This did not make them 'bad' Muslims but, rather, meant that in order to appeal to them, preachers had to ensure the content of lectures was tailored to the audience.

This portrayal of the rural communities underlines the importance of the *kampung* in relation to Salafi *da'wa*. It also links to a particular image of what a *kampung* is and what *kampung* life entails. John Pemberton (1994: 10) suggests that the *kampung* is vested with ideological significance, promoted as a bastion of 'local custom' and a timeless cultural heritage. As Pemberton explains, the *kampung* in Indonesia has a huge amount of cultural capital, although not as a diverse set of social relations but as a set of static, predefined customs. These have imbued its perceived relationship to the central government and urban elite as one based on reliance, as patronage from the government and local political elite mediate the flow of economic and social development initiatives flow and manage political cohesion.

The premise upon which Salafis engage with the *kampung* necessarily follow a similar perception of development, rural communal life, and the 'place' of the *kampung* as a unit of collective tradition and sustenance farming as promoted by the government. Further, the *kampung* remains a cornerstone in the construction of a particular idea of Islamic modernity, as it provides an image of society that Salafi campus activists are attempting to move away from. The anxiety to be a modern Muslim is juxtaposed with the 'backwardness' of the non-university world, and features heavily in many of the tropes utilised by both preachers and activists alike. One's relationship to it, via *pengajian, buku saku* or social welfare, is thus both a form of activism and an act of confirmation in which one distinguishes oneself from a backward past through specific acts.

ITERATION THREE: AN ISLAMIC WOMANHOOD

One of the most important iterations of a modern Salafi subjectivity concerns the construction of proper gender roles and how the genders interact with each other. While my research focused predominantly on male activists, I was able to complement this with a collaborative series of interviews concerning gender relations between male and female members – carried out in conjunction with a female colleague, Nia Rusmiyati.

From what we observed, Salafi men and women each have an idea of what a woman should be through the construction of what they term *kewanitaan* (womanhood). This is complemented by the notion of *sakinah* (tranquillity), a phrase used to denote 'perfect' relations between men and women. As with *kewanitaan, sakinah* is used to promote an alternative to Western forms of gender relations and stereotypes (activists refer to Western perceptions of woman simply by the word *gender*).

Giving substance to these ideas is not an action restricted to *asatidz* but involves women themselves. Women participate in lectures, work in enclaves, and use social media. This creates a parallel structure of businesses and a cadre of religious experts that complement those of their male counterparts. Women thus play an important role in promoting the faith and constructing the ethical boundaries of correct gender relations. Yet as with concepts of being middle class or how to engage with the *kampung*, this too borrows from national ideological narratives of being a modern woman.

Despite insistence by activists that *kewanitaan* and *sakinah* are defined solely through scripture, they remain subject to interpretative variation – and variations tend to coincide with the gender of the interpreter. At its most simplistic, *kewanitaan* as dictated by men involves a return to traditional gender roles, where women are segregated from a male-dominated public sphere and given primary responsibility for educating the family and running the household. When in public, women should wear the *cadar* (full veil) and avoid contact with men, lest they cause *nafsu* (desire) that can lead to *zinah* (illegitimate sexual relationships). This narrative is amplified in *kajian*, as *asatidz* frequently blame gender mixing for social corruption in Indonesia.

The idea that promiscuous women distract hardworking men is hardly new to Indonesia. It has long been part of Islamic and even nationalist oriented discourse. Siegel (1969), Rosen (1984), Mernissi (1987), Ong (1987) and Brenner (1995) have all pointed out that amongst many male Indonesian political leaders and religious ulama, men are viewed as more rational, reasonable, and able to suppress their desires and hold to the Qur'an more consistently than women, who cannot help but tempt men into sin as they are more emotional, sexually active and irrational. Yet as widespread as such presumptions may be, Brenner (1995) and Elmhirst (2000) have both convincingly argued that the idea of self-restrained men and emotional women is not just overtly simplistic but demonstrably false. Salafi women themselves argue that there is a need for segregation, but this is not due to their own sexual promiscuity. Instead, they view *kewanitaan* as part of a modern ethical identity where men's promiscuity (rather than their own) remains a threat to their wellbeing.

Nisa (2012) has noted this in her analysis of Salafi veiling in Yogyakarta. She argues that the practice is linked to a range of emotive processes in one's search for religious purity. It represents a growing sense of *taqwa* (fear and love of Allah) via conscious expressions of docility and shyness that define one's position in this world. She believes that for such women, learning religious principles is not enough; the principles must have an impact on one's outward expressions and habits. Acts of modesty, more than a passive acceptance of principles, indicate an engaged effort to transform oneself through self-scrutiny and daily struggle to apply religious principles to one's behaviour. *Kewanitaan* is thus an ideal type of woman – shy, submissive, devout, intelligent and astute in looking after the welfare of her family – and so signifies an educated and individually responsible selfhood (Wichelen 2010: 53). Female energies can best be put to educating their children, studying religious texts, providing health services to other women, consuming specific products and finding extra income if the family requires it.

This idea of *kewanitaan* reflects an Islamically nuanced version of femininity as described in Indonesian national development narratives. Islamic terminology is the source of the predominant vernacular for *kewanitaan*, but the modern attributes of womanhood remain interwoven with the Indonesian discourse of *ibuism* (motherhood). As Djajadiningrat-Nieuwenhuis (1987: 43–51) has shown, *ibuism* was part of the wider government drive for the *priyayi*sation of society, which in itself was attributable to the government's developmentalist rhetoric.

Simply put, the *priyayi* were Javanese aristocrats who became part of the colonial administration before joining the ranks of the newly formed post-colonial state bureaucracy. The *priyayi* are said to hold several behavioural attributes that distinguish them from their peers. They were *alus* (humble) compared to the *kasar* (rough) nature of the *santri* (pious Muslims), *abangan* (those with syncretic beliefs) and non-Javanese (Geertz 1960: 231–235). Moreover, *priyayi* self-control was meant to represent what Anderson (1972) described as a power or mystical inner strength than enabled an individual to control themselves and their environment without the use of brute force. Such power, it was believed, was finite and could only be acquired through self-discipline and ascetic exercises that contributed to one's potency. Although both the notion of a clearly demarcated *priyayi* class or its hold on mystic power is dubious in modern Indonesia, these understandings of power and Javanese tradition remain popular in Indonesian literature and political discourse.[2]

The image of a humble *priyayi* was not just a source of spiritual power but also of national development. *Priyayi* traits came to represent an ideal type of modern, mild-mannered bureaucratically minded citizenship, based on self-control and discipline. This was strengthened by its extension into national discourses of *ibuism* – the embodiment of an ideal *priyayi* woman. Women, viewed as naturally promiscuous (when left to their own devices) compared to self-restrained men, were meant to discipline themselves and embody the virtues of motherhood for the benefit of the family, the nation and the professional position of their husband. *Ibuism* thus supported 'any action [taken by a woman] provided it is taken as a mother who is looking after her family, a group, a class, a company or the state, without demanding power or prestige in return' (Elmhirst 2000: 489).

---

2 Popular examples can be seen in the literature of Pramoedya Ananta Toer (e.g., *Dia Yang Menyerah* (She who Suffers) from the collection *Cerita Dari Blora* (Stories from Blora).

The model of womanhood was that of a loving mother concerned with the welfare of her family or kin group and any action was conducted first and foremost for the maintenance of social (and family) wellbeing and harmony. This image was reified through state-sanctioned women's associations as well as the village family development board, the Pembinaan Kesejahteraan Keluarga (PKK) (Organisation for Family Welfare). The PKK portrayed women as reproductive agents and carers of future generations, and gentle companions to their producer-husbands (Elmhirst 2000).

It is worth pointing out that not all Indonesians bought into *ibuism*, especially amongst non-Javanese and migrant women (Elmhirst 2000). Furthermore, by the 1980s, the influx of women to universities and the educated workforce challenged the housewife role of *ibuism*. Yet the promotion of women as mothers, albeit mothers now consuming and employed on behalf of the family, remains a strong narrative amongst policymakers in Jakarta. While the resignation of Suharto may have delegitimised the Javanese essence behind *priyayi*sation, elements of conservative indigenism and *ibuism* remain. This is especially so in government welfare institutions and amongst religious conservatives who present it as a return to traditional Islamic gender roles. Proponents of Salafi *kewanitaan* use a similar concept of motherhood, one that is sensitive to the trivialities of modernity, capitalism and communal society. The idea of women being empowered mothers whose agency revolves around the family is key to the way Salafis publicly promote the role of women.

The similarities between national development narratives and *kewanitaan* have informed and justified the ways Salafi women engage with their surroundings in Yogyakarta. Solahuddin frequently referred to women as guardians of the family who look after the children and the health of the community by ensuring all children attend school, and the village and house are clean. Women must be *sopan* (polite), humble and, if necessary, assist family finances by starting collectives that make clothes, offer professional services or otherwise generate income – provided it is done with the family in mind and with the husband's permission. It is also notable that Salafi descriptions of the family often talk about love (between man and woman and woman and child) as a source for social cohesion, and there is little mention of polygamy. Rather, they emphasised the concept of *sakinah* to stress Islam's role in ensuring a loving and monogamous marriage. This concept of the family entails both a loving and actively religious husband and wife who, as several informants urged, must look after each other in private matters as they maintain their commitment to religious values.

Economic and technological transformations along with access to tertiary education have provided women with the skills and means to communicate with each other in new ways. This has had a significant impact on what *kewanitaan* means. Activists have created new virtual tools through which women communicate without the risk of mixing with men. For example, Ummu Syahrial, whose husband is one of the founders of Yufid, has launched a blog where she and others discuss such things as healthy eating, what to expect during menopause and problems women may face after pregnancy. The site is not explicitly religious, but does provide a space where women can ask questions and receive useful tips on managing their health and that of their family. These virtual spaces do not replace physical activities but do nevertheless augment the ability to share information, offer services and organise without hindrance. Ummu Syahrial also has her own social media business and consults as a graphic designer of images and posters for the education of children.

Despite the efflorescence of new online sites, activism also revolves around women-only *da'wa* and the provision of specific women-oriented services. For instance, the YPIA has a women's branch, the Forum Kegiatan Kemuslimahan al-Atsary (al-Atsary forum for Muslimah activities, FKKA). They publish a weekly bulletin amongst woman within university campuses, *Zuhairoh*, which is part of a wider *da'wa* tailored to and deployed by women. In one edition, women are informed that they should use their education so as to understand the implications and meaning of religious knowledge and not act on a Western understanding of 'gender' (FKKA 2012).

Women can also teach or provide health care to children and other women. *Asatidzah* are employed to teach young girls, provide advice for adolescent women and assist as marriage counsellors. More so, the at-Turots runs the Sekolah Tinggi Ilmu Kesehatan Madani (Madani Medical School, Stikes Madani), which actively recruits woman to become nurses and midwives. Much like men, women thus engage in several entrepreneurial and religious roles, forming their own sphere of services, associations and activists, all facilitated via the educational facilities, *kajian*, boarding houses, schools and more recently the Internet.

Kewanitaan in no way counters the idea that women understand that their religion requires them to veil and segregate themselves from men. But its ideological orientation shows how we cannot think of a woman's agency as solely a form of religious submission. Becoming a Salafi woman involves a complex form of learning, through which one segregates oneself from men and maintains a demeanour of shyness and modesty towards others, but actively engages with and questions the meanings of doctrine in one's life. Indeed, women have their own ideas about what modesty and agency should be, and have created parallel forms of authority and action to their male counterparts. While the sphere of women remains less public to that of men, they are prime instigators in promoting a particular understanding of womanhood that appeals to potential female members. By doing so, they relate to the anxieties of being a modern but devout woman in Indonesia, bridging between the idea of returning to a traditional Islamic society, becoming a modern Indonesian woman and being a pious individual.

TOWARDS A YOGYAKARTAN VARIATION OF SALAFISM?

I have so far considered three iterations through which a modern Salafi selfhood has been expressed amongst Yogyakartan activists. These show how agents relate the meaning of religious identity to ideas of Indonesian modernity in ways sensitive to class, gender and development. All three iterations underline the variety of techniques and common tropes used by actors to transform specific religious identities. This process attests to the rhizomatic nature of the movement, as agents strive to create a religious selfhood in tune with the social anxieties present in their own lives and the lives of those they wish to reach. Amongst Yogyakartan Salafis, a process of discursive transformation and adaptation has thus occurred. Urban activists reject non-Islamic elements of lifestyle they have determined to be morally corrupt. Yet they simultaneously promote an Islamic modernity that taps into subcultural concerns popular with the student community. Piety is necessary if one wants to be modern, but no longer must one disassociate oneself from the capitalist economic system, modern technology, secular employment or other forms of social aspiration – as long as one approaches them in religious ways.

Promoting modern Salafism is not without its conceptual challenges. By altering and adapting the emphasis of Salafi doctrine, it is difficult to conceptualise where a pure Salafi global interpretation ends and local norms begin. As more agents inculcate and represent Salafi principles in their habits and da'wa, the potential for divergence from any common point of departure (if one ever existed) continues to grow. An example of this blurriness was evident in Pengusaha Muslim magazine when Ustadz Arif (who we met in Chapter 2) was asked whether one was allowed to work in the military, given that one would have to march to music (considered forbidden by more conservative Muslims). Arif demurred from giving a definitive answer about whether music was permissible, but answered the question in the affirmative. He stated it was beneficial to have good Muslims in the army and, therefore, it was allowed (Pengusaha Muslim 2012).

From a purely academic point of view, the majority of Salafi scholars are unequivocal in their stance that music is haram and one is forbidden to listen to it in any non-religious shape or form (Jawas 2007). Yet for Arif, Islam is a living system that must be available to everyone in society, regardless of professional occupation. By putting its authority behind such readings, Pengusaha Muslim magazine has increased the appeal of this specific religious interpretation, and so altered the ways the movement may be interpreted. It epitomises the spread of Salafi representations and how doctrines are translated into everyday decisions.

This leads me to several final points that are important to an understanding of Salafism in Yogyakarta. Firstly, different preachers, despite sharing similar scholarly references and networks, can disagree. Although there remains a degree of intra-movement cohesion, Salafism spreads through activists whose actions and representations do not follow a blueprint. Rather, they are characterised by a series of experimentations as the movement's doctrine comes into contact with local events and situations.[3] These are not created off the cuff, but are embedded in the locale of Yogyakarta, where they build on and add to popular trajectories and ideas of what living a modern, pious life means.

This brings us to a second point. Salafism in urban Yogyakarta is, as I have argued, not part of any direct or explicit political action, but something much deeper on both a personal and collective scale. It concerns itself with the private transformation of individuals into proper mukmin (pious) Muslims, and with the need to promote these values and implement an

---

3   This would be what Deleuze and Guattari refer to as a map, which they contrast to something already made or pre-defined, what they call a tracing. See Deleuze and Guattari 2004: 13–15.

Islamic lifestyle suitable to such an *umma*. Inculcating a religious selfhood is not limited to internalising religious scripture, but also involves shifting the way one comes to engage with one's surroundings. Agents are the link between religious doctrine and its presumed social significance in ways that mesh with national and economic concepts of progress. Their piety refers not just to scriptural references, but also increasingly to how they do business, live in enclaves and engage with social media ventures. It is linked, as Turner (2011) notes, to broader transformations of contemporary society in which the way one comes to associate and enact religion is fundamentally altered by the forces of modernity.

From this we can draw a final point. Far from decrying an immoral and secular society, Salafis have created a specific idea of what Taylor (2007) calls a religious fullness that comes to rely on non-religious ideas of action and society. Taylor describes such fullness as an activity or condition where life is seen as 'fuller, richer, deeper, more worthwhile and more admirable' (Taylor 2007: 5). Salafis have promoted this religious fullness through a nationally oriented identity that informs their religious selfhood. Inevitably, this builds on social categories present in wider Indonesian discourses of economic progress and national development. Salafi social demarcations not only distinguish between Salafi and non-Salafi, but also identify between nominal Indonesian Muslims, deviant Muslims, urban professionals and rural communities.

A Salafi religious selfhood therefore uses – rather than refutes – a number of national social markers, including class and gender. However, this logic points to a crucial difference between urban Salafism and emancipatory social movements such as the explicitly political Islamic movements of the anti-colonial period. Salafi renewal is void of any mission to actually empower villages as a socio-political or even religious force. As the demarcation between claimed rural and urban intellectual capacity shows, they actively play on class distinctions and, consequently, reify them. Rural and urban members may therefore be equal in the way they are all worthy of becoming proper Muslims, but what this means – in terms of living and intellectual capacity – remains linked to the ideological categories upon which a Salafi subjectivity is constructed.

Accordingly, scripture has become imbued with contextual meanings that assist Salafis in the redrawing of cultural, social, religious and national markers to define religious identity in ways sensitive to the pressures of modernity and the market forces that drive the growing Islamic economy. This process may not aim to directly inform political institutions, but it is nevertheless deeply political. Wearing religious clothes, promoting particular ideas of womanhood, or selling religious goods throw down both religious and increasingly political markers, defining a particular understanding of what it means to be a modern citizen. It is to these broader political consequences that the next chapter will turn.

CHAPTER 6

The Personal as Political: Religious Social Movements in the 21st Century

Firstly, you save yourself; after that you must save your family, and then you must aim to save society —Preacher, at-Turots, February 2012

Religiosity amongst citizens is a strong foundation for the Indonesian people. When our religion is well ... we become stronger
—Activist, Makassar, October 2016

This book has so far provided an account of 21st century Salafism in Indonesia. I have illuminated the sophisticated network of physical spaces, activities and discursive narratives through which a particular form of Salafism has gained popularity in urban centres such as Yogyakarta. As I have stressed throughout the book, localities are the sites where ongoing forces of globalisation occur and so Salafism, instead of representing something foreign, is a dynamic recomposition of a set of religious resources within Indonesia (Hepp 2009). Salafi activists stress that they follow a universal and strict religious tradition that varies little across time and space. But in reality, their behaviour is based on religious interpretations that are interwoven with local and national pressures that provide Salafi doctrine with social meaning. The disconnect between an alleged universalism and local context is hardly unique to Salafism; in fact, we can see a similar drive in numerous global revivalist religious movements. Yet the adeptness shown by activists mentioned in this book has led to significant success in advancing Salafi claims. They have achieved this not just by pragmatically adapting to local anxieties, but through a deeper and more sustained engagement with the cultural politics of Indonesia.

As I have argued throughout this book, Salafism has evolved in concert with global and local socio-political transformations that inform adherents understandings of Islamic identity, citizenship and the global *umma*. I now wish to further expand upon this point to show how these intra-movement transformations influence Indonesia's political sphere, and what this means to our understanding of social movements more broadly. By using a blend of online and face-to-face *da'wa* (propagation) that borrows from both religious and national discourses, Salafis provide an example of a networked social movement working across an array of environments. The movement may have no explicit political demand, but piety nevertheless has deeply political consequences, embedded as it is in local culture and praxis. Yet what does this add to our understanding of a social movements, Islam and their impact on the state?

When it comes to Islamic social movements, Wiktorowitz has provided one of the most definitive academic accounts from which we can draw. In Wiktorowitz's edited volume (2004) that examines Islamic activism around the globe, authors point to the range of political drivers, mobilisers and opportunities that sustain Islamic movements – often against hostile regimes. These analyses, which generally maintain the predominance of the state as the arena for mobilisation and political power as a goal, draw from traditional social movement theories that concentrate on resource mobilisation (McCarthy & Zald 1977), political opportunity structure (McAdam 1982), or cultures and emotion (McAdam 1994; Snow et al. 1986). These social movement theories owe much to empirical studies of trade unions and civil rights movements, believing that the power of social movements lies in the ability of rational actors to come together to make collective demands on a particular system in order to transform it to their benefit (e.g., McAdam 1982).

It has arguably been the concept of 'contentious politics' – popularised by Charles Tilly and Sidney Tarrow (2015) in their book by the same name – that has been the most recent basis for this explicitly political school of social movement theory. In this work, in which they analyse the 2011 Occupy movement and Arab Spring (among others), they outline how contentious politics take account of collective action, politics and familiar social processes of contention. Contentious politics are those 'interactions in which actors make claims bearing on other actors' interests, leading to coordinated efforts on behalf of shared interests or programmes' (*Ibid.*: 7). Contention is shaped by how governments respond (or not) to citizen claims as well as how they regulate the right to protest or protect a particular group in society. If demands are not adequately addressed, particular grievances can lead to a political opportunity structure in which competing interests spill out into a more sustained effort at social change.

There are notable strengths to such a politically focused analysis. For example, Gerry Van Klinken and Su Mon Thazin Aung (2017) have argued that the rise of anti-Muslim violence in Myanmar is due to a social movement of religious nationalists who have capitalised on a contentious political environment caused by political competition between the state's military elite and pro-democracy reformers. There is certainly merit in this analysis. Van Klinken and Aung illuminate how violence, such as that aimed at Muslims in Myanmar, may seem sporadic but is actually systematic and sustained through elite action (or inaction). Yet the primary focus on the state raises a number of problems when attempting to analyse a movement that is more concerned with embodying, enacting and promoting a particular religious lifestyle, as is the case with contemporary Salafis. By foregrounding the primacy of the state, there is an assumption that individuals are driven by rational choices which in turn can ignore one's efforts that go into constructing a religious subjectivity.

There have certainly been a number of sociologists who have approached religion through the prism of rational choice (e.g., Warner 1993; Iannaccone 1998; Finke & Stark 1986), but I suggest these accounts are overly deductive as they focus on economic and material incentive rather than personal sacrifice. Moreover, European concepts of power, the state, accountability and belief remain at the heart of such thinking, taking little account of either the competing notions of power and personhood illuminated by numerous anthropologists, or the cognitive variance at the heart of religious faith that psychologists have pointed to (Van Leeuwen 2014). By omitting the personal pressures, social sacrifices or multiple cognitive interpretations that inform one's life, or the local forms of modernity and power at play (and as seen in the previous chapter), it is difficult to accurately calculate, quantify or define a singular rationality.

A second critique of the above-mentioned social movement theories relates to the state as *the* primary arena through which social movements operate. Salafis interact with state structures (increasingly so) but ultimately transcend them. Their ultimate goal concerns what Giddens (1991) terms 'life politics' rather than the 'emancipatory politics' of the state. This leads us to what have been commonly referred to as new social movement theories, which move away from states and shift our concern to the sustained communal efforts involved in defining a form of identity and idea of reality (Price, Nonini & Tree 2008: 133).

Melucci (1980), one of the scholars at the forefront of the new social movement school, has argued that social movements are not directly focused on the political system, and can be fluid, polycentric and culturally embedded in a given place. These movements are not necessarily concerned with direct political influence but in the creation of a collective solidarity (the formation of which is a political act in itself) that provides meaning to specific forms of living and seeing the world (Melucci 1996). The impetus is not to control resources or change politics, but to alter the plain on which political and personal interpretations and battles are fought.

New social movement theories remain broad, with an emphasis on cultural politics rather than contention. Government decisions may influence the shape and form of a social movement but, ultimately, these movements embody a larger mission: to influence the idea of action and identity within society. In relation to Islamic movements, Bayat (2005; 2007) believes this has led to a shift from a political to post-political Islam, where enthusiasts aim to alter the public sphere to create a shared sense of solidarity. This is in large part due to the growing Islamic knowledge economy in late capitalism, which has caused a turning away from direct political activism to one that is social, economic and often private. In its extremity, this has led to the argument that post-Islamism has led to a more docile political identity. Bryan Turner has, for example, explained that economically inspired avenues of religious behaviour (such as those seen in Chapter 4) create consumer subjects who are predominantly passive and private (Turner 2011). Religious individuals, Turner states, pursue their religious identity through class-based consumption that diminishes the willingness to make sustained demands upon the state.

I agree with these views to a point, but I dispute that a concern with lifestyles and public activism is necessarily post-political. Salafism certainly manifests some of the traits Turner identifies, but this does not necessarily lead to a passive form of citizenship. Seemingly private acts such as growing a beard, donning religious clothing, wearing a t-shirt or carrying a bag bearing a particular religious logo are all as much political as they are personal acts. They catalyse the development of associational patterns, the severing of former identities and the creation of new friendships, which makes any clear distinction between the private, social and political difficult to discern.

As one leading activist at at-Turots succinctly put it, becoming *mukmin* (pious) consists of three stages: 'firstly, you save yourself; after that you must save your family, and then you must aim to save society (*masyarakat*) (Interview, Yogyakarta, 26 February 2012). This line of thought goes beyond urging one to engage in an active form of piety; it is inflected with ideas of reshaping Indonesian society at its grassroots.

SALAFISM AS A SOCIAL MOVEMENT

What does this mean for our analysis of Salafism as social movement? Firstly, as the previous chapters have shown there is significant overlap between private efforts to engage with religious principles, communal social bonds, and concepts of public action. A social movement is not limited to one particular social truth, but spans an array of cognitive iterations and disagreements that are promoted in a series of virtual and physical spaces. There are no defined objectives or boundaries, but rather a sustained effort to inform society that is enriched through multi-layered and multi-directional efforts at social change. It is a multiplicity, with parts of the movements connected to others through a logic of what Deleuze and Guattari (1983) term *agencement* (arrangement), where actors can popularise concepts, become self-sufficient or articulate their doctrine by stressing types of action.

By focussing on *agencement*, we can foreground the role of agents and agency in the way social movements come to create and dispute meanings and shared understandings of action. There is a communal logic at play, which ultimately assists in forming collective languages and solidarities in a given context. Both Fadil and De Koning have shown that the religious selfhoods and moral imaginaries that guide Islamic practice (or non-practice) can often find justification in the development of hermeneutical frameworks that reflect contextual sensitivities and tensions evident in crisscrossing multiple national and religious identities (Fadil 2009; De Koning 2013). As these studies underline, there is ambiguity and anxiety involved in reconciling Islamic orthodoxies and contemporary social dilemmas. The rich debates and conscious choices involved in this process inform how actors and movements ground themselves in a particular time and place.

I see Salafi selfhood as lying within a broader remit of interdependencies; a Salafi identity only becomes possible in a communal setting. In terms of social movement analysis, we must therefore look beyond the religious

163

self as the result of a personal ethical struggle, contention or rational choice, and towards the ongoing efforts of agents to reconcile what Deleuze (as quoted in Isin 2012: 77) refers to as the 'inside' (one's ethical transformation) with the 'outside' forces involved in subject-making. The need to bring the outside back inside is also noted by Al-Mohammad (2010), who uses Deleuze's concept of folding to underline how the formation of a specific selfhood lies within a greater web of relations pertaining to human existence. Building on this, I believe the creation of a Salafi movement relies on the people, events, expectations and experiences that are grounded and rife with tension. In sum, the movement is defined by the communal debates that inform how one must enact Salafism in *this* world.

Salafism is as representative of a global Islamic revival as it is of the ongoing broader cultural disagreements that lie at the heart of Yogyakartan, and indeed Indonesian, postcolonial identity. This leads us to a second and related point; that social movement networks increasingly span physical and online spaces. They transcend territorial borders and traditional ideas of hierarchy. A movement relies on interactions amongst individuals through a series of spaces (such as the mosque sermon or online Yufid platform) where contradictions, struggles and tensions are discussed. It is in these spaces that a set of global resources (such as the work of Islamic scholars) are given broader meaning. This is evident in the lecture material provided by preachers, the way individuals conduct their *da'wa*, and the everyday debates that arise within the movement.

The networked nature of Salafism strengthens the premise that the movement is rhizomatic – an expression I borrow from the lexicon of Deleuze and Guattari. The rhizome here is different from the botanical version as 'there are no points of positions in a rhizome, such as those found in a structure, tree or root' (Deleuze & Guattari 2004: 9). It is instead a multiplicity, with different actors (or 'lines' to draw from Deleuze and Guattari's vocabulary) representing different articulations and actions through which religious meanings are territorialised (or de-territorialised or re-territorialised) as well as enacted and conjoined to new actors/events (Deleuze & Guattari 1983: 18). This is why some Salafis may shun the state while others embrace national discourses of development. It is why, as we see below, Salafi activists in Yogyakarta can engage with ideas of citizenship and political activism, but yet are not necessarily easily understood within the framework of traditional social movement theories. The state has become a performative arena for action, but the movement cannot be defined solely in light of current political developments.

This draws us to our most important point: religious social movements such as Salafism are altering the ways individuals come to think of political subjectivity. This is perhaps obvious, but the point is worth further elaboration as it is fraught with false flag arguments. For example, to its detractors Salafism is seen as a threat towards the power of traditional Islamic organisations such as Nahdlatul Ulama because it represents something foreign (read Saudi Arabian) and not Indonesian. Moreover, it is often viewed from the standpoint of its most extreme (and often violent) elements, such as the Laskar Jihad. Yet while linkages to the Arabian peninsula are certainly important, they can obfuscate the real political transformations that Salafis are both pushing and benefiting from. Salafism offers a challenge to the underlying logic of religious truth in Indonesia not because it is foreign and hostile, but because it draws on deeply local anxieties and discourses formed through a versatile network of individuals, schools and mosques. It is for this reason that Salafism has been able to grow and sustain itself, although I believe this last point requires further elaboration.

CHARITY AND CITIZENSHIP

Subtle yet significant challenges to discourses concerning Islam and class, development and gender (for example) have shown how Salafism has embedded itself in the Indonesian environment, to the point it should no longer be considered a Saudi innovation. Furthermore, the proliferation of new economic ventures highlights how, over the past decade, Salafis have built their own self-sustainable economy. A brief examination of Salafi charity supports this fact. As noted throughout the book, Salafis have amplified their appeal to professional and university-educated Muslims, who in turn now fund specific religious and social welfare initiatives deployed by Salafi foundations. For example, RadioMuslim, which publishes their monthly expenditures and donations, relies almost exclusively on individual donations. Aside from large one-off donations, it asks supporters to set up a monthly direct debit of IDR 50,000 (approximately £2.50). As contributions have increased, so too has the financial strength of RadioMuslim. It rose from receiving approximately IDR 8 million per month in 2011 to over IDR 38 million per month in 2018. This has enabled them to expand their schedule, organise additional *kajian* and, in 2014, build a new FM radio antenna.

The ability to receive and benefit from independent small donations is most evident in local welfare initiatives. The at-Turots runs Peduli Umat (Care for the Umma), the philanthropic wing of its foundation that raises money and delivers relief to disaster-stricken areas in Indonesia. In order to raise funds, it often uses its network of mosques to solicit small donations. In a similar fashion, the YPIA has created the Peduli Muslim (Care for Muslims) to deal with humanitarian issues. With Peduli Muslim, donors can select what type of programme they wish to donate to, ranging from operational costs of a mosque, to welfare initiatives in Indonesia, or to international humanitarian efforts. The funds raised are not insignificant. In 2013, Peduli Muslim raised enough money to send volunteers to Idlib in Syria, where they and employees of Radio Rodja worked together to deliver food and medical supplies to displaced communities. These volunteers uploaded a video about their experience to Yufid on their return, and so ensured the international reach and solidarity of this network was acknowledged by those affiliated with the YPIA and at-Turots.

While the impact of these aid initiatives is limited compared to larger Muslim charities such as Indonesia's Dompet Duafa or the UK's Islamic Relief, they provide a source of symbolic capital that reifies the legitimacy of Indonesian Salafism as a modern religious network with developmentalist aspirations. Not surprisingly, as Salafi activists have grown in economic stature, so too has the reach of their charities. More broadly, however, the increased visibility of such aid initiatives aligns with the overall growth of the Islamic charity sector in Indonesia (Fauzia 2013; Latief 2013; Retsikas 2017). Islamic philanthropy is, as Latief (2016) notes, an important part of contemporary citizenship in Indonesia, providing a way in which (wealthy) Muslims can assist their brethren without relying on state services.

There is historical precedent for such charity. Muhammadiyah was itself established in 1912 to increase the welfare of Muslim communities in light of European colonial discrimination. However, it comes with specific caveats, as Salafis preference the welfare of Muslims over non-Muslims in their charity. In doing so, they allude not only to ideas of Islamic solidarity, but also to the primacy of Muslim welfare over others in Indonesia.

This, in turn, refers to a broader vision of society and the role of Muslims as active citizens within it. The state may not have started as the primary arena for Salafi piety and action, but as activists engage with ideas of aspiration, modernity and religious economies, they increasingly factor these aspects into their rhetoric. Providing justification for action draws from a shared language of religious solidarity that had been common in Indonesia long before Salafism made its initial inroads into the country. Inevitably, the ability to garner funds via donation and enter into political debate underlines a larger and more significant development in contemporary Salafism over the past decade: there is now an increased willingness to tap into and influence public discourses.

THE PERSONAL IS POLITICAL

As mentioned in the previous chapter, activists see themselves as Muslims with an inherently modern and Indonesian outlook. This does more than define the internal dynamics of Salafis; it catalyses an activism that seeks to influence debates concerning religious belonging and identity in Indonesia. Over the course of the 21st century, Salafis have interacted with, and reacted to, the state in numerous ways. During the early years of the Reformasi, Salafis would either join Jafar Umar Thalib in his Laskar Jihad or be drawn to the grassroots factions that promoted Salafism as outside the chaotic world of politics. After a series of bombings by the Al Qaeda inspired Jemaah Islamiyah, Salafis were forced to shift again. They became more transparent by registering their schools with local government bodies and socialising their activities with Indonesian security officials.

The security challenge posed by Jemaah Islamiyah arose in conjunction with an opportunity. The election of Susilo Bambang Yudhoyono to the presidency in 2004 marked a point where Islamic organisations enjoyed increased funds and access to state institutions – particularly through the Majelis Ulama Indonesia (MUI) (Indonesian Ulama Council), then run by Indonesia's current vice-president, Maruf Amin. This gave more life to the already noticeable rise in Islamic banking and economic services, online and TV preachers, and halal commodities. At the same time, the appeal of not just Salafism but Islam more generally became more pronounced within society, transforming university campuses into arenas replete with religious lectures, foundations and study groups. The generation of students who went to university during this period, unlike their Salafi predecessors during the New Order, lived in a more open environment.

Being able to organise openly and in conjunction with state institutions shifted the ways in which activists understood religious tenets. I have already discussed the discursive narratives at play, but we can see broader shifts in the outward focus of Yogyakartan Salafis occurring at the same time. A prime example of this can be seen in at-Turots' joint counter-terror work with the local regency government of Bantul in South Yogyakarta. In an effort to highlight the problem of religious radicalisation, the regency sponsored a number of public talks by at-Turots preachers. In one such lecture, Ustadz Afifi Abdul Wadud argued that terrorism and violence arose out of a misunderstanding of the principle *al-wala' wa-l-bara* (allegiance to Islam and renunciation of unbelievers) and what it meant to one's relations with non-Muslims. He stated that Muslims in Indonesia could not threaten or oppose *kafir* (non-believers), as they did not fall under the category *kafir muharib* (non-believers fighting Muslims) and so could not be threatened (at-Turots 2013).

A notable part of his lecture was how he talked about *al-wala' wa-l-bara'* not through doctrinal references, but as a principle that legitimised the government's position against outright violence against non-Muslims. But this also highlights how non-Muslims in Indonesia have come to be perceived as, first and foremost, *kafir,* rather than Indonesian citizens. Their rights, to the extent that they have any, have been guaranteed by a Muslim majority that ensures they remain protected but nonetheless limited in the social and political domain. Wadud's stance was not a one-off but repeated in different ways amongst many of my interlocutors. It had, for instance, become a common trope amongst Salafis during the anti-Ahok protests of 2016–2017 as well as the 2019 presidential elections. In these cases activists opposed Ahok for being a Christian, and Jokowi for his seemingly 'pluralist' credentials.

These comments are indicative of an opinion held by Salafi activists that Indonesian society is divided between Sunni Muslims and non-Muslims. All have the right to live together, provided non-Muslims do not attempt to convert Muslims and that Muslims remain the dominant political and social figures. Increasingly, this narrative is expressed not through religious doctrine but explanations infused with what Menchik (2016) describes as a Godly Nationalism. Menchik argues that, although Islamic groups have generally come to accept democracy, there remains an emphasis on the need for the community to be respected over the individual, and on the primacy of faith over other values (*Ibid.*). This is the core of Godly Nationalism. He also points out that it is neither institutionalised nor specific in its finer details. Instead, it depends on context and individual interpretation. As such, what Godly Nationalism can entail, apart from agreement that belief in God is inherent to being Indonesian, differs between Muhammadiyah, Nahdlatul Ulama and – ultimately – Salafis. All three may have few issues with Christian Indonesians or ethnic Chinese having access to the social sphere, but they vary significantly as to whether this equates to a right to hold high office, propagate one's religion in public, or receive equal access to welfare when compared to the Muslim majority.

Salafis have incrementally constructed their own version of Godly Nationalism by increasingly drawing comparisons between their own social activism and that of previous generations of Indonesian Muslim reformers, such as those linked to Muhammadiyah and to the *kaum muda* (young group) of Muslim anti-colonial campaigners. Activists believe Indonesian society can be changed through grassroots *da'wa* and appropriate government engagement. One individual who was part of the YPIA stated that the drive for Islamic purity and social advancement in Indonesia began not with Salafis, but with 19th century reformers in West Sumatra. He believed this push had stagnated in the 20th century during the Cold War, but was taken up again by Salafi activists (Interview, Yogyakarta, 6 June 2012). For this reason, they view their movement as a continuation of a pattern of Islamic revivalism in Indonesia. Hence, engaging with the state provides both legitimacy to this claim and a chance to contribute to the Islamisation of the public sphere.

This narrative is further explained by Abu Mujahid, an administrator at a religious *pesantren* in Bandung, in his Sejarah Salafi Indonesia (The History of Salafism in Indonesia, 2012) – a definitive intra-movement historical account of Salafism. He believes the movement was not a reaction to the political conditions during Suharto's New Order, nor was it linked to the DDII. He believes it sprang from a desire for Islamic truth in Indonesia, shared with previous reform movements but purer, given its unwillingness to compromise religious principles for political power. This work is popular amongst Yogyakartan activists, with one interlocutor praising it as the first clear history of their movement (Interview, Yogyakarta, 19 July 2012). Sejarah Salafi Indonesia portrays Salafism as part of Indonesian history despite attributing its doctrine to specific Ulama outside the country. Earlier generations of Indonesian reformers like Ahmad Dahlan or Ahmad

Hassan, while perhaps incorrect in their understanding of scripture, were nevertheless pioneers in providing the space and drive to empower Muslims in Indonesia (Mujahid 2012).

Salafis are thus radically revising their understanding about how they relate to Indonesian history. Ustadz Solahuddin, whom we met in previous chapters, eloquently noted this shift when he argued that we could no longer classify Islam in Indonesia as traditional or reformist. Rather, we must attempt to find out whether a Muslim is good or bad in relation to how they live their life and whether they had *taqwa* (fear and love of God). Both good and bad Muslims are members of Nahdlatul Ulama and Muhammadiyah. While Solahuddin believed non-Salafi Indonesian Muslims might not abide by true (Salafi) doctrine, they could remain good if they did so unknowingly, because they had yet to truly hear about the *manhaj* (method). Salafism, for Solahuddin, was not a movement that appeared in Indonesia during the 1980s; it was an inherent part of every Muslim's search for the truth. It did not attempt to shift people's religious orientation, but pushed them to re-engage with their faith using the tools and teachings that were already available in society (Interview, Yogyakarta, 19 April 2012).

WASATHIYAH: PUSHING A MUSLIM
MAJORITARIANISM

Salafis have come to define their *raison d'être* as a search for religious truth that is, at its core, an Indonesian modernity. In doing so, they are increasingly willing to work with state bodies and even support politicians when they can legitimately argue that doing so is for the good of Muslims. During President Jokowi's tenure, Salafis have increased their nationalist credentials in opposition to what they see as Jokowi's secular vision of modernity and developmentalism. In both the 2014 and 2019 presidential elections, Salafis unsuccessfully opposed Jokowi's campaign, despite several prominent scholars taking to social media and mosques to argue that he and his PDI-P represent the interests of non-Muslims, secularists and Chinese (Putra 2014). These claims were certainly hyperbolic, but they pointed to a trend that many Salafis see as a diminishment of their political influence. This perception grew as both security officials and Islamic organisations such as Nahdlatul Ulama aimed to counter IS extremism, and began to re-ignite familiar tropes that Salafis were foreign and violent.

At this time, several leading Salafi scholars began to adopt the concept of *Wasathiyah*, or moderate Islam. *Wasathiyah* derives from Qur'anic references to the *ummatan wasathan*, or moderate people, and it has featured significantly in both YPIA's lecture schedule and in the public statements of the Makassar-based Wahdah Islamiyah. Amongst Salafis, its use as a label to self-identify where the movement sits in relation to other Muslims is relatively new, emerging in 2016. This is despite the previous popularity of *Wasathiyah* amongst followers of the Muslim Brotherhood and within the preaching of Qatar-based Yusuf Qaradawi (Shavit 2014). As might be obvious, Salafis do not reference such authors in their own definition, preferring to use *Wasathiyah* as a concept to define their increasingly public appeals and how they relate to the state. In this regard, Wahdah Islamiyah announced their support for what they call *demokrasi wasathiyah* (Wahdah Islamiyah 2016), a marked departure from Salafi mores that democracy is a dangerous concept because it promotes the rule of man over God (Jalil 2009).

The use of *Wasathiyah* has been successful in painting Salafism as peaceful, even as or perhaps because the concept remains purposely vague. Instead of elaborating on *Wasathiyah* through particular scholarly works, its introduction into the Salafi lexicon provides an elastic frame to legitimise both their increased public activism and their move toward the centre of the religious field. Certainly, they are not the only ones to use the term. *Wasathiyah* has become a popular notion in efforts by government officials and even the Saudi Arabian religious establishment to distinguish themselves from the jihadism of ISIS and Al Qaeda (Agus 2018). Yet for Indonesian Salafis, *Wasathiyah* represents more than semantics that both government and citizenry might find appealing. It provides a normative framework through which to increase their interventions into the political sphere. It is the culmination of a process that began over a decade ago, when activists began to frame themselves as an inherent part of Indonesian society, and has since become part of a broader effort to turn religious doctrine into practical (and sometimes pragmatic) socio-political mobilisation. This has been characterised by changes to Salafi practices such as the display of Indonesian flags during *kajian* in 2018 (they were absent in 2012), the wearing of batik, and a concern with electoral campaigns and who can protect the interests of Muslims.

The language of *Wasathiyah* also points to a more significant transformation in Indonesian society. As much as *Wasathiyah* represents a frame through which Salafis approach society, it also underscores a broader accommodation by several government officials of conservative norms and the growing awareness by Salafis that their movement can influence political debate. Public concern over religious morality and deviancy has provided a space in which Salafi activists can find common cause with other conservative Muslims and work together on particular issues of morality (IPAC 2016). Several prominent Salafis have joined forces with like-minded conservatives or come to sit in provincial MUI branches. This enables them to talk about moderation on one hand while continuing to emphasise the need to differentiate between true Muslims and other religious minorities, on the other. It is notable, for instance, that neither Solahuddin nor his colleagues extended their concept of moderation to include tolerance for Shi'ism or the GBTQ community. Indeed, while Solahuddin mentioned that even though he had no right to declare another Muslim a non-Muslim, the category of Muslim clearly did not extend to the Shi'a because they rejected basic Islamic tenets and, through Iran, Hezbollah and Assad, were trying to take over Islam's holy sites.

The significance of Solahuddin's statement should not be lost on us. Certainly, Salafi anti-Shi'ism has global dimensions. Many Saudi *shaykh* have condemned all forms of Shi'i belief for its divergence from the true path of the first three generations of Muslims (see Steinberg 2009). Yet Salafis like Solahuddin no longer frame their hostility towards Shi'ism as solely religious, but rather mix this with the impetus to defend Indonesian faith from foreign influence. They are not alone in doing so, as many other socio-conservative Islamic preachers and even government ministers have expressed concern that Shi'a are non-Muslims (HRW 2013: 41).

Condemnation from Salafi *asatidz* plays into a broader narrative about how to define the ethical limits of a legitimate Indonesian religious identity. Accordingly, Salafis and religious intellectuals alike are busy debating and (re-)defining the historical significance of Islam's role in society and its meaning to the nation. Religion is by no means considered a private matter, but one at the very heart of citizenship. To be fully Indonesian, one must follow Sunni Islam or one of the other state-acknowledged official religions. Further, the obsession with Shi'ism is far from an objective assessment of danger either to their own movement or to Indonesia. Instead, it stems from a growing understanding of what it means to be Muslim in contemporary Indonesia, and the ethical boundaries of national identity.

A MODERN RELIGIOUS SUBJECTIVITY

By striving to create a modern Islamic subjectivity, Salafis make claims about what it means to be a modern citizen in contemporary Indonesia, and about what actions must be taken to ensure the position of Muslims remains at the forefront of the public conscience. They do not aim to take political power, nor to enact Sharia law by altering Indonesia's legal system. Rather, they seek to inform local ideas about what is and is not acceptable in the public sphere by conflating national character with religious moral- ity. This inevitably enters the political realm by making acts such as those against Ahok more acceptable and by channelling the ideas that underpin a concept of Indonesian Islam from the fringe to the mainstream. It is for this reason that the eminent scholar of Islam in Indonesia, Sidney Jones, stated in 2013 that 'the biggest issue for Indonesian democracy ... is not terrorism but intolerance, which is moving from the radical fringe to the mainstream' (Jones 2013: 125). Eight years later, I suggest this has occurred more quickly than most imagined.

The growth of the Salafi movement has played a pivotal role in altering the performative and ideological understanding of public religious expres- sion in Indonesia. Ever more vocal and sophisticated demands for public morality and anti-deviancy campaigns have become part of Indonesian dis- course. Far from creating passive citizens, Salafi narratives of development, modernity and the economy have led to a growing desire to change society by building up the Muslim economy and securing religious rights for the presumed majority. Salafism has created a self-sustaining, multi-directional movement whose agents operate across numerous physical and virtual environments through an eclectic mix of activities. While the focus may not relate to a particular political party, or even an attempt to capture state power, it lies at the heart of an evolving and complex religious subjectivity that is shifting how Indonesians contemplate the relationship between religion, history and the state in the 21st century.

173

Conclusion: The End of Pluralism?

I began this book by describing how Salafism is part of a broader process of Islamic revivalism across Indonesia, and it seems fitting to conclude by reflecting briefly on the broader socio-political consequences of such a revival. To be sure, I have provided only a small window into Islamic activism and revival in Indonesia, but hopefully the lack in breadth is offset by the richness and depth of what has been portrayed. As I have outlined throughout the book, Salafi activists have become increasingly astute at utilising a number of platforms and mediums to voice socio-conservative religious values. They may talk primarily about faith and religious practice, but as the resonance of these values grow in Indonesian society, there are adverse political consequences. They have, both discursively and sometimes through direct action, been at the forefront of putting forward a Muslim-majoritarian agenda that seeks to differentiate between Muslim and non-Muslim Indonesians. This has, moreover, gained political currency as religious minorities and the LGBTQ community are increasingly targeted as allegedly 'deviant' as well as somehow not properly Indonesian.

The Salafi movement described within this book is arguably on the vanguard of this trend and, over the past 20 years, it has actively taken advantage of new democratic spaces to develop *da'wa* (propagation) on university campuses, in villages and across the internet. But physical expansion has gone hand-in-hand with discursive maturity, as activists have become ever more reliant on framing the worldly significance of their movement in terms of advancing the moral standing of Indonesian society as a whole. They may refer to far-flung Islamic scholars, but they are not fully global, having brought the nation – in its performative and discursive nature – back into their movement. Part of this development (such as adopting the *yayasan* structure) is pragmatic in nature, but other aspects (such as the use of developmentalist language) underscore a deeper ideological commitment to Indonesian belonging.

Friction is involved in this process, which is why Salafism remains fragmented. But this process also provides Salafis with the versatility described in this book. It is the deeper discursive commitment that has truly allowed Salafism to contribute to the broader growth of Muslim majoritarian discourse. In fact, despite well-rehearsed protestations that they not only are apolitical but must remain so, Salafi activists have subtly pushed this agenda through their mosque sermons and radio shows, often via emotive pleas for Muslim unity.

This majoritarianism truly came to the forefront of national political discourse during the Jakarta gubernatorial elections in 2017, so it is worth turning to this event and its aftermath to show the full extent of how Salafism, alongside other conservative Islamic traditions, have influenced social values. A year prior to the 2017 election, Jakarta's then-incumbent governor, Basuki Tjahaja Purnama (popularly known as Ahok) looked on course to hold onto his office. Ahok had taken over the governorship when Joko Widodo, who had become governor in 2012, was elected president in 2014. As such, he had never actually contested an election as governor, but had nonetheless won applause for his drive to improve the city administration and tackle the city's endemic problems of flooding and traffic congestion. In his two years as governor, he had built a reputation, especially amongst the city's better-off classes, for clean and efficient government.

Ahok was not popular amongst all Jakartans. Since taking office, he had forcibly relocated and evicted approximately 16,000 residents from flood-prone working-class areas, which had caused resentment amongst poorer Jakartans (Wilson 2016). Ahok was also a Christian of ethnic Chinese descent, a background absolutely unacceptable to a range of conservative Muslim organisations. The coalition lined up against Ahok included the vigilante Islamic Defenders Front (Front Pembela Islam, FPI), who had protested against Ahok since 2014, as well as followers of Hizbut Tahrir, the Muslim Brotherhood and a number of Salafi foundations and preachers. As the election approached, these organisations formed an alliance to oppose Ahok and find a suitable Muslim replacement. In June 2016, they organised a series of talks and mosque lectures, initially identifying the businessman-turned-politician Sandiaga Uno as a prospective replacement. These talks cumulated in a mass gathering at Jakarta's Istiqlal Mosque on 18 September, where key speakers reiterated their belief that Muslims were obliged to vote for a Muslim candidate. Several attendees underpinned their reasoning by citing Qur'anic verse al-Maidah 51, which warns Muslims against allying with Christians and Jews.

Amongst Salafi activists, the idea that Ahok was not allowed to rule because he was a non-Muslim seemed natural. As one activist put it, only someone with the correct Muslim *aqida* (creed) was suitable to lead in a predominantly Muslim country (Interview, Makassar, 13 October 2016). Yet these views were not shared by the majority of Jakartans, who at first paid little attention to the gathering anti-Ahok alliance. This changed in late September 2016, however, when Ahok – campaigning in the remote Thousand Islands off the coast of Jakarta – was accused of misquoting *al-Maidah* 51. As a doctored video of Ahok quoting the verse (or, more precisely, hinting that those that used the verse to condemn voting for a Christian were lying) spread, his opponents mobilised against him. The Majelis Ulama Indonesia (MUI) (Indonesian Council of Ulama) denounced Ahok as a blasphemer and demanded that he be held accountable for his 'actions.' In turn, this spurred a series of anti-Ahok demonstrations joined by an estimated 500,000 participants at their peak.

The scale of the demonstrations shocked political commentators. To be certain, civil society and academics had become increasingly concerned about growing religion-based intolerance and the use of so-called morality and blasphemy laws throughout the country over the previous decade. But these demonstrations were the most vivid example of the extent to which conservative preachers could mobilise masses around a sectarian view of politics. More worryingly was the seemingly unproblematic way in which Ahok's political opponents fuelled such anti-pluralist language for their own narrow goals. In the end, Ahok was defeated by Anies Baswedan who, with the backing of Prabowo Subianto, had become the poster-boy for the demonstrators. Ahok also became the first sitting governor to be charged with blasphemy and, in May 2017, he was found guilty and received a sentence of two years.

The short-term causes and consequences of the demonstrations have been discussed extensively by political scientists, journalists and civil society over the past four years. Commentators have, as mentioned, rightly noted that Ahok had already been a target both the FPI and Salafi-inclined scholars like Muhammad Zaitun Rasmin and Bachtiar Nasir years before these demonstrations (Chaplin 2016; IPAC 2018; Setijadi 2017). Observers also noted the overlap of economic grievances and opposition to Ahok, especially amongst Jakartans displaced by Ahok in his attempt to clear illegal settlements along the Ciliwung River (Wilson 2016). Others have pointed to the political alliances and funding that backed the protests, suggesting that the demonstrations were part of a broader political campaign to undermine Ahok (Mietzner & Muhtadi 2018).

Yet the demonstrations revealed something else, too. All of the above-mentioned studies allude to the political potency of Islamic identity in Indonesia, as well as to the heightened anxiety about what being Muslim in modern Indonesia means for one's political leaning. Protestors likely received financial support from political backers, but they were also highly organised in their own right. They deployed a pre-existing network of mosques, social media channels, publication houses and volunteer groups to disseminate their message not just in Jakarta but across the country. As the gubernatorial elections approached, they bussed in thousands of Muslim 'observers' to monitor the vote count at each poll within the city. Consequently, the demonstrators may have coalesced around perceived grievances caused by what Ahok represented, but they also tapped into a pre-existing and arguably expanding network of social anxieties that were circulating in numerous Islamic study circles.

Discursively, while Islam acted as an emotive umbrella for protests, there were larger nationalist arguments also at play. Protest organisers rarely used religious tenets alone when framing their opposition to Ahok. Instead, mosque sermons, social media publications and stump speeches painted the demonstrations as the organic coming-together of Indonesian *pribumi* (native) Muslims in defence of their faith. Muslims, they alleged, had 'had enough' with political rule favourable that they claimed favoured non-Muslims and Chinese business interests. In its place, they demanded a new national consensus based on majoritarian (i.e., Muslim) rule. The fact that this narrative was repeated within an eclectic mix of social classes, educational backgrounds, ethnicities and Islamic doctrines – all of whom joined the protests – underscores how it has grown in potency.

It is for this reason that we must pay close attention to the sustained efforts of Salafis. Indeed, Salafi involvement in the anti-Ahok demonstrations may have been limited compared to other protest groups, but it was important. Some of Indonesia's more active Salafi intellectuals, such as Bachtiar Nasir and Muhammad Zaitun Rasmin, played a leading role in demonstrations. Other Salafi preachers, such as Jafar Umar Thalib, allegedly called for Ahok to be put to death (Rogers 2017). Others – arguably the majority –stayed away from demonstrations, but nonetheless leant their verbal support by urging followers to vote against Ahok. In all cases they sought to re-orient Indonesian political discourse away from civic pluralism and toward an understanding that to be truly representative of Indonesian aspirations, one must be a practicing Muslim.

The economic and nationalist motifs within the demonstrations are similar to the discursive narratives described throughout the book, and they have continued to resonate within Indonesian politics well after Ahok's conviction. What was once a fringe debate over the ethical boundaries of an acceptable Indonesian religious identity has since become a mainstay of political discourse. Politicians have shifted and recast their appearance accordingly. Strikingly, during Joko Widodo's second presidential campaign in 2019, he altered his image and campaign team to accommodate elements of this majoritarian narrative. Gone were the checked shirts symbolic of his previous presidential and gubernatorial campaign images. Jokowi was now pictured on banners across the nation (with the notable exception of Hindu Bali) wearing a white religious shirt with a black *songkok* hat. He was not alone, either, as his then-opponent (and current Minister of Defence) Prabowo Subianto made symbolic overtures to the remnants of the anti-Ahok demonstrations, although they never mobilised behind him like they had against Ahok.

Jokowi's appointment of the Islamic scholar, Ma'ruf Amin, as his selection as vice-president for the 2019 presidential election, also sent a worrying signal to defenders of religious freedoms. While Amin was most likely foist onto Jokowi by his political backers (who saw Amin as too old to run for president himself in 2025; see Fealy 2018) his selection was nonetheless problematic. Amin had been the author of some of the MUI's most controversial *fatawa* against religious minorities during the Susilo Bambang Yudhoyono years, and had strongly influenced the MUI *fatwa* against Ahok in 2016. That neither Jokowi nor his allies cared much over Amin's history points to broader shifts in Indonesia's political calculus over the past decade.

INDONESIA AND SALAFISM IN THE 21ST CENTURY

The increased use of economic and nationalist rhetoric by Salafis underscores the role they play in promoting majoritarianism in Indonesia, and the detrimental affect they – and other Islamic conservatives – are having on the rights of non-Muslims. But if Salafi activists increasingly engage with Indonesian politics and society in local ways, can we ever actually talk about a universal Salafism or a coherent Salafi movement? Is the idea of the religious purity to which Salafis aspire a pipe dream? Does this mean Salafism – as a movement – is moving farther from its goal despite its growing popularity? Answers to these questions depend on how you approach them.

From a strictly religious point of view, Salafis have shown a large degree of cognitive variance when it comes to what doctrine actually means beyond issues of ritual and dress. The conflictual nature of intra-Salafi debate shows there is no clear way to apply Salafism and no one group can claim absolute purity. Yet I would argue that from a sociological perspective, our aim has not been to look for any beginning point from which to measure Salafism. My aim has been to examine how activists engage with religion in their concrete environment. Given their active engagement in cultural and political narratives in Yogyakarta, I would argue that there is no universal Salafi movement, but rather numerous translocal Salafisms held together by a number of institutions, actors, aesthetic markers, shared texts and –importantly – an imagined pan-Salafi solidarity.

No one contests the strong links between Saudi Arabia, its educational institutions and Salafi activists. But as I have shown, Indonesian Salafi work with marked independence from Saudi institutions or authority. Moreover, any idea that the movement would wither without Saudi money does not account for the level of financial independence many Salafi foundations and institutions have developed in the past 20 years. For certain, the movement benefitted from Saudi money (and Gulf money more broadly), but when the Indonesian state pressured several Salafi foundations to curb their receipt foreign financial donations after the rise of the Islamic State, they proved more than capable of continuing their operations.

Nonetheless, the idea that Salafism is a form of Saudisation lingers and has become a popular trope amongst political opponents of Salafism. Leaders of Indonesia's Nahdlatul Ulama often wield this argument as a way of delegitimising the presence of Salafis (as well as other translocal and transnational religious groups). A more recent iteration of this concerns the battle between Indonesian and foreign religious clothing. The former Minister for Religious Affairs and general, Fachrul Razi, had discussed banning the *niqab* and trousers that avoided *isbal* (falling below the ankle) from government offices citing the threat of foreign radicalism.

As I have shown throughout this book, notions that Salafism is a foreign threat are inaccurate. Salafism has been successful precisely because activists are acutely aware and able to interlace religious principles with anxieties about how one should be Indonesian. This poses a theoretical (and doctrinal) conundrum for Salafism. Claims to be a universal and timeless form of Islam that emulates the Prophet Muhammad and his original companions do not hold to the levels of contextualisation we have seen in this book. When I challenged activists directly on this point, they were quick to retort that it was quite impossible to know exactly how the original Muslims would have driven a motorbike or interacted with modern technology – simply because these are new phenomena. They also stated that the appropriate place and use of these aspects of modern life must be determined through careful scrutiny of relevant Islamic works. The purity of Salafism, they maintained, was inevitably upheld through this scrutiny because there was a process of examining Hadith and establishing what activity was valid and what was not.

The time and attention dedicated in Salafi lectures, books and magazines to micro-practices such as brushing one's teeth or what to do when one accidentally hears music while walking on the street, attests to the effort that goes into emulating the original followers. In this regard, Salafis can – on the surface of it – claim to be following a *manhaj* that provides the best possible way to be a literal Muslim. Yet one issue remains. Almost all participants claimed that the correct way to emulate the Prophet was through rigorous scrutiny of religious texts. But if this is the case, why is there so much division and fragmentation amongst Salafis? Why do some activists believe it is acceptable to wear Indonesian batik while others refute this on grounds the Prophet and companions never wore such clothing? Why do others believe television is a permissible form of technology provided it is for religious education, whereas others maintain it must be completely forbidden? For a movement so focused on micro-practices, these issues show how the idea of Salafi purity remains difficult to square.

The existence of contradictory Salafi networks cannot detract from the very deep and personal efforts involved in Salafi activism. Activists are acutely aware that not all of their co-religionists have the same interpretation, but without an identifiable leader or organisational hierarchy, these disputes can be difficult to resolve. On occasion, respected scholars from the Middle East can assist in resolving them but in most cases they end in rupture. Yet the richness of (multiple) interpretations has led to the movement's success. Its rhizomatic nature has proved essential to the spread of Salafism across Indonesia, to its alignment with local anxieties, and to the provision of a diverse range of solutions to the political and social pressures on itself and its followers.

In this regard, my work goes beyond an attempt to offer insight into debates concerning Salafism and Indonesia and thus contributes to the anthropological study of religious mobilisation and social movements more generally. I have built my analysis – especially in terms of understanding contemporary religious agency and renewal – around insightful accounts regarding how religious agents relate to their faith, to social anxieties and to the forces of modernity. I have also attempted to move beyond accounts of religious self-learning and the creation of Islamic selfhood to consider what this means in relation to broader social forces. By looking at Salafism as a translocal social movement, I have attempted to contribute to the literature related to global Islamic renewal by examining how contemporary piety is influenced by the push-and-pulls of urbanisation and global technology, and their effects on culture and religion.

I believe we must look at the forces of globalisation not as a catalyst for deculturation and the erasure of global differences, but as an intensification of global networks and resources that gain significance primarily through the physical spaces and local codes that give them meaning in a particular locale. Globalisation may break down social and cultural boundaries, but it also builds new ones, the finer points of which are worked out through local interactions. Although this suggests that a global Salafism is eclectic in nature – differing across time and space as ideas and principles travel from one locale to the next – it neither renders the movement defunct nor undermines the intensely personal commitments of its activists to create and enact a particular type of Muslimhood. Rather, the process of engaging with religious doctrines can alter the meanings of being a modern Muslim. It is, consequently, a local affair.

Glossary

Adat	Culture
Al-tasfiya wa-l-tarbiya	Purification and education
Al-wala' wa-l-bara'	Allegiance to Islam and renunciation of unbelievers
Akhlak	Morals
Aqida	Islamic creed
Bid'a	Un-Islamic innovations
Da'i	Lay preacher
Daurah	Religious training programme
Da'wa	Propagation, calling one to the Faith
Dukun	Spiritual healer
Fard al-ain	An individual obligation, frequently used to refer to one's obligation to conduct *da'wa*
Fatwa	Islamic legal pronouncement (plural *fatawa*)
Fiqh	Jurisprudence
Fitnah	Sedition
Ghazwul fikr	War of ideas
Gotong royong	Mutual community assistance
Halus	Humble
Haram	Forbidden
Hijrah	The Prophet Muhammad's migrations from Mecca to Madinah. Used to denote young Muslim revivalism in Indonesia

Halaqah	Study circle
Hisba	The commanding of right and forbidding of wrong
Hubbun dunya	Love of the earth (a form of idolatry)
Ibada	Religious practice
Ibuism	Motherhood (as a concept promoted by the New Order)
Ijaza	Accreditation
Ijtihad	Independent reasoning
Isbal	The practice of wearing trousers that do not fall below the ankle
I'tikaf	Where one lives in the mosque to study and pray, common during the final ten days of Ramadan
Ikhlas	Sincerity
Ikhtilath	Mixing of sexes (a form of social corruption)
Jalabiyaa	Islamic Robes
Jemaah	Religious community, Indonesian spelling of *Jama'ah*
Jilbab	Face veil (Indonesian)
Joyoboyo	Javanese zodiac
Kafir	Non-believers
Kajian	Religious lecture
Kajian Akbar	Great religious lecture
Kyai	Indonesian religious scholar linked to Shafi'i school of jurisprudence
Madhhab	School of Jurisprudence, of which there are four in Sunni Islam (Hanbali, Shafi'i, Hanafi and Maliki)
Madrasah	Religious school
Ma'had	Religious school (purely for religious education)

Manhaj	Religious methodology
Muamala	Social conduct
Mukmin	Term for pious Muslim, derives from Arabic word *mu'im*
Murabbi	Religious guide
Nafkah	Livelihood
Nafsu	Desire
Niyya	Intentions
Pengajian	religious lecture, predominantly rural in the context of this book.
Niqab	*Full face veil that leaves only the eyes uncovered*
Pesantren	Religious school (for primary and secondary education)
Sakinah	Tranquillity (used to denote relations between a man and woman in Indonesian Salafism)
Salaf as-Salih	Pious ancestors (specifically the first generations known as the Sahabah, Tabi'un and Tabi' al-Tabi'in)
Salafiyya da'wiyya	Followers of Salafi doctrine who are politically quiet and focus on propagation
Salafiyya harakiyya	Non-violent but political Salafism
Salafiyya jihadiyya	Violent and political Salafism, commonly linked to al-Qaida and Jama'ah Islamiyah
Shaykh	Term used for revered religious scholar based in the Arabian Peninsula
Sholat	Prayer
Syirik	Idolatry
Tabligh Akbar	Great teaching session
Tafakur	Reflection

Taklid	Obedience to religious scholars
Taqwa	Fear and love of God
Tarbiyah	Islamic education
Tawhid	Monotheism and absolute acceptance in the oneness of God and His authority
Umma	The Islamic Community
Ustadz	Religious teacher (plural *asatidz*)
Ustadzah	Female religious teacher (plural *asatidzah*)
Wali al-amr	Obedience to a ruler
Wudhu	Ritual washing before prayer
Yayasan	Foundation, a legal structure in Indonesia
Zakat	Tax and redistribution
Ziarah	Grave visits
Zinah	Illegitimate sexual relationships

References

ADB (2010). *Key Indicators for Asia the Pacific 2010*. (41st Edition). Manila: Asian Development Bank.

Agus, Y. (2018, March 27). Indonesia-Saudi Sepakat Sosialisasikan Islam Wasathiyah. *Republika*.

Al-Albani, M. N. (2000). *Sifat Shalat Nabi*. Yogyakarta: Media Hidayah.

Al-Mohammad, H. (2010). Towards an Ethics of Being-With: Intertwinements of Life in Post-Invasion Basra. *Ethnos*, 75(4), 425–446.

Amnesty (2014). *Prosecuting Beliefs: Indonesia's Blasphemy Laws*. London: Amnesty International.

Anderson, B. (1972). *The Idea of Power in Javanese Culture*. Ithaca, NY: Cornell University Press.

————— (1991). *Imagined Communities: Reflections on the Origin and Spread of Nationalism*. London: Verso.

————— (2001). *Violence and the State in Suharto's Indonesia*. Ithaca, NY: Cornell University Press.

Ansori, M. H. (2009). Consumerism and the Emergence of a New Middle Class in Globalizing Indonesia. *Explorations: A Graduate Student Journal of Southeast Asian Studies*, 9 (Spring).

Antlov, H. P., R, Ibrahim, R., & Van Tujil. (2006). NGO Governance and Accountability in Indonesia: Challenges in a Newly Democratising Country. In L. Jordan and P. Van Tujil (eds), *NGO Accountability: Politics, Principles and Innovations*. London: Earthscan.

Appadurai, A. (2003). Sovereignty without Territoriality: Notes for a Postnational Geography. In S. M. Low and D. Lawrence-Zuniga (eds), *The Anthropology of Space and Place: Locating Culture*. Oxford: Blackwell Publishing, pp. 337–349.

APJII (2019). *Penetrasi & Profil Perilaku Pengguna Internet Indonesia: Survei 2018* (Powerpoint Summary). Jakarta: Indonesia Internet Service Provider Association.

As-Suhaimi, F. bin H. bin R. (2007). *Pokok-Pokok Dakwah Manhaj Salaf.* Jakarta: Griya Ilmu.

As-Sunnah (2011). Bila Si Kecil Susah Buang Air Besar. *As-Sunnah,* 14(8), 12–13.

———— (2012). Memilih Jalanan Sehat Untuk Anak. *As-Sunnah,* 15(3), 13–14.

Aspinall, E. (2005). *Opposing Suharto: Compromise, Resistance, and Regime Change in Indonesia.* Stanford, CA: Stanford University Press.

At-Turots (2013). Sarasehan 'Mencegah Radikalisme dan Terrorisme. Retrieved from binbaz.or.id/berita/37-kabar-berita/183-sarasehan-qpencegahan-radikalisme-dan-terorismeq (accessed 15 November 2013).

Badri, M. A. (2012). Siapa Ambil Untung Dari Perayaan Idul Fitri? *Pengusaha Muslim,* 30, 42–45.

Baits, A. N. (2014). Apakah Zakat Non Muslim Ditermina? *Tanya Ustadz.* Yufid

Banker, C. (2019a). Kampung Hijrah: Enabling Environments for Salafism on University Campuses in Yogyakarta, Indonesia, Tufts University, PhD thesis.

———— (2019b). The Changing Face of Indonesian Islam. *The Diplomat.* Retrieved from thediplomat.com/2019/12/the-changing-face-of-indonesian-islam/ (accessed 20 January 2020).

Barker, J. (2005). Engineers and Political Dreams: Indonesia in the Satellite Age. *Current Anthropology,* 46(5), 703–727.

Basyier, A. U. (2011a). *Ada Apa Dengan Salafi.* Surakarta, Indonesia: Rumah Dzikir.

———— (2011b). *Indonesia Negeri Para Pendengki.* Surabaya, Indonesia: Shafa Publika.

Bayat, A. (2002). Piety, Privelage and Egyptian Youth. *ISIM Newsletter,* 10(1), 23.

———— (2005). Islamism and Social Movement Theory. *Third World Quarterly,* 26(6), 891–908.

———— (2007). *Making Islam Democractic: Social Movements and the Post-Islamist Turn.* Stanford, CA: Stanford University Press.

Beatty, A. (1999). *Varieties of Javanese Religion: An Anthropological Account.* Cambridge: Cambridge University Press.

———— (2009). *A Shadow Falls in the Heart of Java.* London: Faber and Faber.

Benda, H. (1958). Christiaan Snouck Hurgronje and the Foundation of Dutch Islamic Policy in Indonesia. *The Journal of Modern History,* 30(4), 338–347.

Bonnefoy, L. (2011). *Salafism in Yemen: Transnationalism and Religious Identity.* London: Hurst and Company.

Bourchier, D. (1998). Indonesianising Indonesia: Conservative Indigenism in an Age of Globalisation. *Social Semiotics,* 8(2/3), 203–214.

———— (2014). *Illiberal Democracy in Indonesia:The Ideology of the Family.* London; Routledge.

Bowen, J. R. (1993). *Muslims Through Discourse.* Princeton, NJ: Princeton University Press.

Brenner, S. (1995). Why Women Rule the Roost: Rethinking Javanese Ideologies of Gender and Self Control. In A. Ong and M. G. Peletz (eds), *Betwitching Women, Pious Men: Gender and Body Politics in Southeast Asia.* London: University of California Press.

———— (1996). Reconstructing Self and Society: Javanese Women and "The Veil." *American Ethnologist,* 23(4), 673–697.

Bubalo, A., G. Fealy and W Mason. (2008). *Zealous Democrats: Islamism and Democracy in Egypt, Indonesia and Turkey.* Sydney, NSW: Lowy Institute for International Policy.

Buehler, M. (2016). *The Politics of Shari'a Law: Islamist Activists and the State in Democratizing Indonesia.* Cambridge: Cambridge University Press.

Buehler, M., and E. Pisani. (2016). Why do Indonesian Politicians Promote Shari'a Laws? An Analytic Framework for Muslim-Majority Democracies. *Third World Quarterly,* 1–19.

Burhanudin, J., and K. van Djik. (2013). Islam in Indonesia: Constrasting Images and Interpretations. Amsterdam, Netherlands: Amsterdam University Press.

Bush, R. (2015). Religious politics and minority rights during the Yudhoyono presidency. In E. Aspinall, M. Mietzner, and D. Tomsa (eds), *The*

Yudhoyono Presidency: Indonesia's Decade of Stability and Stagnation. Singapore: Institute of Southeast Asian Studies, pp. 239–257.

Callon, M. (1986). Some Elements of a Sociology of Translation: Domestication of the Scallops and the Fishermen of St. Brieue Bay. In J. Law (ed.), *Power, Action and Belief: A New Sociology of Knowledge?* London: Routledge, pp. 196–223.

Castells, M. (2010). *The Rise of the Network Society.* Oxford: Oxford University Press.

Chaplin, C. (2016). Stuck in the immoderate middle. *New Mandala.* Retrieved from www.newmandala.org/stuck-immoderate-middle/ (accessed 8 November 2016)

——— (2018). Salafi De Koning, M. (2012). The "Other" Political Islam: Understanding Salafi Politics. In O. Roy and A. Boubekeur (eds), *Whatever Happened to the Islamists? Salafs, Heavy Metal Muslims and the Lure of Consumerist Islam.* London: Hurst Publishers, pp. 153–178.

Islamic Piety vs Civic Activism: Wahdah Islamiyah and Differentiated Citizenship in Indonesia. *Citizenship Studies,* 22(2), 208–223.

——— (2013). How should I Live as a "True" Muslim? Regimes of Living among Dutch Muslims in the Salafi Movement. *Etnofoor,* 25(2), 53–72.

Deeb, L. (2006). *The Enchanted Modern: Gender and Public Piety in Shi'i Lebanon.* Princeton, NJ: Princeton University Press.

Deleuze, G. (2016). *Foucault.* London: Bloomsbury Publishing.

Deleuze, G., and Guattari, F. (1983). *On the Line.* New York: Semiotext(e).

——— (2004). *A Thousand Plateaus: Capitalism and Schizophrenia.* London: Continuum.

Dijk, C. van. (1981). *Rebellion Under the Banner of Islam: The Darul Islam in Indonesia.* The Hague: Martinus Nijhoff.

Djik, K. van, and Kaptein, N. J. G. (2016). *Islam, Politics and Change: The Indonesian Experience after the Fall of Suharto.* Leiden: Leiden University Press.

Djajadingrat-Nieuwenhuis, M. (1987). Ibuism and Priyayisation: Path to Power? In E. Locher-Scholten and A. Niehof (eds), *Indonesian Women in Focus: Past and Present Notions.* Dordrecht, Netherlands: Foris.

Edwards, G. (2014). *Social Movements and Protest*. Cambridge: Cambridge University Press.

Effendy, B. (2003). *Islam and the State in Indonesia*. Singapore: Institute for Southeast Asian Studies (ISEAS).

Eickelman, D, and J. Piscatori. (1996). *Muslim Politics*. Princeton, NJ: Princeton University Press.

Eickelman, D., and J. Anderson. (2003). New Media in the Muslim World: The Emerging Public Sphere. In M. Tessler (ed.), *Indiana Series in Middle East Studies*. Bloomington, IN: Indiana University Press.

Elmhirst, R. (2000). A Javanese Diaspora? Gender and Identity Politics in Indonesia's Transmigration Resettlement Programme. *Women's Studies International Forum*, 23(4), 487–500.

Esposito, J. L. (2003). *The Oxford Dictionary of Islam*. Oxford: Oxford University Press.

Fadil, N. (2009). Managing Affects and Sensibilities: The Case of Not-Handshaking and Not-Fasting. *Social Anthropology*, 17(4), 439–454.

Fauzia, A. (2013). *Faith and the State: A History of Islamic Philanthropy in Indonesia*. Leiden: Brill.

Fealy, G. (2008). Consuming Islam: Commodified Religion and Aspirational Pietism in Contemporary Indonesia. In G. Fealy and S. White (eds), *Expressing Islam: Religious Life and Politics in Indonesia*. Singapore: Institute for Southeast Asian Studies (ISEAS).

———— (2018). Jokowi's Vice-Presidential Turmoil. *The Strategist*: Australia Strategic Policy Institute. Retrieved from www.aspistrategist.org.au/jokowis-vice-presidential-turmoil/ (accessed 8 June 2020)

Fealy, G., and S. White. (2008). Expressing Islam: Religious Life and Politics in Indonesia. Singapore: Institute for Southeast Asian Studies (ISEAS).

Finke, R., and R. Stark. (1986). Turning Pews into People: Estimating 19th Century Church Membership. *Journal for the Scientific Study of Religion*, 25, 180–192.

Fischer, J. (2008). *Proper Islamic Consumption: Shopping Among the Malays in Modern Malaysia*. Copenhagen: NIAS Press.

FKKA (Forum Kegiatan Kemulihanan al-Atsari). (2012). Mengenal Allah Jalan Menuju KeBahagian. *Zuhairoh*.

Fradkin, H. (2008). *The History and Unwritten Future of Salafism*. Washington, DC: The Hudson Institute.

Frisk, S. (2009). *Submitting to God: Women and Islam in Urban Malaysia*. Copenhagen: NIAS Press.

Gade, F. (2013). Indonesia Valentine's Protest: "Sex Holiday" Decried by Muslim Officials. *Huffington Post*. Retrieved from www. huffingtonpost.com/2013/02/14/indonesia-valentines-protest-sex-holiday-muslim-officials__n_2685327.html (accessed 15 March 2013)

Gaonkar, D. P. (2002). Toward New Imaginaries: An Introduction. *Public Culture*, 14(1), 1–19.

Geertz, C. (1960). *The Religion of Java*. Chicago, IL: The Free Press of Glencoe.

Giddens, A. (1991). *Modernity and Self-Identity: Self and Society in the Late Modern Age*. Cambridge: Polity Press.

Gledhill, J (2000). *Power and its Disguises: Anthropological Perspectives on Politics*. (2nd Edition). London: Pluto Press.

Goffman, E. (1972). *Interaction Rituals: Essays in Face-to-Face Behaviour*. London: Penguin Books.

Google Books (2019). Ngram Viewer Search on 'Salafi' within Corpus of English Books (1980–2008). (accessed 15 September 2019).

Gupta, A, and J. Ferguson. (1992). Beyond 'Culture': Space, Identity and the Politics of Difference. *Cultural Anthropology*, 7(1), 6–23.

Habib, A. R. (2012). Kelabu di Hari Valentine. *At-Tauhid*, 7.

Hadiz, V. R. (2015). *Islamic Populism in Indonesia and the Middle East*. Cambridge: Cambridge University Press.

Harsono, A. (2014). Undoing Yudhoyono's Sectarian Legacy. *New Mandala*. Retrieved from www.newmandala.org/undoing-yudhoyonos-sectarian-legacy/ (accessed 29 June 2018).

Hasan, N. (2006). *Laskar Jihad: Islam, Militancy and the Quest for Identity in Post New Order Indonesia*. Ithaca, NY: Cornell University Press.

———— (2007). The Salafi Movement in Indonesia: Transnational Dynamics and Local Development. *Comparative Studies of South Asia, Africa and the Middle East*, 27(1), 83–94.

————— (2010). The Failure of the Wahhabi Campaign: Transnational Islam and the Salafi Madrasa in post-9/11 Indonesia. *South East Asia Research*, 18(4), 675–705.

————— (2014). Between the Global and the Local: Negotiating Islam and Democracy in Provincial Indonesia. In G. van Klinken and W. Berenschot (eds), *In Search of Middle Indonesia: Middle Classes in Provincial Towns*. Leiden: Brill.

Hasan, N., I. Abubakar, I., and W. Weck. (2011). *Islam in the Public Sphere: The Politics of Identity and The Future of Democracy in Indonesia*. Jakarta: Centre for the Study of Religion and Culture, Universitas Islam Negeri Syarif Hidayatullah.

Hasbullah, M. (2000). Cultural Presentation of the Muslim Middle Class in Contemporary Indonesia. *Studi Islamika*, 7(2), 1–58.

HASMI. (2011). *Bahaya Syirik*. Bogor, Indonesia: Lajnah Ilmiah Hasmi.

Hassim, E. (2010). *The Origins of Salafism in Indonesia*. Leipzig: Lambert Academic Publishing.

Haykel, B. (2009). On the Nature of Salafi Thought and Action. In R. Meijer (ed.), *Global Salafism: Islam's New Religious Movement*. London: Hurst and Company.

Hecker, P. (2010). Heavy Metal in the Middle East: New Urban Spaces in a Translocal Underground. In A. Bayat and L. Herrera (eds), *Being Young and Muslim*. Oxford: Oxford University Press, pp. 325–339.

Hefner, R. (1997). Print Islam: Mass Media and Ideological Rivalries among Indonesian Muslims. *Indonesia*, 64, 77–104.

————— (1999). Civic Pluralism Denied? The New Media and Jihadi Violence in Indonesia. In J. Anderson and D. Eickelman (eds), *New Media in the Muslim World*. Bloomington, IN: Indiana University Press.

————— (2000). *Civil Islam: Muslims and Democratisation in Indonesia*. Princeton, NJ: Princeton University Press.

Heiphetz, L., E.S. Spelke, E. S., and M.R. Banaji. (2014). What do Different Beliefs Tell Us? An Examination of Factual, Opinion-based, and Religious Beliefs. *Cognitive Development*, 30, 15–29.

Hepp, A. (2009). Localities of Diasporic Communicative Spaces: Material Aspects of Translocal Mediated Networking. *The Communication Review*, 12(4), 327–348.

Hill, M., and K.F. Lian. (2013). *The Politics of Nation Building and Citizenship in Singapore*. London: Routledge.

Hirschkind, C. (2009). *The Ethical Soundscape: Cassette Sermons and Islamic Counterpublics*. New York: Columbia University Press.

Hoesterey, J. B. (2012). Prophetic Cosmopolitanism: Islam, Pop Psychology, and Civic Virtue in Indonesia. *City and Space*, 24(1), 38–61.

———— (2015). *Rebranding Islam: Piety, Prosperity, and a Self-Help Guru*. Stanford, CA: Stanford University Press.

Hooker, M. B. (2003). *Indonesian Islam: Social Change Through Contemporary Fatawa*. Honolulu, HA: University of Hawaii Press.

Hooker, V., and G. Fealy. (2006). Country Overviews and Context of Southeast Asian Islam – Indonesia. In V. Hooker (ed.), *Voices of Islam in Southeast Asia: A Contemporary Sourcebook*. Singapore: Institute of Southeast Asian Studies (ISEAS).

HRW. (2013). *In Religion's Name: Abuses Against Religious Minorities in Indonesia*. USA: Human Rights Watch.

Iannaccone, L. (1998). Introduction to the Economics of Religion. *Journal of Economic Literature*, 36, 1465–1496.

ICG (2000). *Indonesia's Maluku Crisis: The Issues*. Asia Briefing No. 2. Brussels: International Crisis Group.

———— (2002). *Indonesia Backgrounder: How the Jemaah Islamiyah Terrorist Network Operates*. Asia Report No. 43. Brussels: International Crisis Group.

———— (2004). *Indonesia Backgrounder: Why Salafism and Terrorism Mostly Don't Mix*. Asia Report No. 83. Brussels: Internationl Crisis Group.

———— (2008). *Indonesia: Implications of the Ahmadiyah Decree*. Asia Briefing No. 78. Brussels: International Crisis Group.

Idahram (2011). *Sejarah berdarah sekte Salafi Wahabi: Mereka membunuh semuanya, termasuk para ulama*. Yogyakarta, Indonesia: Pustaka Pesantren.

Ihza, Y. (1995). Combining Activism and Intellectualism: The Biography of Mohammad Natsir. *Studi Islamika*, 2(1), 111–147.

Inden, R. (1990). *Imagining India*. Oxford: Blackwell.

Inge, A. (2017). *The Making of a Salafi Muslim Woman: Paths to Conversion.* Oxford: Oxford University Press.

IPAC (2016). *The Anti-Shi'a Movement in Indonesia.* IPAC Report No. 27. Jakarta: Institute for Policy Analysis of Conflict.

———— (2018). *After Ahok: The Islamist Agenda in Indonesia.* IPAC Report No. 44. Jakarta: Institute for Policy Analysis of Conflict.

———— (2018). *Puritan Political Engagement: The Evolution of Salafism in Malaysia.* IPAC Report No. 52. Jakarta: Institute for Policy Analysis of Conflict.

Iqtidar, H. (2011). *Secularizing Islamists? Jama'at-e-Islami and Jama'at-ud-da'wa in Urban Pakistan.* Chicago, IL: University of Chicago Press.

Isin, E. F. (2012). *Citizens Without Frontiers.* London: Bloomsbury.

Jakarta Post. (2014a). Muslim Organisations Warn of "Dark World" of Valentine's Day. *The Jakarta Post.* Retrieved from www.thejakartapost.com/news/2014/02/13/muslim-organisations-warn-dark-world-valentine-s-day.html (accessed 25 February 2014).

———— (2014b). Number of RI Internet Users Increases to 71.19 Million in 2013: ARJII. *The Jakarta Post.* Retrieved from www.thejakartapost.com/news/2014/01/15/number-ri-internet-users-increases-7119-million-2013-apjii.html (accessed 25 February 2014).

Jawas, Y. bin A. Q. (2004). *Penjelasan dan Nasehat Serta Bantahan Kepada Jafar Umar Thalib.* Podcast recorded 22 August 2004, Surabaya, Indonesia.

———— (2007). *Hukum Lagu, Musik dan Nasyid Menurut Syari'at Islam.* Bogor, Indonesia: Pustaka at-Taqwa.

———— (2011). Kuburan Bukan Tempat Membaca Al-Qur'an. *As-Sunnah,* 15(3).

Jones, C. (2007). Fashion and Faith in Urban Indonesia. *Fashion Theory,* 11(2/3), 211–232.

Jones, S. (2013). Indonesian Government Approaches to Radical Islam Since 1998. In M. Kunkler and A. Stepan (eds), *Democracy and Islam in Indonesia.* New York: Columbia University Press.

Juhannis, H. (2006). The Struggle for Formalist Islam in South Sulawesi: From Darul Islam to Komite Persiapan Penegakan Syariat Islam.

Faculty of Asian Studies, Australian National University, Canberra, PhD thesis.

Juris, J. S. (2007). Practicing Militant Ethnography With the Movement for Global Resistance in Barcelona. In S. Shukaitis and D. Graeber (eds), *Constituent Imagination: Militant Investigation, Collective Theorisation.* Oakland, CA: AK Press, pp. 164–176.

Juris, J. S., and A. Khasnabish. (2013). Ethnography and Activism within Networked Spaces of Transnational Ecounter. In J. S. Juris and A. Khasnabish (eds), *Insurgent Encounters: Transnational Activism, Ethnography, and the Political.* Durham, NC: Duke University Press, pp. 1–28.

Kersten, C. (2015). *Islam in Indonesia: The Contest for Society, Ideas and Values.* London: Hurst and Company.

Kim, H. (2010). Praxis and Religious Authority in Islam: The Case of Ahmad Dahlan, Founder of Muhammadiyah. *Studi Islamika,* 17(1), 69–92.

King, R. (1999). *Orientalism and Religion: Post-Colonial Theory, India and The Mystic East.* New York: Routledge.

Kitiarsa, P (ed.) (2008). *Religious Commodifications in Asia: Marketing Gods.* London: Routledge.

Lacroix, S. (2011). *Awakening Islam: The Politics of Religious Dissent in Contemporary Saudi Arabia.* Cambridge, MA: Harvard University Press.

Latief, H. (2013). Islam and Humanitarian Affairs: The Middle Class and New Patterns of Islamic Activism. In J. Burhanudin and K. van Djik (eds), *Islam in Indonesia: Constrasting Images and Interpretations.* Amsterdam: Amsterdam University Press, pp. 173–194.

——— (2016). Philanthropy and "Muslim Citizenship" in Post-Suharto Indonesia. *Southeast Asian Studies,* 5(2), 269–286.

Latif, Y. (2005). The Rupture of Young Muslim Intelligentsia in the Modernisation of Indonesia. *Studi Islamika,* 12(3), 373–420.

Lefebvre, H. (1991). *The Production of Space.* Oxford: Blackwell.

Lehmann, D., and B. Siebzehner. (2006). *Remaking Israeli Judaism: The Challenge of the Shas.* London: Hurst and Company.

——— (2010). Rational Choice and the Sociology of Religion. In B. S. Turner (ed.), *The New Blackwell Companion to the Sociology of Religion.* Oxford: Blackwell Publishing Ltd.

Leslie, S. W., and R. Kargon. (2006). Exporting MIT: Science, Technology, and Nation-Building in India and Iran. *Osiris*, 21, 110–130.

Lipman, V. (2012). The World's Most Active Twitter City? You Won't Guess It. *Forbes*. Retrieved from www.forbes.com/sites/victorlipman/2012/12/30/the-worlds-most-active-twitter-city-you-wont-guess-it/ (accessed 25 February 2014).

Lukens-Bull, R. (2008). Commodification of Religion and the "Religification" of Commodities: Youth Culture and Religious Identity. In P. Kitiarsa, (ed.), *Religious Commodifications in Asia: Marketing Gods*. London: Routledge.

Lukito, R. (2012). *Resisting the Inbetweeness: State Identity and the Current Islamisation of Law in Indonesia*.

Madinier, R. (2015). *Islam and Politics in Indonesia: The Masyumi Party Between Democracy and Integralism*. Singapore: NUS Press.

Mahmood, S. (2001). Rehearsed Spontaneity and the Conventionality of Ritual: Discipline of Salat. *American Ethnologist*, 28(4), 827–853.

——— (2005). *Politics of Piety: The Islamic Revival and the Feminist Subject*. Princeton, NJ: Princeton University Press.

Mandaville, P. (2007). *Global Political Islam*. Oxford: Routledge.

Massey, D. (1994). *Space, Place and Gender*. Cambridge: Polity Press.

McAdam, D. (1994). Culture and Social Movements. In Larana, E., H. Johnston, and J. R. Gusfield (eds), *New Social Movements: From Ideology to Identity*. Philadelphia, PA: Temple University Press, pp. 36–57.

——— (1982). *Political Process and the Development of Black Insurgency, 1930–1970*. Chicago, IL: University of Chicago Press.

McCarthy, J. D., and M. N. Zald. (1977). Resource Mobilisation and Social Movements: A Partial Theory. *American Journal of Sociology*, 82(6), 1212–1241.

Media Indonesia (2012), Menag Tegarskan Bertentangan dengan Islam. *Media Indonesia*. Retrieved from www.mediaindonesia.com/read/2012/01/25/293947/293/14/Menag-Tegaskan-Syiah-Bertentangan-dengan-Islam (accessed 20 March 2015).

Meijer, R. (2010). Salafism: Doctrine, Diversity and Practice. In K. Hroub (ed.), *Political Islam: Context vs Ideology*. London: London Middle East Institute.

Melucci, A. (1980). New Social Movements: A Theoretical Approach. *Social Science Information*, 19(2), 199–226.

——— (1989). *Nomads of the Present: Social Movements and Individual Needs in Contemporary Society*. London: Hutchinson Radius.

——— (1996). *Challenging Codes*. Cambridge: Cambridge University Press.

Menchik, J. (2016). *Islam and Democracy in Indonesia: Tolerance without Liberalism*. Cambridge: Cambridge University Press.

Mersinnia, F. (1987). *Beyond the Veil: Male-Female Dynamics in Modern Muslim Society*. Bloomington, IN: Indiana University Press.

Mietzner, M. (2009). *Military Politics, Islam and the State in Indonesia: From Turbulent Transition to Democractic Consolidation*. Singapore: Institute for Southeast Asian Studies (ISEAS).

Mietzner, M., and B. Muhtadi. (2018). Explaining the 2016 Islamic Mobilisation in Indonesia: Religious Intolerance, Militant Groups and the Politics of Accommodation. *Asian Studies Review*, 42(3), 479–497.

Minhal, A. (2011). Kekayaan Bukan Tanda Kemuliaan, Kemiskinan Bukan Petunjuk Kehinaan. *As-Sunnah*, 15(3).

Morris, R. (2000). *In the Place of Origins: Modernity and its Mediums in Northern Thaliand*. Durham, NC: Duke University Press.

Muzakki, A. (2008). Islam as a Symbolic Commodity: Transmitting and Consuming Islam Through Public Sermons in Indonesia. In P. Kitiarsa (ed.), *Religious Commodifications in Asia: Marketing Gods*. London: Routledge.

——— (2012). *Sejarah Salafi Indonesia*. Bandung, Indonesia: TooBagus Publishing.

Nisa, E. F. (2012). Embodied Faith: Agency and Obedience among Face-Veiled University Students in Indonesia. *The Asia Pacific Journal of Anthropology*, 13(4), 366–381.

Oberschall, A. (1995). *Social Movements: Ideologies, Interests, and Identities*. New Brunswick, NJ: Transaction Publishers.

Ong, A. (1987). *Spirits of Resistance and Capitalist Discipline: Factory Women in Malaysia*. Albany, NY: SUNY Press.

Osman, M. N. M (2019). Insight: Is Hizbut Tahrir a Threat to Indonesia? *The Jakarta Post*. Retrieved from www.thejakartapost.com/academia/2019/06/20/is-hizbut-tahrir-a-threat-to-indonesia.html (accessed 20 June 2019).

Pall, Z. (2013). *Lebanese Salafis between the Gulf and Europe: Development, Fractionalisation and Transnational Networks of Salafism in Lebanon.* Amsterdam: Amsterdam University Press.

Pemberton, J. (1994). *On the Subject of "Java".* Ithaca, NY: Cornell University Press.

Pengusaha Muslim (2012). Tanya-Jawab Syariah: Hukum Bekerja Sebagai Tentara. *Pengusaha Muslim.* Retrieved from pengusahamuslim.com/tamyajawab-syariah-hukum-1535 (accessed 25 May 2012).

Price, C., D. Nonini, and E. F. Tree. (2008). Grounded Utopian Movements: Subjects of Neglect. *Anthropological Quarterly,* 81(1), 127–159.

Putra, A. P. (2014). Tolak Golput, Dai Salafi Pilih Pasangan Ini untuk Pilpres 2014, *Republika,* 24 May 2014.

Retsikas, K. (2013). Becoming Sacred: Humanity and Divinity in East Java, Indonesia. In M. Marsden and K. Retsikas (eds), *Articulating Islam: Anthropological Approaches to Muslim Worlds.* London: Springer, pp. 119–138.

Retsikas, K. (2017). The Gift of Future Time: Islamic Welfare and Entrepreneurship in 21st Century Indonesia. *South East Asia Research,* 25(3), 284–300.

Robinson, K. (2008). Islamic Cosmopolitics, Human Rights and Anti-Violence Strategies in Indonesia. In P. Werbner (ed.), *Anthropology and the New Cosmopolitanism.* Oxford: Berg Publishers.

Rogers, B. (2017, May 29). Stop Calling Indonesia a Role Model. It's Stopped Being One. *The Diplomat.* Retrieved from thediplomat.com/2017/05/stop-calling-indonesia-a-role-model-its-stopped-being-one/ (accessed 5 July 2018).

Rokhman, M. A. (2011). Relationship between Indonesian and Western Characters in Galang Lufityanto's novel Bule Celup. *26th ASEASUK Conference.* University of Cambridge.

Rosen, L. (1984). *Bargaining for Reality: The Construction of Social Relations in a Muslim Community.* Chicago, IL: University of Chicago Press.

Roy, O. (2004). *Globalised Islam: The Search for a New Umma.* London: Hurst and Company.

Rudnyckyj, D. (2009a). Market Islam in Indonesia. *Journal of the Royal Anthropological Institute,* 15(1), 183–201.

——— (2009b). Spiritual Economies: Islam and Neoliberalism in Contemporary Indonesia. *Cultural Anthropology,* 24(1), 104–141.

Said, E. (2001). Traveling Theory. In M. Bayoumi and A. Rubin (eds), *The Edward Said Reader*. London: Granta Publications, pp. 195–217.

Saifullah. (2011). Menyibak Hakikat Hizbut Tahrir. *Al Furqon*, 118.

Samad, T. (2012). *Indonesia's Urban Development: Towards Inclusive and Sustainable Economic Growth*. World Bank.

Schulte-Nordholt, H. (2011). Modernity and Cultural Citizenship in the Netherlands Indies: An Illustrated Hypothesis. *Journal of Southeast Asian Studies*, 42(3), 435–457.

Schulze, K. E. (2017). The "Ethnic" nn Indonesia's Communal Conflicts: Violence in Ambon, Poso, and Sambas. *Ethnic and Racial Studies*, 40(12), 2096–2114.

Scott, M. (2016). Indonesia: The Saudis are Coming. New York: The New York Review of Books.

SerambiMadinah (2011). Unofficial Indonesian Alumni Website, Islamic University of Madinah. Retrieved from www.serambimadinah.com (accessed 6 October 2011).

Setijadi, C. (2017). Ahok's Downfall and the Rise of Islamist Populism in Indonesia, *ISEAS Perspectives* (38), 1–9.

Shavit, U. (2014). Can Muslims Befriend Non-Muslims? Debating al-wala' wa-al-bara (Loyalty and Disavowal) in Theory and Practice. *Islam and Christian Muslim Relations*, 25(1), 67–88.

Shehabi, S. (2008). The Role of Religious Ideology in the Expansionist Policies of Saudi Arabia. In M. Al-Rasheed (ed.), *Kingdom Withouth Borders: Saud Arabia's Politics, Religious and Media Frontiers*. New York: Columbia University Press.

Sidel, J. (2006). *Riots, Pogroms and Jihad: Religious Violence in Indonesia*. Ithaca, NY: Cornell University Press.

Siegel, J. (1969). *The Rope of God*. Berkeley, CA: University of California Press.

——— (1998). *A New Criminal Type in Jakarta: Counter-Revolution Today*. Durham, NC: Duke University Press.

——— (2006). *Naming the Witch*. Stanford, CA: Stanford University Press.

Sivan, E. (1995). The Enclave Culture. In M. Marty and S. R. Appleby (eds), *Fundamentalisms Comprehended*. Chicago, IL: Chicago University Press.

Smith-Hefner, N. J. (2005). The New Muslim Romance: Changing Patterns of Courtship and Marriage Among Educated Javanese Youth. *Journal of Southeast Asian Studies*, 36(3), 441–459.

Snow, D. A., B. Rochford, S. K. Worden, and R. D. Benford. (1986). Frame Alignment Processes, Micromobilisation and Movement Participation. *American Sociological Review*, 51(4), 464–481.

Solahudin. (2011). *NII Sampai JI: Salafy Jihadisme di Indonesia*. Depok, Indonesia: Komunitas Bambu.

Spencer, J. (2007). *Anthropology, Politics, and the State: Democracy and Violence in South Asia*. Cambridge: Cambridge University Press.

Sperber, D. (1985). Anthropology and Psychology: Towards an Epidemiology of Representations. *Man* (NS), 20(1), 72–89.

———(1996). *Explaining Culture: A Naturalistic Approach*. Oxford: Blackwell Publishing.

Steinberg, G. (2009). Jihadi-Salafism and the Shi'is: Remarks about the Intellectual Roots of Anti-Shi'ism. In R. Meijer (ed.), *Global Salafism: Islam's New Religious Movement*. London: Hurst and Company.

Sullivan, J. (1992). *Local Government and Community in Java: An Urban Case Study*. Oxford: Oxford University Press.

Sunarwoto. (2016). Salafi Dakwah Radio: A Contest for Religious Authority. *Archipel*, 91, 203–230.

Surya (2011). Pengelola Radio-NU Sepakat Berdamai. *Surya*. Retrieved from www.surya.co.id/2011/10/01/pengelola-radio-nu-sepakat-berdamai (accessed 23 January 2012)

Syamhudi, K. (2012). Membongkar Akar Orientalisme. *As-Sunnah*, 15(10).

Syamsuddin, D. (1995). The Muhammadiyah Da'wah and Allocative Politics in the New Order Indonesia. *Studi Islamika*, 2(2), 35–71.

Tarrow, S. (2012). *Strangers at the Gates: Movements and States in Contentious Politics*. Cambridge: Cambridge University Press.

Tarrow, S., and C. Tilly. (2009). Contentious Politics and Social Movements. In C. Boix and S. C. Stokes (eds), *The Oxford Handbook of Comparative Politics*. Oxford: Oxford University Press.

Taylor, C. (2002). Modern Social Imaginaries. *Public Culture*, 14(1), 91–124.

———— (2007). *A Secular Age*. Cambridge, MA: Harvard University Press.

Telegraph (2013). Islamic Radicals Protest "Sexy" Valentine's Day in Indonesia. *The Telegraph*.

Thalib, J. U. (1998). Dakwah Salafiyah Merupakan Perjuangan Reformasi Rakyat. *Salafy, 28*, 10–15.

Tilly, C and S. Tarrow (2015) *Contentious Politics*, 2nd Edition. Oxford: Oxford University Press.

Touraine, A. (1992). Beyond Social Movements? *Theory, Culture and Society,* 9(1), 125–145.

Tsing, A. L. (2005). *Friction: An Ethnography of Global Connection*. Princeton, NJ: Princeton University Press.

Turner, B. (2009). Goods Not Gods: New Spiritualities, Consumerism and Religious Markets. In I. R. Jones, P. Higgs, and D. J. Ekerdt (eds), *Consumption and Generational Change: The Rise of Consumer Lifestyles*. New Brunswick, NJ: Transaction Publishers.

———— (2011). *Religion and Modern Society: Citizenship, Secularisation and the State*. Cambridge: Cambridge University Press.

Uttu (2006). Distro. *Inside Indonesia*. Australia National University. Retrieved from www.insideindonesia.org/feature-editions/distro (accessed 10 January 2021).

Van Bruinessen, M. (2002). The Geneologies of Islamic Radicalism in post-Suharto Indonesia. *South East Asia Research*, 10(2), 117–154.

———— (2013a). Ghazwul Fikri or Arabisation? Indonesian Muslims Responses to Globalisation. In K. Miichi and O. Farouk (eds), *Dynamics of Southeast Asian Muslims in the Era of Globalisation*. Tokyo: Japan International Cooperation Agency Research Institute.

———— (ed.) (2013b). *Contemporary Developments in Indonesian Islam: Explaining the "Conservative Turn"*. Singapore: Institute for Southeast Asian Studies (ISEAS).

Van Klinken, G, and M.T Su Aung. (2017). The Contentious Politics of Anti-Muslim Scapegoating in Myanmar. *Journal of Contemporary Asia,* 14(3), 353–375.

Van Klinken, G, and W. Berenschot. (2014). In Search of Middle Indonesia: Middle Classes in Provincial Towns. Leiden, Netherlands: Brill.

Van Leeuwen, N. (2014). Religious Credence is not Factual Belief. *Cognition*, 133, 698–715.

Varagur, K. (2020). *The Call: Inside the Global Saudi Religious Project*. New York: Columbia Global Reports.

Wahdah Islamiyah. (2016). *10 Rekomendasi Eksternal Muktamar III Wahdah Islamiyah*. Makassar.

Wagemakers, J. (2016). Revisiting Wiktorowicz: Categorising and Defining the Branches of Salafism. In F. Cavatorta and F. Merone (eds), *Salafism After the Arab Awakening: Contending with People's Power*. London: Hurst Publishers, pp. 7–24.

Wahid, A. B. (2006). *Salafi Da'wa Movement after the Dissolution of Laskar Jihad*. UIN Sunan Kalijaga.

Wahid, D. (2014). Nurturing the Salafi Manhaj: A Study of Salafi Pesantrens in Contemporary Indonesia. Utrecht University, PhD thesis.

Warner, S. (1993). Working in Progress Towards a New Paradigm for the Sociological Study of Religion in the US. *American Journal of Sociology*, 98(5), 1044–1093.

Werve, J. (2006). *The Corruption Notebook 2006: Stories from the World-wide Struggle Against Abuses of Power*. Washington, DC: Global Integrity.

White, B. (2017). The myth of the harmonious village. *Inside Indonesia*, 128.

Wichelen, S. Van. (2010). *Religion, Politics and Gender in Indonesia: Disputing the Muslim Body*. New York: Routledge.

Widodo, A. (2008). Writing for God. *Inside Indonesia*. Australia National University. Retrieved from www.insideindonesia.org/writing-for-god

Wiktorowicz, Q. (2004). *Islamic Activism: A Social Movement Theory Approach*. Bloomington, IN: Indiana University Press.

——— (2006). Anatomy of the Salafi Movement. *Studies in Conflict and Terrorism*, 29(3), 207–239.

Wilson, I. D. (2016). Making enemies out of friends. *New Mandala*. Retrieved from www.newmandala.org/making-enemies-friends/ (accessed 5 November 2016)

Woodward, M. (1989). *Islam in Java: Normative Piety and Mysticism in the Sultanate of Yogyakarta*. Tucson, AZ: University of Arizona Press.

———— (2011). *Java, Indonesia and Islam*. London: Springer.

Zulkifli, A., A. A. Kuswardono, D. Sepriyossa, A. Sutarwijono, and R. Fajri. (2000). Milisi Sipil Dan Pesta Senayan. *Tempo*, 22(XXIX), 22–26.

Index

Printed by Printforce, United Kingdom